# Mastering Linux - Networking

A catalogue record for this book is available from the Hong Kong Public Libraries.

Published in Hong Kong by Samurai Media Limited.

Email: info@samuraimedia.org

ISBN 978-988-8406-21-0

# Table of Contents

# List of Tables

# Part I. network management

# Table of Contents

# Chapter 1. general networking

While this chapter is not directly about **Linux**, it does contain general networking concepts that will help you in troubleshooting networks on **Linux**.

# 1.1. network layers

## 1.1.1. seven OSI layers

When talking about protocol layers, people usually mention the seven layers of the **osi** protocol (Application, Presentation, Session, Transport, Network, Data Link and Physical). We will discuss layers 2 and 3 in depth, and focus less on the other layers. The reason is that these layers are important for understanding networks. You will hear administrators use words like "this is a layer 2 device" or "this is a layer 3 broadcast", and you should be able to understand what they are talking about.

## 1.1.2. four DoD layers

The **DoD** (or tcp/ip) model has only four layers, roughly mapping its **network access layer** to OSI layers 1 and 2 (Physical and Datalink), its **internet** (IP) layer to the OSI **network layer**, its **host-to-host** (tcp, udp) layer to OSI layer 4 (transport) and its **application layer** to OSI layers 5, 6 and 7.

Below an attempt to put OSI and DoD layers next to some protocols and devices.

| OSI Model | DoD Model | protocols | | devices/apps |
|---|---|---|---|---|
| layer 5, 6, 7 | application | dns, dhcp, ntp, snmp, https, ftp, ssh, telnet, http, pop3... others | | web server, mail server, browser, mail client... |
| layer 4 | host-to-host | tcp | udp | gateway |
| layer 3 | internet | ip, icmp, igmp | | router, firewall layer 3 switch |
| layer 2 | network access | arp (mac), rarp | | bridge layer 2 switch |
| layer 1 | | ethernet, token ring | | hub |

### 1.1.3. short introduction to the physical layer

The physical layer, or **layer 1**, is all about voltage, electrical signals and mechanical connections. Some networks might still use **coax** cables, but most will have migrated to **utp** (cat 5 or better) with **rj45** connectors.

Devices like **repeaters** and **hubs** are part of this layer. You cannot use software to 'see' a **repeater** or **hub** on the network. The only thing these devices are doing is amplifying electrical signals on cables. **Passive hubs** are multiport amplifiers that amplify an incoming electrical signal on all other connections. **Active hubs** do this by reading and retransmitting bits, without interpreting any meaning in those bits.

Network technologies like **csma/cd** and **token ring** are defined on this layer.

This is all we have to say about **layer 1** in this book.

### 1.1.4. short introduction to the data link layer

The data link layer, or **layer 2** is about frames. A frame has a **crc** (cyclic redundancy check). In the case of ethernet (802.3), each network card is identifiable by a unique 48-bit **mac** address (media access control address).

On this layer we find devices like bridges and switches. A bridge is more intelligent than a hub because a **bridge** can make decisions based on the mac address of computers. A **switch** also understands mac addresses.

In this book we will discuss commands like **arp** and **ifconfig** to explore this layer.

### 1.1.5. short introduction to the network layer

**Layer 3** is about ip packets. This layer gives every host a unique 32-bit ip address. But **ip** is not the only protocol on this layer, there is also icmp, igmp, ipv6 and more. A complete list can be found in the **/etc/protocols** file.

On this layer we find devices like **routers** and layer 3 switches, devices that know (and have) an ip address.

In tcp/ip this layer is commonly referred to as the **internet layer**.

### 1.1.6. short introduction to the transport layer

We will discuss the **tcp** and **udp** protocols in the context of layer 4. The DoD model calls this the host-to-host layer.

### 1.1.7. layers 5, 6 and 7

The tcp/ip application layer includes layers 5, 6 and 7. Details on the difference between these layers are out of scope of this course.

## 1.1.8. network layers in this book

Stacking of layers in this book is based on the **Protocols in Frame** explanation in the **wireshark** sniffer. When sniffing a dhcp packet, we notice the following in the sniffer.

```
[Protocols in Frame: eth:ip:udp:bootp]
```

Sniffing for ntp (Network Time Protocol) packets gives us this line, which makes us conclude to put **ntp** next to **bootp** in the protocol chart below.

```
[Protocols in Frame: eth:ip:udp:ntp]
```

Sniffing an **arp** broadcast makes us put arp next to **ip**. All these protocols are explained later in this chapter.

```
[Protocols in Frame: eth:arp]
```

Below is a protocol chart based on wireshark's knowledge. It contains some very common protocols that are discussed in this book. The chart does not contain all protocols.

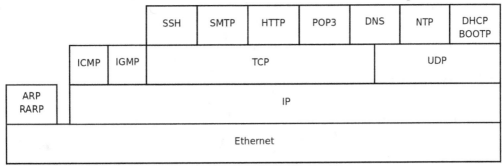

# 1.2. unicast, multicast, broadcast, anycast

## 1.2.1. unicast

A **unicast** communication originates from one computer and is destined for exactly one other computer (or host). It is common for computers to have many **unicast** communications.

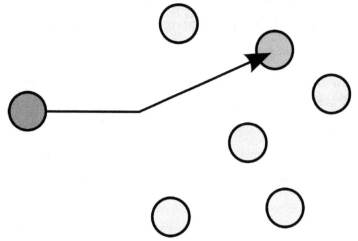

## 1.2.2. multicast

A **multicast** is destined for a group (of computers).

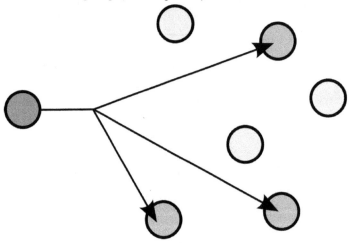

Some examples of **multicast** are Realplayer (.sdp files) and **ripv2** (a routing protocol).

## 1.2.3. broadcast

A **broadcast** is meant for everyone.

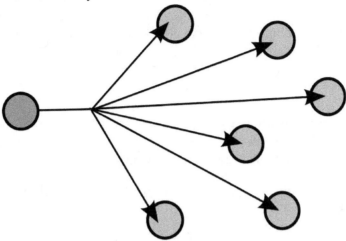

Typical example here is the BBC (British Broadcasting Corporation) broadcasting to everyone. In datacommunications a broadcast is most common confined to the **lan**.

Careful, a **layer 2 broadcast** is very different from a **layer 3 broadcast**. A layer two broadcast is received by all network cards on the same segment (it does not pass any router), whereas a layer 3 broadcast is received by all hosts in the same ip subnet.

## 1.2.4. anycast

The **root name servers** of the internet use **anycast**. An **anycast** signal goes the the (geographically) nearest of a well defined group.

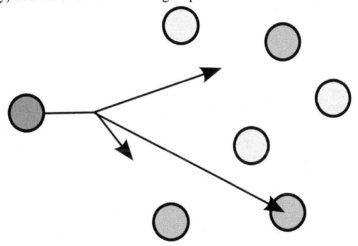

With thanks to the nice anonymous wikipedia contributor to put these pictures in the public domain.

# 1.3. lan-wan-man

The term **lan** is used for local area networks, as opposed to a **wan** for wide area networks. The difference between the two is determined by the **distance** between the computers, and not by the number of computers in a network. Some protocols like **atm** are designed for use in a **wan**, others like **ethernet** are designed for use in a **lan**.

## 1.3.1. lan

A **lan** (Local Area Network) is a local network. This can be one room, or one floor, or even one big building. We say **lan** as long as computers are **close** to each other. You can also define a **lan** when all computers are **ethernet** connected.

A **lan** can contain multiple smaller **lan**'s. The picture below shows three **lan**'s that together make up one **lan**.

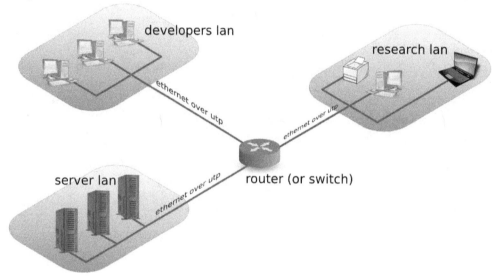

## 1.3.2. man

A **man** (Metropolitan Area Network) is something inbetween a **lan** and a **wan**, often comprising several buildings on the same campus or in the same city. A **man** can use **fddi** or **ethernet** or other protocols for connectivity.

### 1.3.3. wan

A **wan** (Wide Area Network) is a network with a lot of distance between the computers (or hosts). These hosts are often connected by **leased lines**. A **wan** does not use **ethernet**, but protocols like **fddi**, **frame relay**, **ATM** or **X.25** to connect computers (and networks).

The picture below shows a branch office that is connected through **Frame Relay** with headquarters.

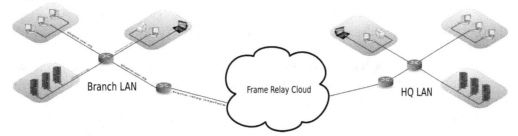

The acronym **wan** is also used for large surface area networks like the **internet**.

**Cisco** is known for their **wan** technology. They make **routers** that connect many **lan** networks using **wan** protocols.

### 1.3.4. pan-wpan

Your home network is called a **pan** (Personal Area Network). A wireless **pan** is a **wpan**.

# 1.4. internet - intranet - extranet

The **internet** is a global network. It connects many networks using the **tcp/ip** protocol stack.

The origin of the **internet** is the **arpanet**. The **arpanet** was created in 1969, that year only four computers were connected in the network. In 1971 the first **e-mail** was sent over the **arpanet**. **E-mail** took 75 percent of all **arpanet** traffic in 1973. 1973 was also the year **ftp** was introduced, and saw the connection of the first European countries (Norway and UK). In 2009 the internet was available to 25 percent of the world population. In 2011 it is estimated that only a quarter of internet webpages are in English.

An **intranet** is a private **tcp/ip** network. An **intranet** uses the same protocols as the **internet**, but is only accessible to people from within one organization.

An **extranet** is similar to an **intranet**, but some trusted organizations (partners/clients/suppliers/...) also get access.

# 1.5. tcp/ip

## 1.5.1. history of tcp/ip

In the Sixties development of the **tcp/ip** protocol stack was started by the US Department of Defense. In the Eighties a lot of commercial enterprises developed their own protocol stack: IBM created **sna**, Novell had **ipx/spx**, Microsoft completed **netbeui** and Apple worked with **appletalk**. All the efforts from the Eighties failed to survive the Nineties. By the end of the Nineties, almost all computers in the world were able to speak tcp/ip.

In my humble opinion, the main reason for the survival of **tcp/ip** over all the other protocols is its openness. Everyone is free to develop and use the tcp/ip protocol suite.

## 1.5.2. rfc (request for comment)

The protocols that are used on the internet are defined in **rfc's**. An rfc or **request for comment** describes the inner working of all internet protocols. The **IETF** (Internet Engineering Task Force) is the sole publisher of these protocols since 1986.

The official website for the rfc's is **http://www.rfc-editor.org**. This website contains all rfc's in plain text, for example rfc2132 (which defines dhcp and bootp) is accessible at http://www.rfc-editor.org/rfc/rfc2132.txt.

## 1.5.3. many protocols

For reliable connections, you use **tcp**, whereas **udp** is connectionless but faster. The **icmp** error messages are used by **ping**, multicast groups are managed by **igmp**.

These protocols are visible in the protocol field of the ip header, and are listed in the **/etc/protocols** file.

```
paul@debian5:~$ grep tcp /etc/protocols
tcp      6       TCP             # transmission control protocol
```

## 1.5.4. many services

Network cards are uniquely identified by their **mac address**, hosts by their **ip address** and applications by their **port number**.

Common application level protocols like smtp, http, ssh, telnet and ftp have fixed **port numbers**. There is a list of **port numbers** in **/etc/services**.

```
paul@ubu1010:~$ grep ssh /etc/services
ssh             22/tcp                  # SSH Remote Login Protocol
ssh             22/udp
```

# Chapter 2. interface configuration

This chapter explains how to configure **network interface cards** to work with **tcp/ip**.

# 2.1. to gui or not to gui

Recent Linux distributions often include a graphical application to configure the network. Some people complain that these applications mess networking configurations up when used simultaneously with command line configurations. Notably **Network Manager** (often replaced by **wicd**) and **yast** are known to not care about configuration changes via the command line.

Since the goal of this course is **server** administration, we will assume our Linux servers are always administered through the command line.

This chapter only focuses on using the command line for network interface configuration!

Unfortunately there is no single combination of Linux commands and **/etc** files that works on all Linux distributions. We discuss networking on two (large but distinct) Linux distribution families.

We start with **Debian** (this should also work on Ubuntu and Mint), then continue with **RHEL** (which is identical to CentOS and Fedora).

# 2.2. Debian nic configuration

## 2.2.1. /etc/network/interfaces

The **/etc/network/interfaces** file is a core network interface card configuration file on **debian**.

### dhcp client

The screenshot below shows that our computer is configured for **dhcp** on **eth0** (the first network interface card or nic).

```
paul@debian8:~$ cat /etc/network/interfaces
# This file describes the network interfaces available on your system
# and how to activate them. For more information, see interfaces(5).

# The loopback network interface
auto lo
iface lo inet loopback

auto eth0
iface eth0 inet dhcp
```

Configuring network cards for **dhcp** is good practice for clients, but servers usually require a **fixed ip address**.

### fixed ip

The screenshot below shows **/etc/network/interfaces** configured with a **fixed ip address**.

```
root@debian7~# cat /etc/network/interfaces
auto lo
iface lo inet loopback

auto  eth0
iface eth0 inet static
address   10.42.189.198
broadcast 10.42.189.207
netmask   255.255.255.240
gateway   10.42.189.193
```

The screenshot above also shows that you can provide more configuration than just the ip address. See **interfaces(5)** for help on setting a **gateway**, **netmask** or any of the other options.

## 2.2.2. /sbin/ifdown

It is adviced (but not mandatory) to down an interface before changing its configuration. This can be done with the **ifdown** command.

The command will not give any output when downing an interface with a fixed ip address. However **ifconfig** will no longer show the interface.

```
root@ubu1104srv:~# ifdown eth0
root@ubu1104srv:~# ifconfig
lo    Link encap:Local Loopback
      inet addr:127.0.0.1  Mask:255.0.0.0
      inet6 addr: ::1/128 Scope:Host
      UP LOOPBACK RUNNING  MTU:16436  Metric:1
      RX packets:106 errors:0 dropped:0 overruns:0 frame:0
      TX packets:106 errors:0 dropped:0 overruns:0 carrier:0
      collisions:0 txqueuelen:0
      RX bytes:11162 (11.1 KB)  TX bytes:11162 (11.1 KB)
```

An interface that is down cannot be used to connect to the network.

## 2.2.3. /sbin/ifup

Below a screenshot of **ifup** bringing the **eth0** ethernet interface up using dhcp. (Note that this is a Ubuntu 10.10 screenshot, Ubuntu 11.04 omits **ifup** output by default.)

```
root@ubu1010srv:/etc/network# ifup eth0
Internet Systems Consortium DHCP Client V3.1.3
Copyright 2004-2009 Internet Systems Consortium.
All rights reserved.
For info, please visit https://www.isc.org/software/dhcp/

Listening on LPF/eth0/08:00:27:cd:7f:fc
Sending on   LPF/eth0/08:00:27:cd:7f:fc
Sending on   Socket/fallback
DHCPREQUEST of 192.168.1.34 on eth0 to 255.255.255.255 port 67
DHCPNAK from 192.168.33.100
DHCPDISCOVER on eth0 to 255.255.255.255 port 67 interval 3
DHCPOFFER of 192.168.33.77 from 192.168.33.100
DHCPREQUEST of 192.168.33.77 on eth0 to 255.255.255.255 port 67
DHCPACK of 192.168.33.77 from 192.168.33.100
bound to 192.168.33.77 -- renewal in 95 seconds.
ssh stop/waiting
ssh start/running, process 1301
root@ubu1010srv:/etc/network#
```

The details of **dhcp** are covered in a separate chapter in the **Linux Servers** course.

# 2.3. RHEL nic configuration

## 2.3.1. /etc/sysconfig/network

The **/etc/sysconfig/network** file is a global (across all network cards) configuration file. It allows us to define whether we want networking (NETWORKING=yes|no), what the hostname should be (HOSTNAME=) and which gateway to use (GATEWAY=).

```
[root@rhel6 ~]# cat /etc/sysconfig/network
NETWORKING=yes
HOSTNAME=rhel6
GATEWAY=192.168.1.1
```

There are a dozen more options settable in this file, details can be found in **/usr/share/doc/ initscripts-*/sysconfig.txt**.

Note that this file contains no settings at all in a default RHEL7 install (with networking enabled).

```
[root@rhel71 ~]# cat /etc/sysconfig/network
# Created by anaconda
```

## 2.3.2. /etc/sysconfig/network-scripts/ifcfg-

Each network card can be configured individually using the **/etc/sysconfig/network-scripts/ ifcfg-*** files. When you have only one network card, then this will probably be **/etc/ sysconfig/network-scripts/ifcfg-eth0**.

### dhcp client

Below a screenshot of **/etc/sysconfig/network-scripts/ifcfg-eth0** configured for dhcp (BOOTPROTO="dhcp"). Note also the NM_CONTROLLED paramater to disable control of this nic by **Network Manager**. This parameter is not explained (not even mentioned) in **/usr/share/doc/initscripts-*/sysconfig.txt**, but many others are.

```
[root@rhel6 ~]# cat /etc/sysconfig/network-scripts/ifcfg-eth0
DEVICE="eth0"
HWADDR="08:00:27:DD:0D:5C"
NM_CONTROLLED="no"
BOOTPROTO="dhcp"
ONBOOT="yes"
```

The BOOTPROTO variable can be set to either **dhcp** or **bootp**, anything else will be considered **static** meaning there should be no protocol used at boot time to set the interface values.

RHEL7 adds **ipv6** variables to this file.

```
[root@rhel71 network-scripts]# cat ifcfg-enp0s3
TYPE="Ethernet"
BOOTPROTO="dhcp"
DEFROUTE="yes"
PEERDNS="yes"
PEERROUTES="yes"
IPV4_FAILURE_FATAL="no"
```

```
IPV6INIT="yes"
IPV6_AUTOCONF="yes"
IPV6_DEFROUTE="yes"
IPV6_PEERDNS="yes"
IPV6_PEERROUTES="yes"
IPV6_FAILURE_FATAL="no"
NAME="enp0s3"
UUID="9fa6a83a-2f8e-4ecc-962c-5f614605f4ee"
DEVICE="enp0s3"
ONBOOT="yes"
[root@rhel71 network-scripts]#
```

## fixed ip

Below a screenshot of a **fixed ip** configuration in **/etc/sysconfig/network-scripts/ifcfg-eth0**.

```
[root@rhel6 ~]# cat /etc/sysconfig/network-scripts/ifcfg-eth0
DEVICE="eth0"
HWADDR="08:00:27:DD:0D:5C"
NM_CONTROLLED="no"
BOOTPROTO="none"
IPADDR="192.168.1.99"
NETMASK="255.255.255.0"
GATEWAY="192.168.1.1"
ONBOOT="yes"
```

The HWADDR can be used to make sure that each network card gets the correct name when multiple network cards are present in the computer. It can not be used to assign a **mac address** to a network card. For this, you need to specify the MACADDR variable. Do not use HWADDR and MACADDR in the same **ifcfg-ethx** file.

The BROADCAST= and NETWORK= parameters from previous RHEL/Fedora versions are obsoleted.

# 2.3.3. nmcli

On RHEL7 you should run **nmcli connection reload** if you changed configuration files in **/etc/sysconfig/** to enable your changes.

The **nmcli** tool has many options to configure networking on the command line in RHEL7/CentOS7

```
man nmcli
```

# 2.3.4. nmtui

Another recommendation for RHEL7/CentOS7 is to use **nmtui**. This tool will use a 'windowed' interface in command line to manage network interfaces.

```
nmtui
```

## 2.3.5. /sbin/ifup and /sbin/ifdown

The **ifup** and **ifdown** commands will set an interface up or down, using the configuration discussed above. This is identical to their behaviour in Debian and Ubuntu.

```
[root@rhel6 ~]# ifdown eth0 && ifup eth0
[root@rhel6 ~]# ifconfig eth0
eth0 Link encap:Ethernet  HWaddr 08:00:27:DD:0D:5C
     inet addr:192.168.1.99  Bcast:192.168.1.255  Mask:255.255.255.0
     inet6 addr: fe80::a00:27ff:fedd:d5c/64 Scope:Link
     UP BROADCAST RUNNING MULTICAST  MTU:1500  Metric:1
     RX packets:2452 errors:0 dropped:0 overruns:0 frame:0
     TX packets:1881 errors:0 dropped:0 overruns:0 carrier:0
     collisions:0 txqueuelen:1000
     RX bytes:257036 (251.0 KiB)  TX bytes:184767 (180.4 KiB)
```

# 2.4. ifconfig

The use of **/sbin/ifconfig** without any arguments will present you with a list of all active network interface cards, including wireless and the loopback interface. In the screenshot below **eth0** has no ip address.

```
root@ubu1010:~# ifconfig
eth0 Link encap:Ethernet  HWaddr 00:26:bb:5d:2e:52
     UP BROADCAST MULTICAST  MTU:1500  Metric:1
     RX packets:0 errors:0 dropped:0 overruns:0 frame:0
     TX packets:0 errors:0 dropped:0 overruns:0 carrier:0
     collisions:0 txqueuelen:1000
     RX bytes:0 (0.0 B)  TX bytes:0 (0.0 B)
     Interrupt:43 Base address:0xe000

eth1 Link encap:Ethernet  HWaddr 00:26:bb:12:7a:5e
     inet addr:192.168.1.30  Bcast:192.168.1.255  Mask:255.255.255.0
     inet6 addr: fe80::226:bbff:fe12:7a5e/64 Scope:Link
     UP BROADCAST RUNNING MULTICAST  MTU:1500  Metric:1
     RX packets:11141791 errors:202 dropped:0 overruns:0 frame:11580126
     TX packets:6473056 errors:3860 dropped:0 overruns:0 carrier:0
     collisions:0 txqueuelen:1000
     RX bytes:3476531617 (3.4 GB)  TX bytes:2114919475 (2.1 GB)
     Interrupt:23

lo   Link encap:Local Loopback
     inet addr:127.0.0.1  Mask:255.0.0.0
     inet6 addr: ::1/128 Scope:Host
     UP LOOPBACK RUNNING  MTU:16436  Metric:1
     RX packets:2879 errors:0 dropped:0 overruns:0 frame:0
     TX packets:2879 errors:0 dropped:0 overruns:0 carrier:0
     collisions:0 txqueuelen:0
     RX bytes:486510 (486.5 KB)  TX bytes:486510 (486.5 KB)
```

You can also use **ifconfig** to obtain information about just one network card.

```
[root@rhel6 ~]# ifconfig eth0
eth0 Link encap:Ethernet  HWaddr 08:00:27:DD:0D:5C
     inet addr:192.168.1.99  Bcast:192.168.1.255  Mask:255.255.255.0
     inet6 addr: fe80::a00:27ff:fedd:d5c/64 Scope:Link
     UP BROADCAST RUNNING MULTICAST  MTU:1500  Metric:1
     RX packets:2969 errors:0 dropped:0 overruns:0 frame:0
     TX packets:1918 errors:0 dropped:0 overruns:0 carrier:0
     collisions:0 txqueuelen:1000
```

```
         RX bytes:335942 (328.0 KiB)  TX bytes:190157 (185.7 KiB)
```

When **/sbin** is not in the **$PATH** of a normal user you will have to type the full path, as seen here on Debian.

```
paul@debian5:~$ /sbin/ifconfig eth3
eth3 Link encap:Ethernet  HWaddr 08:00:27:ab:67:30
      inet addr:192.168.1.29  Bcast:192.168.1.255  Mask:255.255.255.0
      inet6 addr: fe80::a00:27ff:feab:6730/64 Scope:Link
      UP BROADCAST RUNNING MULTICAST  MTU:1500  Metric:1
      RX packets:27155 errors:0 dropped:0 overruns:0 frame:0
      TX packets:30527 errors:0 dropped:0 overruns:0 carrier:0
      collisions:0 txqueuelen:1000
      RX bytes:13095386 (12.4 MiB)  TX bytes:25767221 (24.5 MiB)
```

## 2.4.1. up and down

You can also use **ifconfig** to bring an interface up or down. The difference with **ifup** is that **ifconfig eth0 up** will re-activate the nic keeping its existing (current) configuration, whereas **ifup** will read the correct file that contains a (possibly new) configuration and use this config file to bring the interface up.

```
[root@rhel6 ~]# ifconfig eth0 down
[root@rhel6 ~]# ifconfig eth0 up
[root@rhel6 ~]# ifconfig eth0
eth0 Link encap:Ethernet  HWaddr 08:00:27:DD:0D:5C
      inet addr:192.168.1.99  Bcast:192.168.1.255  Mask:255.255.255.0
      inet6 addr: fe80::a00:27ff:fedd:d5c/64 Scope:Link
      UP BROADCAST RUNNING MULTICAST  MTU:1500  Metric:1
      RX packets:2995 errors:0 dropped:0 overruns:0 frame:0
      TX packets:1927 errors:0 dropped:0 overruns:0 carrier:0
      collisions:0 txqueuelen:1000
      RX bytes:339030 (331.0 KiB)  TX bytes:191583 (187.0 KiB)
```

## 2.4.2. setting ip address

You can **temporary** set an ip address with **ifconfig**. This ip address is only valid until the next **ifup/ifdown** cycle or until the next **reboot**.

```
[root@rhel6 ~]# ifconfig eth0 | grep 192
      inet addr:192.168.1.99  Bcast:192.168.1.255  Mask:255.255.255.0
[root@rhel6 ~]# ifconfig eth0 192.168.33.42 netmask 255.255.0.0
[root@rhel6 ~]# ifconfig eth0 | grep 192
      inet addr:192.168.33.42  Bcast:192.168.255.255  Mask:255.255.0.0
[root@rhel6 ~]# ifdown eth0 && ifup eth0
[root@rhel6 ~]# ifconfig eth0 | grep 192
      inet addr:192.168.1.99  Bcast:192.168.1.255  Mask:255.255.255.0
```

## 2.4.3. setting mac address

You can also use **ifconfig** to set another **mac address** than the one hard coded in the network card. This screenshot shows you how.

```
[root@rhel6 ~]# ifconfig eth0 | grep HWaddr
eth0 Link encap:Ethernet  HWaddr 08:00:27:DD:0D:5C
[root@rhel6 ~]# ifconfig eth0 hw ether 00:42:42:42:42:42
[root@rhel6 ~]# ifconfig eth0 | grep HWaddr
eth0 Link encap:Ethernet  HWaddr 00:42:42:42:42:42
```

# 2.5. ip

The **ifconfig** tool is deprecated on some systems. Use the **ip** tool instead.

To see ip addresses on RHEL7 for example, use this command:

```
[root@rhel71 ~]# ip a
1: lo: <LOOPBACK,UP,LOWER_UP> mtu 65536 qdisc noqueue state UNKNOWN
    link/loopback 00:00:00:00:00:00 brd 00:00:00:00:00:00
    inet 127.0.0.1/8 scope host lo
       valid_lft forever preferred_lft forever
    inet6 ::1/128 scope host
       valid_lft forever preferred_lft forever
2: enp0s3: <BROADCAST,MULTICAST,UP,LOWER_UP> mtu 1500 qdisc pfifo_fast state UP qlen 1000
    link/ether 08:00:27:89:22:33 brd ff:ff:ff:ff:ff:ff
    inet 192.168.1.135/24 brd 192.168.1.255 scope global dynamic enp0s3
       valid_lft 6173sec preferred_lft 6173sec
    inet6 fe80::a00:27ff:fe89:2233/64 scope link
       valid_lft forever preferred_lft forever
[root@rhel71 ~]#
```

# 2.6. dhclient

Home and client Linux desktops often have **/sbin/dhclient** running. This is a daemon that enables a network interface to lease an ip configuration from a **dhcp server**. When your adapter is configured for **dhcp** or **bootp**, then **/sbin/ifup** will start the **dhclient** daemon.

When a lease is renewed, **dhclient** will override your **ifconfig** set ip address!

# 2.7. hostname

Every host receives a **hostname**, often placed in a **DNS name space** forming the **fqdn** or Fully Qualified Domain Name.

This screenshot shows the **hostname** command and the configuration of the hostname on Red Hat/Fedora.

```
[root@rhel6 ~]# grep HOSTNAME /etc/sysconfig/network
HOSTNAME=rhel6
[root@rhel6 ~]# hostname
rhel6
```

Starting with RHEL7/CentOS7 this file is empty. The hostname is configured in the standard **/etc/hostname** file.

```
[root@rhel71 ~]# cat /etc/hostname
rhel71.linux-training.be
[root@rhel71 ~]#
```

Ubuntu/Debian uses the **/etc/hostname** file to configure the **hostname**.

```
paul@debian8:~$ cat /etc/hostname
server42
paul@debian8:~$ hostname
server42
```

On all Linux distributions you can change the **hostname** using the **hostname $newname** command. This is not a permanent change.

```
[root@rhel6 ~]# hostname server42
[root@rhel6 ~]# hostname
server42
```

On any Linux you can use **sysctl** to display and set the hostname.

```
[root@rhel6 ~]# sysctl kernel.hostname
kernel.hostname = server42
[root@rhel6 ~]# sysctl kernel.hostname=rhel6
kernel.hostname = rhel6
[root@rhel6 ~]# sysctl kernel.hostname
kernel.hostname = rhel6
[root@rhel6 ~]# hostname
rhel6
```

# 2.8. arp

The **ip to mac** resolution is handled by the **layer two broadcast** protocol **arp**. The **arp table** can be displayed with the **arp tool**. The screenshot below shows the list of computers that this computer recently communicated with.

```
root@barry:~# arp -a
? (192.168.1.191) at 00:0C:29:3B:15:80 [ether] on eth1
agapi (192.168.1.73) at 00:03:BA:09:7F:D2 [ether] on eth1
anya (192.168.1.1) at 00:12:01:E2:87:FB [ether] on eth1
faith (192.168.1.41) at 00:0E:7F:41:0D:EB [ether] on eth1
kiss (192.168.1.49) at 00:D0:E0:91:79:95 [ether] on eth1
laika (192.168.1.40) at 00:90:F5:4E:AE:17 [ether] on eth1
pasha (192.168.1.71) at 00:03:BA:02:C3:82 [ether] on eth1
shaka (192.168.1.72) at 00:03:BA:09:7C:F9 [ether] on eth1
root@barry:~#
```

*Anya is a Cisco Firewall, faith is a laser printer, kiss is a Kiss DP600, laika is a laptop and Agapi, Shaka and Pasha are SPARC servers. The question mark is a Red Hat Enterprise Linux server running on a virtual machine.*

You can use **arp -d** to remove an entry from the **arp table**.

```
[root@rhel6 ~]# arp
Address              HWtype  HWaddress           Flags Mask      Iface
ubu1010              ether   00:26:bb:12:7a:5e   C               eth0
anya                 ether   00:02:cf:aa:68:f0   C               eth0
[root@rhel6 ~]# arp -d anya
[root@rhel6 ~]# arp
Address              HWtype  HWaddress           Flags Mask      Iface
ubu1010              ether   00:26:bb:12:7a:5e   C               eth0
anya                         (incomplete)                        eth0
[root@rhel6 ~]# ping anya
PING anya (192.168.1.1) 56(84) bytes of data.
64 bytes from anya (192.168.1.1): icmp_seq=1 ttl=254 time=10.2 ms
...
[root@rhel6 ~]# arp
Address              HWtype  HWaddress           Flags Mask      Iface
ubu1010              ether   00:26:bb:12:7a:5e   C               eth0
anya                 ether   00:02:cf:aa:68:f0   C               eth0
```

# 2.9. route

You can see the computer's local routing table with the **/sbin/route** command (and also with **netstat -r** ).

```
root@RHEL4b ~]# netstat -r
Kernel IP routing table
Destination     Gateway     Genmask         Flags   MSS Window  irtt Iface
192.168.1.0     *           255.255.255.0   U         0 0          0 eth0
[root@RHEL4b ~]# route
Kernel IP routing table
Destination     Gateway     Genmask         Flags Metric Ref    Use Iface
192.168.1.0     *           255.255.255.0   U     0      0        0 eth0
[root@RHEL4b ~]#
```

It appears this computer does not have a **gateway** configured, so we use **route add default gw** to add a **default gateway** on the fly.

```
[root@RHEL4b ~]# route add default gw 192.168.1.1
[root@RHEL4b ~]# route
Kernel IP routing table
Destination     Gateway     Genmask         Flags Metric Ref    Use Iface
192.168.1.0     *           255.255.255.0   U     0      0        0 eth0
default         192.168.1.1 0.0.0.0         UG    0      0        0 eth0
[root@RHEL4b ~]#
```

Unless you configure the gateway in one of the **/etc/** file from the start of this chapter, your computer will forget this **gateway** after a reboot.

# 2.10. ping

If you can **ping** to another host, then **tcp/ip** is configured.

```
[root@RHEL4b ~]# ping 192.168.1.5
PING 192.168.1.5 (192.168.1.5) 56(84) bytes of data.
64 bytes from 192.168.1.5: icmp_seq=0 ttl=64 time=1004 ms
64 bytes from 192.168.1.5: icmp_seq=1 ttl=64 time=1.19 ms
64 bytes from 192.168.1.5: icmp_seq=2 ttl=64 time=0.494 ms
64 bytes from 192.168.1.5: icmp_seq=3 ttl=64 time=0.419 ms

--- 192.168.1.5 ping statistics ---
4 packets transmitted, 4 received, 0% packet loss, time 3009ms
rtt min/avg/max/mdev = 0.419/251.574/1004.186/434.520 ms, pipe 2
[root@RHEL4b ~]#
```

# 2.11. optional: ethtool

To display or change network card settings, use **ethtool**. The results depend on the capabilities of your network card. The example shows a network that auto-negotiates it's bandwidth.

```
root@laika:~# ethtool eth0
Settings for eth0:
 Supported ports: [ TP ]
 Supported link modes:   10baseT/Half 10baseT/Full
                         100baseT/Half 100baseT/Full
                         1000baseT/Full
 Supports auto-negotiation: Yes
 Advertised link modes:  10baseT/Half 10baseT/Full
                         100baseT/Half 100baseT/Full
                         1000baseT/Full
 Advertised auto-negotiation: Yes
 Speed: 1000Mb/s
 Duplex: Full
 Port: Twisted Pair
 PHYAD: 0
 Transceiver: internal
 Auto-negotiation: on
 Supports Wake-on: pumbg
 Wake-on: g
 Current message level: 0x00000033 (51)
 Link detected: yes
```

This example shows how to use ethtool to switch the bandwidth from 1000Mbit to 100Mbit and back. Note that some time passes before the nic is back to 1000Mbit.

```
root@laika:~# ethtool eth0 | grep Speed
 Speed: 1000Mb/s
root@laika:~# ethtool -s eth0 speed 100
root@laika:~# ethtool eth0 | grep Speed
 Speed: 100Mb/s
root@laika:~# ethtool -s eth0 speed 1000
root@laika:~# ethtool eth0 | grep Speed
 Speed: 1000Mb/s
```

# 2.12. practice: interface configuration

1. Verify whether **dhclient** is running.

2. Display your current ip address(es).

3. Display the configuration file where this **ip address** is defined.

4. Follow the **nic configuration** in the book to change your ip address from **dhcp client** to **fixed**. Keep the same **ip address** to avoid conflicts!

5. Did you also configure the correct **gateway** in the previous question ? If not, then do this now.

6. Verify that you have a gateway.

7. Verify that you can connect to the gateway, that it is alive.

8. Change the last two digits of your **mac address**.

9. Which ports are used by http, pop3, ssh, telnet, nntp and ftp ?

10. Explain why e-mail and websites are sent over **tcp** and not **udp**.

11. Display the **hostname** of your computer.

12. Which ip-addresses did your computer recently have contact with ?

# 2.13. solution: interface configuration

1. Verify whether **dhclient** is running.

```
paul@debian5:~$ ps fax | grep dhclient
```

2. Display your current ip address(es).

```
paul@debian5:~$ /sbin/ifconfig | grep 'inet '
      inet addr:192.168.1.31  Bcast:192.168.1.255  Mask:255.255.255.0
      inet addr:127.0.0.1  Mask:255.0.0.0
```

3. Display the configuration file where this **ip address** is defined.

```
Ubuntu/Debian: cat /etc/network/interfaces
Redhat/Fedora: cat /etc/sysconfig/network-scripts/ifcfg-eth*
```

4. Follow the **nic configuration** in the book to change your ip address from **dhcp client** to **fixed**. Keep the same **ip address** to avoid conflicts!

```
Ubuntu/Debian:
ifdown eth0
vi /etc/network/interfaces
ifup eth0

Redhat/Fedora:
ifdown eth0
vi /etc/sysconfig/network-scripts/ifcfg-eth0
ifup eth0
```

5. Did you also configure the correct **gateway** in the previous question ? If not, then do this now.

6. Verify that you have a gateway.

```
paul@debian5:~$ /sbin/route
Kernel IP routing table
Destination    Gateway        Genmask        Flags Metric Ref  Use Iface
192.168.1.0    *              255.255.255.0  U     0      0     0 eth0
default        192.168.1.1    0.0.0.0        UG    0      0     0 eth0
```

7. Verify that you can connect to the gateway, that it is alive.

```
paul@debian5:~$ ping -c3 192.168.1.1
PING 192.168.1.1 (192.168.1.1) 56(84) bytes of data.
64 bytes from 192.168.1.1: icmp_seq=1 ttl=254 time=2.28 ms
64 bytes from 192.168.1.1: icmp_seq=2 ttl=254 time=2.94 ms
64 bytes from 192.168.1.1: icmp_seq=3 ttl=254 time=2.34 ms

--- 192.168.1.1 ping statistics ---
3 packets transmitted, 3 received, 0% packet loss, time 2008ms
rtt min/avg/max/mdev = 2.283/2.524/2.941/0.296 ms
```

8. Change the last two digits of your **mac address**.

```
[root@rhel6 ~]# ifconfig eth0 hw ether 08:00:27:ab:67:XX
```

9. Which ports are used by http, pop3, ssh, telnet, nntp and ftp ?

```
root@rhel6 ~# grep ^'http ' /etc/services
```

```
http          80/tcp          www www-http     # WorldWideWeb HTTP
http          80/udp          www www-http     # HyperText Transfer Protocol
root@rhel6 ~# grep ^'smtp ' /etc/services
smtp          25/tcp          mail
smtp          25/udp          mail
root@rhel6 ~# grep ^'ssh ' /etc/services
ssh           22/tcp                           # The Secure Shell (SSH) Protocol
ssh           22/udp                           # The Secure Shell (SSH) Protocol
root@rhel6 ~# grep ^'telnet ' /etc/services
telnet        23/tcp
telnet        23/udp
root@rhel6 ~# grep ^'nntp ' /etc/services
nntp          119/tcp         readnews untp    # USENET News Transfer Protocol
nntp          119/udp         readnews untp    # USENET News Transfer Protocol
root@rhel6 ~# grep ^'ftp ' /etc/services
ftp           21/tcp
ftp           21/udp          fsp fspd
```

10. Explain why e-mail and websites are sent over **tcp** and not **udp**.

```
Because tcp is reliable and udp is not.
```

11. Display the **hostname** of your computer.

```
paul@debian5:~$ hostname
debian5
```

12. Which ip-addresses did your computer recently have contact with ?

```
root@rhel6 ~# arp -a
? (192.168.1.1) at 00:02:cf:aa:68:f0 [ether] on eth2
? (192.168.1.30) at 00:26:bb:12:7a:5e [ether] on eth2
? (192.168.1.31) at 08:00:27:8e:8a:a8 [ether] on eth2
```

# Chapter 3. network sniffing

A network administrator should be able to use a sniffer like **wireshark** or **tcpdump** to troubleshoot network problems.

A student should often use a sniffer to learn about networking. This chapter introduces you to **network sniffing**.

# 3.1. wireshark

## 3.1.1. installing wireshark

This example shows how to install **wireshark** on **.deb** based distributions (including Debian, Mint, Xubuntu, and others).

```
root@debian8:~# apt-get install wireshark
Reading package lists... Done
Building dependency tree
Reading state information... Done
... (output truncated)
```

On **.rpm** based distributions like CentOS, RHEL and Fedora you can use **yum** to install **wireshark**.

```
[root@centos7 ~]# yum install wireshark
Loaded plugins: fastestmirror
Loading mirror speeds from cached hostfile
... (output truncated)
```

## 3.1.2. selecting interface

When you start **wireshark** for the first time, you will need to select an interface. You will see a dialog box that looks similar to this one.

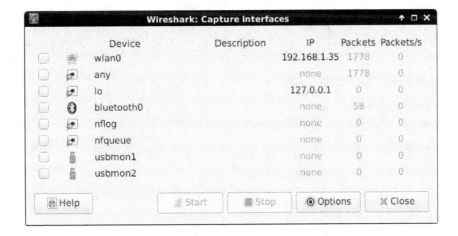

It is possible that there are no interfaces available because some distributions only allow root to sniff the network. You may need to use **sudo wireshark**.

Or you can follow the general advice to sniff using **tcpdump** or any other tool, and save the capture to a file. Any saved capture can be analyzed using **wireshark** at a later time.

## 3.1.3. minimize traffic

Sniffing a network can generate many thousands of packets in a very short time. This can be overwhelming. Try to mitigate by isolating your sniffer on the network. Preferably sniff an isolated virtual network interface over which you control all traffic.

If you are at home to learn sniffing, then it could help to close all network programs on your computer, and disconnect other computers and devices like smartphones and tablets to minimize the traffic.

Even more important than this is the use of **filters** which will be discussed in this chapter.

## 3.1.4. sniffing ping

I started the sniffer and captured all packets while doing these three **ping** commands (there is no need for root to do this):

```
root@debian7:~# ping -c2 ns1.paul.local
PING ns1.paul.local (10.104.33.30) 56(84) bytes of data.
64 bytes from 10.104.33.30: icmp_req=1 ttl=64 time=0.010 ms
64 bytes from 10.104.33.30: icmp_req=2 ttl=64 time=0.023 ms

--- ns1.paul.local ping statistics ---
2 packets transmitted, 2 received, 0% packet loss, time 1001ms
rtt min/avg/max/mdev = 0.010/0.016/0.023/0.007 ms
root@debian7:~# ping -c3 linux-training.be
PING linux-training.be (188.93.155.87) 56(84) bytes of data.
64 bytes from antares.ginsys.net (188.93.155.87): icmp_req=1 ttl=56 time=15.6 ms
64 bytes from antares.ginsys.net (188.93.155.87): icmp_req=2 ttl=56 time=17.8 ms
64 bytes from antares.ginsys.net (188.93.155.87): icmp_req=3 ttl=56 time=14.7 ms

--- linux-training.be ping statistics ---
3 packets transmitted, 3 received, 0% packet loss, time 2003ms
rtt min/avg/max/mdev = 14.756/16.110/17.881/1.309 ms
root@debian7:~# ping -c1 centos7.paul.local
PING centos7.paul.local (10.104.33.31) 56(84) bytes of data.
64 bytes from 10.104.33.31: icmp_req=1 ttl=64 time=0.590 ms

--- centos7.paul.local ping statistics ---
1 packets transmitted, 1 received, 0% packet loss, time 0ms
rtt min/avg/max/mdev = 0.590/0.590/0.590/0.000 ms
```

In total more than 200 packets were sniffed from the network. Things become clearer when you enter **icmp** in the filter field and press the **apply** button.

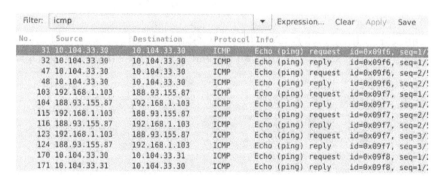

## 3.1.5. sniffing ping and dns

Using the same capture as before, but now with a different **filter**. We want to see both **dns** and **icmp** traffic, so we enter both in the filter field.

We put **dns or icmp** in the filter to achieve this. Putting **dns and icmp** would render nothing because there is no packet that matches both protocols.

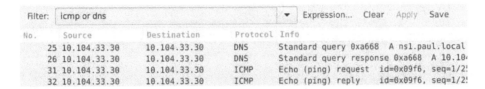

In the screenshot above you can see that packets 25 and 26 both have 10.104.33.30 as **source** and **destination** ip address. That is because the dns client is the same computer as the dns server.

The same is true for packets 31 and 32, since the machine is actually pinging itself.

## 3.1.6. specific ip address

This is a screenshot that filters for **dns** packets that contain a certain **ip address**. The filter in use is **ip.addr==10.104.33.30 and dns**. The **and** directive forces each displayed packet to match both conditions.

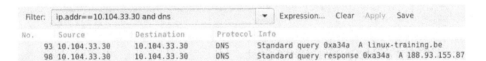

Packet 93 is the **dns query** for the A record of linux-training.be. Packet 98 is the response from the **dns server**. What do you think happened in the packets between 93 and 98 ? Try to answer this before reading on (it always helps to try to predict what you will see, and then checking your prediction).

## 3.1.7. filtering by frame

The correct technical term for a **packet** as sniffed is a **frame** (because we sniff on layer two). So to display packets with certain numbers, we use **frame.number** in the filter.

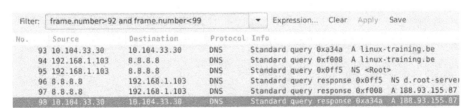

## 3.1.8. looking inside packets

The middle pane can be expanded. When selecting a line in this pane, you can see the corresponding bytes in the frame in the bottom panel.

This screenshot shows the middle pane with the source address of my laptop selected.

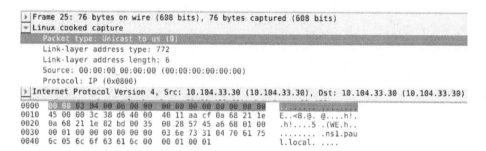

Note that the above works fine when sniffing one interface. When sniffing with for example **tcpdump -i any** you will end up with **Linux cooked** at this level.

## 3.1.9. other filter examples

You can combine two protocols with a logical **or** between them. The example below shows how to filter only **arp** and **bootp** (or **dhcp**) packets.

This example shows how to filter for **dns** traffic containing a certain **ip address**.

# 3.2. tcpdump

Sniffing on the command line can be done with **tcpdump**. Here are some examples.

Using the **tcpdump host $ip** command displays all traffic with one host (192.168.1.38 in this example).

```
root@ubuntu910:~# tcpdump host 192.168.1.38
tcpdump: verbose output suppressed, use -v or -vv for full protocol decode
listening on eth0, link-type EN10MB (Ethernet), capture size 96 bytes
```

Capturing only ssh (tcp port 22) traffic can be done with **tcpdump tcp port $port**. This screenshot is cropped to 76 characters for readability in the pdf.

```
root@deb503:~# tcpdump tcp port 22
tcpdump: verbose output suppressed, use -v or -vv for full protocol decode
listening on eth1, link-type EN10MB (Ethernet), capture size 96 bytes
14:22:20.716313 IP deb503.local.37973 > rhel53.local.ssh: P 666050963:66605
14:22:20.719936 IP rhel53.local.ssh > deb503.local.37973: P 1:49(48) ack 48
14:22:20.720922 IP rhel53.local.ssh > deb503.local.37973: P 49:113(64) ack
14:22:20.721321 IP rhel53.local.ssh > deb503.local.37973: P 113:161(48) ack
14:22:20.721820 IP deb503.local.37973 > rhel53.local.ssh: . ack 161 win 200
14:22:20.722492 IP rhel53.local.ssh > deb503.local.37973: P 161:225(64) ack
14:22:20.760602 IP deb503.local.37973 > rhel53.local.ssh: . ack 225 win 200
14:22:23.108106 IP deb503.local.54424 > ubuntu910.local.ssh: P 467252637:46
14:22:23.116804 IP ubuntu910.local.ssh > deb503.local.54424: P 1:81(80) ack
14:22:23.116844 IP deb503.local.54424 > ubuntu910.local.ssh: . ack 81 win 2
^C
10 packets captured
10 packets received by filter
0 packets dropped by kernel
```

Same as above, but write the output to a file with the **tcpdump -w $filename** command.

```
root@ubuntu910:~# tcpdump -w sshdump.tcpdump tcp port 22
tcpdump: listening on eth0, link-type EN10MB (Ethernet), capture size 96 bytes
^C
17 packets captured
17 packets received by filter
0 packets dropped by kernel
```

With **tcpdump -r $filename** the file created above can be displayed.

```
root@ubuntu910:~# tcpdump -r sshdump.tcpdump
```

Many more examples can be found in the manual page of **tcpdump**.

# 3.3. practice: network sniffing

1. Install wireshark on your computer (not inside a virtual machine).

2. Start a ping between your computer and another computer.

3. Start sniffing the network.

4. Display only the ping echo's in the top pane using a filter.

5. Now ping to a name (like www.linux-training.be) and try to sniff the DNS query and response. Which DNS server was used ? Was it a tcp or udp query and response ?

6. Find an amateur/hobby/club website that features a login prompt. Attempt to login with user 'paul' and password 'hunter2' while your sniffer is running. Now find this information in the sniffer.

# 3.4. solution: network sniffing

1. Install wireshark on your computer (not inside a virtual machine).

```
Debian/Ubuntu: aptitude install wireshark
```

```
Red Hat/Mandriva/Fedora: yum install wireshark
```

2. Start a ping between your computer and another computer.

```
ping $ip_address
```

3. Start sniffing the network.

```
(sudo) wireshark
```

```
select an interface (probably eth0)
```

4. Display only the ping echo's in the top pane using a filter.

```
type 'icmp' (without quotes) in the filter box, and then click 'apply'
```

5. Now ping to a name (like www.linux-training.be) and try to sniff the DNS query and response. Which DNS server was used ? Was it a tcp or udp query and response ?

```
First start the sniffer.
```

```
Enter 'dns' in the filter box and click apply.
```

```
root@ubuntu910:~# ping www.linux-training.be
PING www.linux-training.be (88.151.243.8) 56(84) bytes of data.
64 bytes from fosfor.openminds.be (88.151.243.8): icmp_seq=1 ttl=58 time=14.9 ms
64 bytes from fosfor.openminds.be (88.151.243.8): icmp_seq=2 ttl=58 time=16.0 ms
^C
--- www.linux-training.be ping statistics ---
2 packets transmitted, 2 received, 0% packet loss, time 1002ms
rtt min/avg/max/mdev = 14.984/15.539/16.095/0.569 ms
```

The wireshark screen should look something like this.

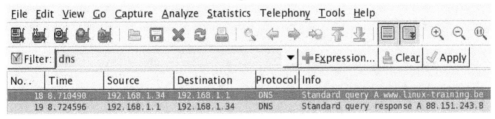

The details in wireshark will say the DNS query was inside a udp packet.

6. Find an amateur/hobby/club website that features a login prompt. Attempt to login with user 'paul' and password 'hunter2' while your sniffer is running. Now find this information in the sniffer.

# Chapter 4. binding and bonding

Sometimes a server needs more than one **ip address** on the same network card, we call this **binding** ip addresses.

Linux can also activate multiple network cards behind the same **ip address**, this is called **bonding**.

This chapter will teach you how to configure **binding** and **bonding** on the most common Linux distributions.

# 4.1. binding on Redhat/Fedora

## 4.1.1. binding extra ip addresses

To bind more than one **ip address** to the same interface, use **ifcfg-eth0:0**, where the last zero can be anything else. Only two directives are required in the files.

```
[root@rhel6 ~]# cat /etc/sysconfig/network-scripts/ifcfg-eth0:0
DEVICE="eth0:0"
IPADDR="192.168.1.133"
[root@rhel6 ~]# cat /etc/sysconfig/network-scripts/ifcfg-eth0:1
DEVICE="eth0:0"
IPADDR="192.168.1.142"
```

## 4.1.2. enabling extra ip-addresses

To activate a virtual network interface, use **ifup**, to deactivate it, use **ifdown**.

```
[root@rhel6 ~]# ifup eth0:0
[root@rhel6 ~]# ifconfig | grep 'inet '
          inet addr:192.168.1.99  Bcast:192.168.1.255  Mask:255.255.255.0
          inet addr:192.168.1.133  Bcast:192.168.1.255  Mask:255.255.255.0
          inet addr:127.0.0.1  Mask:255.0.0.0
[root@rhel6 ~]# ifup eth0:1
[root@rhel6 ~]# ifconfig | grep 'inet '
          inet addr:192.168.1.99  Bcast:192.168.1.255  Mask:255.255.255.0
          inet addr:192.168.1.133  Bcast:192.168.1.255  Mask:255.255.255.0
          inet addr:192.168.1.142  Bcast:192.168.1.255  Mask:255.255.255.0
          inet addr:127.0.0.1  Mask:255.0.0.0
```

## 4.1.3. verifying extra ip-addresses

Use **ping** from another computer to check the activation, or use **ifconfig** like in this screenshot.

```
[root@rhel6 ~]# ifconfig
eth0    Link encap:Ethernet  HWaddr 08:00:27:DD:0D:5C
        inet addr:192.168.1.99  Bcast:192.168.1.255  Mask:255.255.255.0
        inet6 addr: fe80::a00:27ff:fedd:d5c/64 Scope:Link
        UP BROADCAST RUNNING MULTICAST  MTU:1500  Metric:1
        RX packets:1259 errors:0 dropped:0 overruns:0 frame:0
        TX packets:545 errors:0 dropped:0 overruns:0 carrier:0
        collisions:0 txqueuelen:1000
        RX bytes:115260 (112.5 KiB)  TX bytes:84293 (82.3 KiB)

eth0:0 Link encap:Ethernet  HWaddr 08:00:27:DD:0D:5C
        inet addr:192.168.1.133  Bcast:192.168.1.255  Mask:255.255.255.0
        UP BROADCAST RUNNING MULTICAST  MTU:1500  Metric:1

eth0:1 Link encap:Ethernet  HWaddr 08:00:27:DD:0D:5C
        inet addr:192.168.1.142  Bcast:192.168.1.255  Mask:255.255.255.0
        UP BROADCAST RUNNING MULTICAST  MTU:1500  Metric:1
```

# 4.2. binding on Debian/Ubuntu

## 4.2.1. binding extra ip addresses

The configuration of multiple ip addresses on the same network card is done in **/etc/network/ interfaces** by adding **eth0:x** devices. Adding the **netmask** is mandatory.

```
debian5:~# cat /etc/network/interfaces
# This file describes the network interfaces available on your system
# and how to activate them. For more information, see interfaces(5).

# The loopback network interface
auto lo
iface lo inet loopback

# The primary network interface
iface eth0 inet static
address 192.168.1.34
network 192.168.1.0
netmask 255.255.255.0
gateway 192.168.1.1
auto eth0

auto eth0:0
iface eth0:0 inet static
address 192.168.1.233
netmask 255.255.255.0

auto eth0:1
iface eth0:1 inet static
address 192.168.1.242
netmask 255.255.255.0
```

## 4.2.2. enabling extra ip-addresses

Use **ifup** to enable the extra addresses.

```
debian5:~# ifup eth0:0
debian5:~# ifup eth0:1
```

## 4.2.3. verifying extra ip-addresses

Use **ping** from another computer to check the activation, or use **ifconfig** like in this screenshot.

```
debian5:~# ifconfig | grep 'inet '
      inet addr:192.168.1.34  Bcast:192.168.1.255  Mask:255.255.255.0
      inet addr:192.168.1.233  Bcast:192.168.1.255  Mask:255.255.255.0
      inet addr:192.168.1.242  Bcast:192.168.1.255  Mask:255.255.255.0
      inet addr:127.0.0.1  Mask:255.0.0.0
```

# 4.3. bonding on Redhat/Fedora

We start with **ifconfig -a** to get a list of all the network cards on our system.

```
[root@rhel6 network-scripts]# ifconfig -a | grep Ethernet
eth0      Link encap:Ethernet  HWaddr 08:00:27:DD:0D:5C
eth1      Link encap:Ethernet  HWaddr 08:00:27:DA:C1:49
eth2      Link encap:Ethernet  HWaddr 08:00:27:40:03:3B
```

In this demo we decide to bond **eth1** and **eth2**.

We will name our bond **bond0** and add this entry to **modprobe** so the kernel can load the **bonding module** when we bring the interface up.

```
[root@rhel6 network-scripts]# cat /etc/modprobe.d/bonding.conf
alias bond0 bonding
```

Then we create **/etc/sysconfig/network-scripts/ifcfg-bond0** to configure our **bond0** interface.

```
[root@rhel6 network-scripts]# pwd
/etc/sysconfig/network-scripts
[root@rhel6 network-scripts]# cat ifcfg-bond0
DEVICE=bond0
IPADDR=192.168.1.199
NETMASK=255.255.255.0
ONBOOT=yes
BOOTPROTO=none
USERCTL=no
```

Next we create two files, one for each network card that we will use as slave in **bond0**.

```
[root@rhel6 network-scripts]# cat ifcfg-eth1
DEVICE=eth1
BOOTPROTO=none
ONBOOT=yes
MASTER=bond0
SLAVE=yes
USERCTL=no
[root@rhel6 network-scripts]# cat ifcfg-eth2
DEVICE=eth2
BOOTPROTO=none
ONBOOT=yes
MASTER=bond0
SLAVE=yes
USERCTL=no
```

Finally we bring the interface up with **ifup bond0**.

```
[root@rhel6 network-scripts]# ifup bond0
[root@rhel6 network-scripts]# ifconfig bond0
bond0     Link encap:Ethernet  HWaddr 08:00:27:DA:C1:49
          inet addr:192.168.1.199  Bcast:192.168.1.255  Mask:255.255.255.0
          inet6 addr: fe80::a00:27ff:feda:c149/64 Scope:Link
          UP BROADCAST RUNNING MASTER MULTICAST  MTU:1500  Metric:1
          RX packets:251 errors:0 dropped:0 overruns:0 frame:0
          TX packets:21 errors:0 dropped:0 overruns:0 carrier:0
          collisions:0 txqueuelen:0
          RX bytes:39852 (38.9 KiB)  TX bytes:1070 (1.0 KiB)
```

The **bond** should also be visible in **/proc/net/bonding**.

```
[root@rhel6 network-scripts]# cat /proc/net/bonding/bond0
Ethernet Channel Bonding Driver: v3.5.0 (November 4, 2008)

Bonding Mode: load balancing (round-robin)
MII Status: up
MII Polling Interval (ms): 0
Up Delay (ms): 0
Down Delay (ms): 0

Slave Interface: eth1
MII Status: up
Link Failure Count: 0
Permanent HW addr: 08:00:27:da:c1:49

Slave Interface: eth2
MII Status: up
Link Failure Count: 0
Permanent HW addr: 08:00:27:40:03:3b
```

# 4.4. bonding on Debian/Ubuntu

We start with **ifconfig -a** to get a list of all the network cards on our system.

```
debian5:~# ifconfig -a | grep Ethernet
eth0      Link encap:Ethernet  HWaddr 08:00:27:bb:18:a4
eth1      Link encap:Ethernet  HWaddr 08:00:27:63:9a:95
eth2      Link encap:Ethernet  HWaddr 08:00:27:27:a4:92
```

In this demo we decide to bond **eth1** and **eth2**.

We also need to install the **ifenslave** package.

```
debian5:~# aptitude search ifenslave
p ifenslave     - Attach and detach slave interfaces to a bonding device
p ifenslave-2.6 - Attach and detach slave interfaces to a bonding device
debian5:~# aptitude install ifenslave
Reading package lists... Done
...
```

Next we update the **/etc/network/interfaces** file with information about the **bond0** interface.

```
debian5:~# tail -7 /etc/network/interfaces
iface bond0 inet static
 address 192.168.1.42
 netmask 255.255.255.0
 gateway 192.168.1.1
 slaves eth1 eth2
 bond-mode active-backup
 bond_primary eth1
```

On older version of Debian/Ubuntu you needed to **modprobe bonding**, but this is no longer required. Use **ifup** to bring the interface up, then test that it works.

```
debian5:~# ifup bond0
debian5:~# ifconfig bond0
bond0     Link encap:Ethernet  HWaddr 08:00:27:63:9a:95
          inet addr:192.168.1.42  Bcast:192.168.1.255  Mask:255.255.255.0
          inet6 addr: fe80::a00:27ff:fe63:9a95/64 Scope:Link
          UP BROADCAST RUNNING MASTER MULTICAST  MTU:1500  Metric:1
          RX packets:212 errors:0 dropped:0 overruns:0 frame:0
          TX packets:39 errors:0 dropped:0 overruns:0 carrier:0
          collisions:0 txqueuelen:0
          RX bytes:31978 (31.2 KiB)  TX bytes:6709 (6.5 KiB)
```

The **bond** should also be visible in **/proc/net/bonding**.

```
debian5:~# cat /proc/net/bonding/bond0
Ethernet Channel Bonding Driver: v3.2.5 (March 21, 2008)

Bonding Mode: fault-tolerance (active-backup)
Primary Slave: eth1
Currently Active Slave: eth1
MII Status: up
MII Polling Interval (ms): 0
Up Delay (ms): 0
Down Delay (ms): 0

Slave Interface: eth1
MII Status: up
Link Failure Count: 0
```

```
Permanent HW addr: 08:00:27:63:9a:95

Slave Interface: eth2
MII Status: up
Link Failure Count: 0
Permanent HW addr: 08:00:27:27:a4:92
```

# 4.5. practice: binding and bonding

1. Add an extra **ip address** to one of your network cards. Test that it works (have your neighbour ssh to it)!

2. Use **ifdown** to disable this extra **ip address**.

3. Make sure your neighbour also succeeded in **binding** an extra ip address before you continue.

4. Add an extra network card (or two) to your virtual machine and use the theory to **bond** two network cards.

# 4.6. solution: binding and bonding

1. Add an extra **ip address** to one of your network cards. Test that it works (have your neighbour ssh to it)!

```
Redhat/Fedora:
add an /etc/sysconfig/network-scripts/ifcfg-ethX:X file
as shown in the theory

Debian/Ubuntu:
expand the /etc/network/interfaces file
as shown in the theory
```

2. Use **ifdown** to disable this extra **ip address**.

```
ifdown eth0:0
```

3. Make sure your neighbour also succeeded in **binding** an extra ip address before you continue.

```
ping $extra_ip_neighbour
or
ssh $extra_ip_neighbour
```

4. Add an extra network card (or two) to your virtual machine and use the theory to **bond** two network cards.

```
Redhat/Fedora:
add ifcfg-ethX and ifcfg-bondX files in /etc/sysconfig/network-scripts
as shown in the theory
and don't forget the modprobe.conf

Debian/Ubuntu:
expand the /etc/network/interfaces file
as shown in the theory
and don't forget to install the ifenslave package
```

# Chapter 5. ssh client and server

The **secure shell** or **ssh** is a collection of tools using a secure protocol for communications with remote Linux computers.

This chapter gives an overview of the most common commands related to the use of the **sshd** server and the **ssh** client.

# 5.1. about ssh

## 5.1.1. secure shell

Avoid using **telnet**, **rlogin** and **rsh** to remotely connect to your servers. These older protocols do not encrypt the login session, which means your user id and password can be sniffed by tools like **wireshark** or **tcpdump**. To securely connect to your servers, use **ssh**.

The **ssh protocol** is secure in two ways. Firstly the connection is **encrypted** and secondly the connection is **authenticated** both ways.

An ssh connection always starts with a cryptographic handshake, followed by **encryption** of the transport layer using a symmetric cypher. In other words, the tunnel is encrypted before you start typing anything.

Then **authentication** takes place (using user id/password or public/private keys) and communication can begin over the encrypted connection.

The **ssh protocol** will remember the servers it connected to (and warn you in case something suspicious happened).

The **openssh** package is maintained by the **OpenBSD** people and is distributed with a lot of operating systems (it may even be the most popular package in the world).

## 5.1.2. /etc/ssh/

Configuration of **ssh** client and server is done in the **/etc/ssh** directory. In the next sections we will discuss most of the files found in **/etc/ssh/**.

## 5.1.3. ssh protocol versions

The **ssh** protocol has two versions (1 and 2). Avoid using version 1 anywhere, since it contains some known vulnerabilities. You can control the protocol version via **/etc/ssh/ ssh_config** for the client side and **/etc/ssh/sshd_config** for the openssh-server daemon.

```
paul@ubu1204:/etc/ssh$ grep Protocol ssh_config
#    Protocol 2,1
paul@ubu1204:/etc/ssh$ grep Protocol sshd_config
Protocol 2
```

## 5.1.4. public and private keys

The **ssh** protocol uses the well known system of **public and private keys**. The below explanation is succinct, more information can be found on wikipedia.

```
http://en.wikipedia.org/wiki/Public-key_cryptography
```

Imagine Alice and Bob, two people that like to communicate with each other. Using **public and private keys** they can communicate with **encryption** and with **authentication**.

When Alice wants to send an encrypted message to Bob, she uses the **public key** of Bob. Bob shares his **public key** with Alice, but keeps his **private key** private! Since Bob is the only one to have Bob's **private key**, Alice is sure that Bob is the only one that can read the encrypted message.

When Bob wants to verify that the message came from Alice, Bob uses the **public key** of Alice to verify that Alice signed the message with her **private key**. Since Alice is the only one to have Alice's **private key**, Bob is sure the message came from Alice.

## 5.1.5. rsa and dsa algorithms

This chapter does not explain the technical implementation of cryptographic algorithms, it only explains how to use the ssh tools with **rsa** and **dsa**. More information about these algorithms can be found here:

```
http://en.wikipedia.org/wiki/RSA_(algorithm)
http://en.wikipedia.org/wiki/Digital_Signature_Algorithm
```

# 5.2. log on to a remote server

The following screenshot shows how to use **ssh** to log on to a remote computer running Linux. The local user is named **paul** and he is logging on as user **admin42** on the remote system.

```
paul@ubu1204:~$ ssh admin42@192.168.1.30
The authenticity of host '192.168.1.30 (192.168.1.30)' can't be established.
RSA key fingerprint is b5:fb:3c:53:50:b4:ab:81:f3:cd:2e:bb:ba:44:d3:75.
Are you sure you want to continue connecting (yes/no)?
```

As you can see, the user **paul** is presented with an **rsa** authentication fingerprint from the remote system. The user can accepts this bu typing **yes**. We will see later that an entry will be added to the **~/.ssh/known_hosts** file.

```
paul@ubu1204:~$ ssh admin42@192.168.1.30
The authenticity of host '192.168.1.30 (192.168.1.30)' can't be established.
RSA key fingerprint is b5:fb:3c:53:50:b4:ab:81:f3:cd:2e:bb:ba:44:d3:75.
Are you sure you want to continue connecting (yes/no)? yes
Warning: Permanently added '192.168.1.30' (RSA) to the list of known hosts.
admin42@192.168.1.30's password:
Welcome to Ubuntu 12.04 LTS (GNU/Linux 3.2.0-26-generic-pae i686)

 * Documentation:  https://help.ubuntu.com/

1 package can be updated.
0 updates are security updates.

Last login: Wed Jun  6 19:25:57 2012 from 172.28.0.131
admin42@ubuserver:~$
```

The user can get log out of the remote server by typing **exit** or by using **Ctrl-d**.

```
admin42@ubuserver:~$ exit
logout
Connection to 192.168.1.30 closed.
paul@ubu1204:~$
```

# 5.3. executing a command in remote

This screenshot shows how to execute the **pwd** command on the remote server. There is no need to **exit** the server manually.

```
paul@ubu1204:~$ ssh admin42@192.168.1.30 pwd
admin42@192.168.1.30's password:
/home/admin42
paul@ubu1204:~$
```

# 5.4. scp

The **scp** command works just like **cp**, but allows the source and destination of the copy to be behind **ssh**. Here is an example where we copy the **/etc/hosts** file from the remote server to the home directory of user paul.

```
paul@ubu1204:~$ scp admin42@192.168.1.30:/etc/hosts /home/paul/serverhosts
admin42@192.168.1.30's password:
hosts                                       100%  809     0.8KB/s   00:00
```

Here is an example of the reverse, copying a local file to a remote server.

```
paul@ubu1204:~$ scp ~/serverhosts admin42@192.168.1.30:/etc/hosts.new
admin42@192.168.1.30's password:
serverhosts                                 100%  809     0.8KB/s   00:00
```

# 5.5. setting up passwordless ssh

To set up passwordless ssh authentication through public/private keys, use **ssh-keygen** to generate a key pair without a passphrase, and then copy your public key to the destination server. Let's do this step by step.

In the example that follows, we will set up ssh without password between Alice and Bob. Alice has an account on a Red Hat Enterprise Linux server, Bob is using Ubuntu on his laptop. Bob wants to give Alice access using ssh and the public and private key system. This means that even if Bob changes his password on his laptop, Alice will still have access.

## 5.5.1. ssh-keygen

The example below shows how Alice uses **ssh-keygen** to generate a key pair. Alice does not enter a passphrase.

```
[alice@RHEL5 ~]$ ssh-keygen -t rsa
Generating public/private rsa key pair.
Enter file in which to save the key (/home/alice/.ssh/id_rsa):
Created directory '/home/alice/.ssh'.
Enter passphrase (empty for no passphrase):
Enter same passphrase again:
Your identification has been saved in /home/alice/.ssh/id_rsa.
Your public key has been saved in /home/alice/.ssh/id_rsa.pub.
The key fingerprint is:
9b:ac:ac:56:c2:98:e5:d9:18:c4:2a:51:72:bb:45:eb alice@RHEL5
[alice@RHEL5 ~]$
```

You can use **ssh-keygen -t dsa** in the same way.

## 5.5.2. ~/.ssh

While **ssh-keygen** generates a public and a private key, it will also create a hidden **.ssh** directory with proper permissions. If you create the **.ssh** directory manually, then you need to chmod 700 it! Otherwise ssh will refuse to use the keys (world readable private keys are not secure!).

As you can see, the **.ssh** directory is secure in Alice's home directory.

```
[alice@RHEL5 ~]$ ls -ld .ssh
drwx------ 2 alice alice 4096 May  1 07:38 .ssh
[alice@RHEL5 ~]$
```

Bob is using Ubuntu at home. He decides to manually create the **.ssh** directory, so he needs to manually secure it.

```
bob@laika:~$ mkdir .ssh
bob@laika:~$ ls -ld .ssh
drwxr-xr-x 2 bob bob 4096 2008-05-14 16:53 .ssh
bob@laika:~$ chmod 700 .ssh/
bob@laika:~$
```

## 5.5.3. id_rsa and id_rsa.pub

The **ssh-keygen** command generate two keys in .ssh. The public key is named ~/.ssh/**id_rsa.pub**. The private key is named ~/.ssh/**id_rsa**.

```
[alice@RHEL5 ~]$ ls -l .ssh/
total 16
-rw------- 1 alice alice 1671 May  1 07:38 id_rsa
-rw-r--r-- 1 alice alice  393 May  1 07:38 id_rsa.pub
```

The files will be named **id_dsa** and **id_dsa.pub** when using **dsa** instead of **rsa**.

## 5.5.4. copy the public key to the other computer

To copy the public key from Alice's server tot Bob's laptop, Alice decides to use **scp**.

```
[alice@RHEL5 .ssh]$ scp id_rsa.pub bob@192.168.48.92:~/.ssh/authorized_keys
bob@192.168.48.92's password:
id_rsa.pub                                    100%  393    0.4KB/s   00:00
```

Be careful when copying a second key! Do not overwrite the first key, instead append the key to the same ~/.**ssh/authorized_keys** file!

```
cat id_rsa.pub >> ~/.ssh/authorized_keys
```

Alice could also have used **ssh-copy-id** like in this example.

```
ssh-copy-id -i .ssh/id_rsa.pub bob@192.168.48.92
```

## 5.5.5. authorized_keys

In your ~/.ssh directory, you can create a file called **authorized_keys**. This file can contain one or more public keys from people you trust. Those trusted people can use their private keys to prove their identity and gain access to your account via ssh (without password). The example shows Bob's authorized_keys file containing the public key of Alice.

```
bob@laika:~$ cat .ssh/authorized_keys
ssh-rsa AAAAB3NzaC1yc2EAAAABIwAAAQEApCQ9xzyLzJes1sR+hPyqW2vyzt1D4zTLqk\
MDWBR4mMFuUZD/O583I3Lg/Q+JIq0RSksNzaL/BNLDou1jMpBe2Dmf/u22u4KmqlJBfDhe\
yTmGSBzeNYCYRSMq78CT919a+y6x/shucwhaILsy8A2XfJ9VCggkVtu7XlWFDL2cum08/0\
mRFwVrfc/uPsAn5XkkTscl4g21mQbnp9wJC40pGSJXXMuFOk8MgCb5ieSnpKFniAKM+tEo\
/vjDGSi3F/bxu691jscrU0VUdIoOSo98HUfEf7jKBRikxGAC7I4HLa+/zX73OIvRFAb2hv\
tUhn6RHrBtUJUjbSGiYeFTLDfcTQ== alice@RHEL5
```

## 5.5.6. passwordless ssh

Alice can now use ssh to connect passwordless to Bob's laptop. In combination with **ssh**'s capability to execute commands on the remote host, this can be useful in pipes across different machines.

```
[alice@RHEL5 ~]$ ssh bob@192.168.48.92 "ls -l .ssh"
total 4
-rw-r--r-- 1 bob bob 393 2008-05-14 17:03 authorized_keys
[alice@RHEL5 ~]$
```

# 5.6. X forwarding via ssh

Another popular feature of **ssh** is called **X11 forwarding** and is implemented with **ssh -X**.

Below an example of X forwarding: user paul logs in as user greet on her computer to start the graphical application mozilla-thunderbird. Although the application will run on the remote computer from greet, it will be displayed on the screen attached locally to paul's computer.

```
paul@debian5:~/PDF$ ssh -X greet@greet.dyndns.org -p 55555
Warning: Permanently added the RSA host key for IP address \
'81.240.174.161' to the list of known hosts.
Password:
Linux raika 2.6.8-2-686 #1 Tue Aug 16 13:22:48 UTC 2005 i686 GNU/Linux

Last login: Thu Jan 18 12:35:56 2007
greet@raika:~$ ps fax | grep thun
greet@raika:~$ mozilla-thunderbird &
[1] 30336
```

# 5.7. troubleshooting ssh

Use **ssh -v** to get debug information about the ssh connection attempt.

```
paul@debian5:~$ ssh -v bert@192.168.1.192
OpenSSH_4.3p2 Debian-8ubuntu1, OpenSSL 0.9.8c 05 Sep 2006
debug1: Reading configuration data /home/paul/.ssh/config
debug1: Reading configuration data /etc/ssh/ssh_config
debug1: Applying options for *
debug1: Connecting to 192.168.1.192 [192.168.1.192] port 22.
debug1: Connection established.
debug1: identity file /home/paul/.ssh/identity type -1
debug1: identity file /home/paul/.ssh/id_rsa type 1
debug1: identity file /home/paul/.ssh/id_dsa type -1
debug1: Remote protocol version 1.99, remote software version OpenSSH_3
debug1: match: OpenSSH_3.9p1 pat OpenSSH_3.*
debug1: Enabling compatibility mode for protocol 2.0
...
```

# 5.8. sshd

The ssh server is called **sshd** and is provided by the **openssh-server** package.

```
root@ubu1204~# dpkg -l openssh-server | tail -1
ii  openssh-server   1:5.9p1-5ubuntu1    secure shell (SSH) server,...
```

# 5.9. sshd keys

The public keys used by the sshd server are located in **/etc/ssh** and are world readable. The private keys are only readable by root.

```
root@ubu1204~# ls -l /etc/ssh/ssh_host_*
-rw-------  1 root root  668 Jun  7 2011 /etc/ssh/ssh_host_dsa_key
-rw-r--r--  1 root root  598 Jun  7 2011 /etc/ssh/ssh_host_dsa_key.pub
-rw-------  1 root root 1679 Jun  7 2011 /etc/ssh/ssh_host_rsa_key
-rw-r--r--  1 root root  390 Jun  7 2011 /etc/ssh/ssh_host_rsa_key.pub
```

# 5.10. ssh-agent

When generating keys with **ssh-keygen**, you have the option to enter a passphrase to protect access to the keys. To avoid having to type this passphrase every time, you can add the key to **ssh-agent** using **ssh-add**.

Most Linux distributions will start the **ssh-agent** automatically when you log on.

```
root@ubu1204~# ps -ef | grep ssh-agent
paul    2405 2365  0 08:13 ?        00:00:00 /usr/bin/ssh-agent...
```

This clipped screenshot shows how to use **ssh-add** to list the keys that are currently added to the **ssh-agent**

```
paul@debian5:~$ ssh-add -L
ssh-rsa AAAAB3NzaC1yc2EAAAABIwAAAQEAvgI+Vx5UrIsusZPl8da8URHGsxG7yivv3/\
...
wMGqa48Kelwom8TGb4Sgcwpp/VO/ldA5m+BGCw== paul@deb503
```

# 5.11. practice: ssh

0. Make sure that you have access to **two Linux computers,** or work together with a partner for this exercise. For this practice, we will name one of the machines the server.

1. Install **sshd** on the server

2. Verify in the ssh configuration files that only protocol version 2 is allowed.

3. Use **ssh** to log on to the server, show your current directory and then exit the server.

4. Use **scp** to copy a file from your computer to the server.

5. Use **scp** to copy a file from the server to your computer.

6. (optional, only works when you have a graphical install of Linux) Install the xeyes package on the server and use ssh to run xeyes on the server, but display it on your client.

7. (optional, same as previous) Create a bookmark in firefox, then quit firefox on client and server. Use **ssh -X** to run firefox on your display, but on your neighbour's computer. Do you see your neighbour's bookmark ?

8. Use **ssh-keygen** to create a key pair without passphrase. Setup passwordless ssh between you and your neighbour. (or between your client and your server)

9.Verify that the permissions on the server key files are correct; world readable for the public keys and only root access for the private keys.

10. Verify that the **ssh-agent** is running.

11. (optional) Protect your keypair with a **passphrase**, then add this key to the **ssh-agent** and test your passwordless ssh to the server.

# 5.12. solution: ssh

0. Make sure that you have access to **two Linux computers**, or work together with a partner for this exercise. For this practice, we will name one of the machines the server.

1. Install **sshd** on the server

```
apt-get install openssh-server (on Ubuntu/Debian)
yum -y install openssh-server (on Centos/Fedora/Red Hat)
```

2. Verify in the ssh configuration files that only protocol version 2 is allowed.

```
grep Protocol /etc/ssh/ssh*_config
```

3. Use **ssh** to log on to the server, show your current directory and then exit the server.

```
user@client$ ssh user@server-ip-address
user@server$ pwd
/home/user
user@server$ exit
```

4. Use **scp** to copy a file from your computer to the server.

```
scp localfile user@server:~
```

5. Use **scp** to copy a file from the server to your computer.

```
scp user@server:~/serverfile .
```

6. (optional, only works when you have a graphical install of Linux) Install the xeyes package on the server and use ssh to run xeyes on the server, but display it on your client.

```
on the server:
apt-get install xeyes
on the client:
ssh -X user@server-ip
xeyes
```

7. (optional, same as previous) Create a bookmark in firefox, then quit firefox on client and server. Use **ssh -X** to run firefox on your display, but on your neighbour's computer. Do you see your neighbour's bookmark ?

8. Use **ssh-keygen** to create a key pair without passphrase. Setup passwordless ssh between you and your neighbour. (or between your client and your server)

```
See solution in book "setting up passwordless ssh"
```

9. Verify that the permissions on the server key files are correct; world readable for the public keys and only root access for the private keys.

```
ls -l /etc/ssh/ssh_host_*
```

10. Verify that the **ssh-agent** is running.

```
ps fax | grep ssh-agent
```

11. (optional) Protect your keypair with a **passphrase**, then add this key to the **ssh-agent** and test your passwordless ssh to the server.

```
man ssh-keygen
man ssh-agent
man ssh-add
```

# Chapter 6. introduction to nfs

The **network file system** (or simply **nfs**) enables us since the Eighties to share a directory with other computers on the network.

In this chapter we see how to setup an **nfs** server and an **nfs** client computer.

# 6.1. nfs protocol versions

The older **nfs** versions 2 and 3 are stateless (**udp**) by default (but they can use **tcp**). The more recent **nfs version 4** brings a stateful protocol with better performance and stronger security.

NFS version 4 was defined in **rfc 3010** in 2000 and **rfc 3530** in 2003 and requires tcp (port 2049). It also supports **Kerberos** user authentication as an option when mounting a share. NFS versions 2 and 3 authenticate only the host.

# 6.2. rpcinfo

Clients connect to the server using **rpc** (on Linux this can be managed by the **portmap** daemon). Look at **rpcinfo** to verify that **nfs** and its related services are running.

```
root@RHELv4u2:~# /etc/init.d/portmap status
portmap (pid 1920) is running...
root@RHELv4u2:~# rpcinfo -p
program vers proto   port
100000    2   tcp     111  portmapper
100000    2   udp     111  portmapper
100024    1   udp   32768  status
100024    1   tcp   32769  status
root@RHELv4u2:~# service nfs start
Starting NFS services:                        [  OK  ]
Starting NFS quotas:                          [  OK  ]
Starting NFS daemon:                          [  OK  ]
Starting NFS mountd:                          [  OK  ]
```

The same **rpcinfo** command when **nfs** is started.

```
root@RHELv4u2:~# rpcinfo -p
program vers proto   port
100000    2   tcp     111  portmapper
100000    2   udp     111  portmapper
100024    1   udp   32768  status
100024    1   tcp   32769  status
100011    1   udp     985  rquotad
100011    2   udp     985  rquotad
100011    1   tcp     988  rquotad
100011    2   tcp     988  rquotad
100003    2   udp    2049  nfs
100003    3   udp    2049  nfs
100003    4   udp    2049  nfs
100003    2   tcp    2049  nfs
100003    3   tcp    2049  nfs
100003    4   tcp    2049  nfs
100021    1   udp   32770  nlockmgr
100021    3   udp   32770  nlockmgr
100021    4   udp   32770  nlockmgr
100021    1   tcp   32789  nlockmgr
100021    3   tcp   32789  nlockmgr
100021    4   tcp   32789  nlockmgr
100005    1   udp    1004  mountd
100005    1   tcp    1007  mountd
100005    2   udp    1004  mountd
100005    2   tcp    1007  mountd
100005    3   udp    1004  mountd
100005    3   tcp    1007  mountd
```

# 6.3. server configuration

**nfs** is configured in **/etc/exports**. You might want some way (**ldap**?) to synchronize userid's across computers when using **nfs** a lot.

The **rootsquash** option will change UID 0 to the UID of a **nobody** (or similar) user account. The **sync** option will write writes to disk before completing the client request.

# 6.4. /etc/exports

Here is a sample **/etc/exports** to explain the syntax:

```
paul@laika:~$ cat /etc/exports
# Everyone can read this share
/mnt/data/iso  *(ro)

# Only the computers named pasha and barry can readwrite this one
/var/www pasha(rw) barry(rw)

# same, but without root squashing for barry
/var/ftp pasha(rw) barry(rw,no_root_squash)

# everyone from the netsec.local domain gets access
/var/backup        *.netsec.local(rw)

# ro for one network, rw for the other
/var/upload   192.168.1.0/24(ro) 192.168.5.0/24(rw)
```

More recent incarnations of **nfs** require the **subtree_check** option to be explicitly set (or unset with **no_subtree_check**). The **/etc/exports** file then looks like this:

```
root@debian6 ~# cat /etc/exports
# Everyone can read this share
/srv/iso  *(ro,no_subtree_check)

# Only the computers named pasha and barry can readwrite this one
/var/www pasha(rw,no_subtree_check) barry(rw,no_subtree_check)

# same, but without root squashing for barry
/var/ftp pasha(rw,no_subtree_check) barry(rw,no_root_squash,no_subtree_check)
```

# 6.5. exportfs

You don't need to restart the nfs server to start exporting your newly created exports. You can use the **exportfs -va** command to do this. It will write the exported directories to **/var/lib/nfs/etab**, where they are immediately applied.

```
root@debian6 ~# exportfs -va
exporting pasha:/var/ftp
exporting barry:/var/ftp
exporting pasha:/var/www
exporting barry:/var/www
exporting *:/srv/iso
```

# 6.6. client configuration

We have seen the **mount** command and the **/etc/fstab** file before.

```
root@RHELv4u2:~# mount -t nfs barry:/mnt/data/iso /home/project55/
root@RHELv4u2:~# cat /etc/fstab | grep nfs
barry:/mnt/data/iso    /home/iso              nfs      defaults    0 0
root@RHELv4u2:~#
```

Here is another simple example. Suppose the project55 people tell you they only need a couple of CD-ROM images, and you already have them available on an **nfs** server. You could issue the following command to mount this storage on their **/home/project55** mount point.

```
root@RHELv4u2:~# mount -t nfs 192.168.1.40:/mnt/data/iso /home/project55/
root@RHELv4u2:~# ls -lh /home/project55/
total 3.6G
drwxr-xr-x  2 1000 1000 4.0K Jan 16 17:55 RHELv4u1
drwxr-xr-x  2 1000 1000 4.0K Jan 16 14:14 RHELv4u2
drwxr-xr-x  2 1000 1000 4.0K Jan 16 14:54 RHELv4u3
drwxr-xr-x  2 1000 1000 4.0K Jan 16 11:09 RHELv4u4
-rw-r--r--  1 root root 1.6G Oct 13 15:22 sled10-vmwarews5-vm.zip
root@RHELv4u2:~#
```

# 6.7. practice: introduction to nfs

1. Create two directories with some files. Use **nfs** to share one of them as read only, the other must be writable. Have your neighbour connect to them to test.

2. Investigate the user owner of the files created by your neighbour.

3. Protect a share by ip-address or hostname, so only your neighbour can connect.

# Chapter 7. introduction to networking

# 7.1. introduction to iptables

## 7.1.1. iptables firewall

The Linux kernel has a built-in stateful firewall named **iptables**. To stop the **iptables** firewall on Red Hat, use the service command.

```
root@RHELv4u4:~# service iptables stop
Flushing firewall rules:                              [  OK  ]
Setting chains to policy ACCEPT: filter               [  OK  ]
Unloading iptables modules:                           [  OK  ]
root@RHELv4u4:~#
```

The easy way to configure iptables, is to use a graphical tool like KDE's **kmyfirewall** or **Security Level Configuration Tool**. You can find the latter in the graphical menu, somewhere in System Tools - Security, or you can start it by typing **system-config-securitylevel** in bash. These tools allow for some basic firewall configuration. You can decide whether to enable or disable the firewall, and what typical standard ports are allowed when the firewall is active. You can even add some custom ports. When you are done, the configuration is written to **/etc/sysconfig/iptables** on Red Hat.

```
root@RHELv4u4:~# cat /etc/sysconfig/iptables
# Firewall configuration written by system-config-securitylevel
# Manual customization of this file is not recommended.
*filter
:INPUT ACCEPT [0:0]
:FORWARD ACCEPT [0:0]
:OUTPUT ACCEPT [0:0]
:RH-Firewall-1-INPUT - [0:0]
-A INPUT -j RH-Firewall-1-INPUT
-A FORWARD -j RH-Firewall-1-INPUT
-A RH-Firewall-1-INPUT -i lo -j ACCEPT
-A RH-Firewall-1-INPUT -p icmp --icmp-type any -j ACCEPT
-A RH-Firewall-1-INPUT -p 50 -j ACCEPT
-A RH-Firewall-1-INPUT -p 51 -j ACCEPT
-A RH-Firewall-1-INPUT -p udp --dport 5353 -d 224.0.0.251 -j ACCEPT
-A RH-Firewall-1-INPUT -p udp -m udp --dport 631 -j ACCEPT
-A RH-Firewall-1-INPUT -m state --state ESTABLISHED,RELATED -j ACCEPT
-A RH-F...NPUT -m state --state NEW -m tcp -p tcp --dport 22 -j ACCEPT
-A RH-F...NPUT -m state --state NEW -m tcp -p tcp --dport 80 -j ACCEPT
-A RH-F...NPUT -m state --state NEW -m tcp -p tcp --dport 21 -j ACCEPT
-A RH-F...NPUT -m state --state NEW -m tcp -p tcp --dport 25 -j ACCEPT
-A RH-Firewall-1-INPUT -j REJECT --reject-with icmp-host-prohibited
COMMIT
root@RHELv4u4:~#
```

To start the service, issue the **service iptables start** command. You can configure iptables to start at boot time with chkconfig.

```
root@RHELv4u4:~# service iptables start
Applying iptables firewall rules:                     [  OK  ]
root@RHELv4u4:~# chkconfig iptables on
root@RHELv4u4:~#
```

One of the nice features of iptables is that it displays extensive **status** information when queried with the **service iptables status** command.

```
root@RHELv4u4:~# service iptables status
Table: filter
Chain INPUT (policy ACCEPT)
target       prot opt source            destination
RH-Firewall-1-INPUT  all  --  0.0.0.0/0          0.0.0.0/0

Chain FORWARD (policy ACCEPT)
target       prot opt source            destination
RH-Firewall-1-INPUT  all  --  0.0.0.0/0          0.0.0.0/0

Chain OUTPUT (policy ACCEPT)
target       prot opt source            destination

Chain RH-Firewall-1-INPUT (2 references)
target    prot opt source        destination
ACCEPT    all  --  0.0.0.0/0     0.0.0.0/0
ACCEPT    icmp --  0.0.0.0/0     0.0.0.0/0     icmp type 255
ACCEPT    esp  --  0.0.0.0/0     0.0.0.0/0
ACCEPT    ah   --  0.0.0.0/0     0.0.0.0/0
ACCEPT    udp  --  0.0.0.0/0     224.0.0.251  udp dpt:5353
ACCEPT    udp  --  0.0.0.0/0     0.0.0.0/0     udp dpt:631
ACCEPT    all  --  0.0.0.0/0     0.0.0.0/0     state RELATED,ESTABLISHED
ACCEPT    tcp  --  0.0.0.0/0     0.0.0.0/0     state NEW tcp dpt:22
ACCEPT    tcp  --  0.0.0.0/0     0.0.0.0/0     state NEW tcp dpt:80
ACCEPT    tcp  --  0.0.0.0/0     0.0.0.0/0     state NEW tcp dpt:21
ACCEPT    tcp  --  0.0.0.0/0     0.0.0.0/0     state NEW tcp dpt:25
REJECT    all  --  0.0.0.0/0     0.0.0.0/0     reject-with icmp-host-prohibited

root@RHELv4u4:~#
```

Mastering firewall configuration requires a decent knowledge of tcp/ip. Good iptables tutorials can be found online here http://iptables-tutorial.frozentux.net/iptables-tutorial.html and here http://tldp.org/HOWTO/IP-Masquerade-HOWTO/.

# 7.2. practice : iptables

1. Verify whether the firewall is running.

2. Stop the running firewall.

# 7.3. solution : iptables

### 1. Verify whether the firewall is running.

```
root@rhel55 ~# service iptables status | head
Table: filter
Chain INPUT (policy ACCEPT)
num  target      prot opt source                destination
1    RH-Firewall-1-INPUT  all  --  0.0.0.0/0             0.0.0.0/0

Chain FORWARD (policy ACCEPT)
num  target      prot opt source                destination
1    RH-Firewall-1-INPUT  all  --  0.0.0.0/0             0.0.0.0/0

Chain OUTPUT (policy ACCEPT)
```

### 2. Stop the running firewall.

```
root@rhel55 ~# service iptables stop
Flushing firewall rules:                            [  OK  ]
Setting chains to policy ACCEPT: filter             [  OK  ]
Unloading iptables modules:                         [  OK  ]
root@rhel55 ~# service iptables status
Firewall is stopped.
```

# 7.4. xinetd and inetd

## 7.4.1. the superdaemon

Back when resources like RAM memory were limited, a super-server was devised to listen to all sockets and start the appropriate daemon only when needed. Services like **swat**, **telnet** and **ftp** are typically served by such a super-server. The **xinetd** superdaemon is more recent than **inetd**. We will discuss the configuration both daemons.

Recent Linux distributions like RHEL5 and Ubuntu10.04 do not activate **inetd** or **xinetd** by default, unless an application requires it.

## 7.4.2. inetd or xinetd

First verify whether your computer is running **inetd** or **xinetd**. This Debian 4.0 Etch is running **inetd**.

```
root@barry:~# ps fax | grep inet
 3870 ?        Ss     0:00 /usr/sbin/inetd
```

This Red Hat Enterprise Linux 4 update 4 is running **xinetd**.

```
[root@RHEL4b ~]# ps fax | grep inet
 3003 ?        Ss     0:00 xinetd -stayalive -pidfile /var/run/xinetd.pid
```

Both daemons have the same functionality (listening to many ports, starting other daemons when they are needed), but they have different configuration files.

## 7.4.3. xinetd superdaemon

The **xinetd** daemon is often called a superdaemon because it listens to a lot of incoming connections, and starts other daemons when they are needed. When a connection request is received, **xinetd** will first check TCP wrappers (/etc/hosts.allow and /etc/hosts.deny) and then give control of the connection to the other daemon. This superdaemon is configured through **/etc/xinetd.conf** and the files in the directory **/etc/xinetd.d**. Let's first take a look at /etc/xinetd.conf.

```
paul@RHELv4u2:~$ cat /etc/xinetd.conf
#
# Simple configuration file for xinetd
#
# Some defaults, and include /etc/xinetd.d/

defaults
{
instances               = 60
log_type                = SYSLOG authpriv
log_on_success          = HOST PID
log_on_failure          = HOST
cps                     = 25 30
```

```
}

includedir /etc/xinetd.d

paul@RHELv4u2:~$
```

According to the settings in this file, xinetd can handle 60 client requests at once. It uses the **authpriv** facility to log the host ip-address and pid of successful daemon spawns. When a service (aka protocol linked to daemon) gets more than 25 cps (connections per second), it holds subsequent requests for 30 seconds.

The directory **/etc/xinetd.d** contains more specific configuration files. Let's also take a look at one of them.

```
paul@RHELv4u2:~$ ls /etc/xinetd.d
amanda     chargen-udp echo       klogin      rexec   talk
amandaidx  cups-lpd    echo-udp   krb5-telnet rlogin  telnet
amidxtape  daytime     eklogin    kshell      rsh     tftp
auth       daytime-udp finger     ktalk       rsync   time
chargen    dbskkd-cdb  gssftp     ntalk       swat    time-udp
paul@RHELv4u2:~$ cat /etc/xinetd.d/swat
# default: off
# description: SWAT is the Samba Web Admin Tool. Use swat \
#              to configure your Samba server. To use SWAT, \
#              connect to port 901 with your favorite web browser.
service swat
{
port            = 901
socket_type     = stream
wait            = no
only_from       = 127.0.0.1
user            = root
server          = /usr/sbin/swat
log_on_failure  += USERID
disable         = yes
}
paul@RHELv4u2:~$
```

The services should be listed in the **/etc/services** file. Port determines the service port, and must be the same as the port specified in /etc/services. The **socket_type** should be set to **stream** for tcp services (and to dgram for udp). The **log_on_failure** += concats the userid to the log message formatted in /etc/xinetd.conf. The last setting **disable** can be set to yes or no. Setting this to **no** means the service is enabled!

Check the xinetd and xinetd.conf manual pages for many more configuration options.

## 7.4.4. inetd superdaemon

This superdaemon has only one configuration file **/etc/inetd.conf**. Every protocol or daemon that it is listening for, gets one line in this file.

```
root@barry:~# grep ftp /etc/inetd.conf
tftp dgram udp wait nobody /usr/sbin/tcpd /usr/sbin/in.tftpd /boot/tftp
root@barry:~#
```

You can disable a service in inetd.conf above by putting a # at the start of that line. Here an example of the disabled vmware web interface (listening on tcp port 902).

```
paul@laika:~$ grep vmware /etc/inetd.conf
#902 stream tcp nowait root /usr/sbin/vmware-authd vmware-authd
```

# 7.5. practice : inetd and xinetd

1. Verify on all systems whether they are using xinetd or inetd.

2. Look at the configuration files.

3. (If telnet is installable, then replace swat in these questions with telnet) Is swat installed ? If not, then install swat and look at the changes in the (x)inetd configuration. Is swat enabled or disabled ?

4. Disable swat, test it. Enable swat, test it.

# 7.6. network file system

## 7.6.1. protocol versions

The older **nfs** versions 2 and 3 are stateless (udp) by default, but they can use tcp. Clients connect to the server using **rpc** (on Linux this is controlled by the **portmap** daemon. Look at **rpcinfo** to verify that **nfs** and its related services are running.

```
root@RHELv4u2:~# /etc/init.d/portmap status
portmap (pid 1920) is running...
root@RHELv4u2:~# rpcinfo -p
program vers proto   port
100000    2   tcp    111  portmapper
100000    2   udp    111  portmapper
100024    1   udp  32768  status
100024    1   tcp  32769  status
root@RHELv4u2:~# service nfs start
Starting NFS services:                            [  OK  ]
Starting NFS quotas:                              [  OK  ]
Starting NFS daemon:                              [  OK  ]
Starting NFS mountd:                              [  OK  ]
```

The same **rpcinfo** command when **nfs** is started.

```
root@RHELv4u2:~# rpcinfo -p
program vers proto   port
100000    2   tcp    111  portmapper
100000    2   udp    111  portmapper
100024    1   udp  32768  status
100024    1   tcp  32769  status
100011    1   udp    985  rquotad
100011    2   udp    985  rquotad
100011    1   tcp    988  rquotad
100011    2   tcp    988  rquotad
100003    2   udp   2049  nfs
100003    3   udp   2049  nfs
100003    4   udp   2049  nfs
100003    2   tcp   2049  nfs
100003    3   tcp   2049  nfs
100003    4   tcp   2049  nfs
100021    1   udp  32770  nlockmgr
100021    3   udp  32770  nlockmgr
100021    4   udp  32770  nlockmgr
100021    1   tcp  32789  nlockmgr
100021    3   tcp  32789  nlockmgr
100021    4   tcp  32789  nlockmgr
100005    1   udp   1004  mountd
100005    1   tcp   1007  mountd
100005    2   udp   1004  mountd
100005    2   tcp   1007  mountd
100005    3   udp   1004  mountd
100005    3   tcp   1007  mountd
root@RHELv4u2:~#
```

**nfs version 4** requires tcp (port 2049) and supports **Kerberos** user authentication as an option. **nfs** authentication only takes place when mounting the share. **nfs** versions 2 and 3 authenticate only the host.

## 7.6.2. server configuration

**nfs** is configured in **/etc/exports**. Here is a sample **/etc/exports** to explain the syntax. You need some way (NIS domain or LDAP) to synchronize userid's across computers when using **nfs** a lot. The **rootsquash** option will change UID 0 to the UID of the nfsnobody user account. The **sync** option will write writes to disk before completing the client request.

```
paul@laika:~$ cat /etc/exports
# Everyone can read this share
/mnt/data/iso  *(ro)

# Only the computers barry and pasha can readwrite this one
/var/www pasha(rw) barry(rw)

# same, but without root squashing for barry
/var/ftp pasha(rw) barry(rw,no_root_squash)

# everyone from the netsec.lan domain gets access
/var/backup      *.netsec.lan(rw)

# ro for one network, rw for the other
/var/upload   192.168.1.0/24(ro) 192.168.5.0/24(rw)
```

You don't need to restart the nfs server to start exporting your newly created exports. You can use the **exportfs -va** command to do this. It will write the exported directories to **/var/lib/nfs/etab**, where they are immediately applied.

## 7.6.3. client configuration

We have seen the **mount** command and the **/etc/fstab** file before.

```
root@RHELv4u2:~# mount -t nfs barry:/mnt/data/iso /home/project55/
root@RHELv4u2:~# cat /etc/fstab | grep nfs
barry:/mnt/data/iso   /home/iso              nfs     defaults    0 0
root@RHELv4u2:~#
```

Here is another simple example. Suppose the project55 people tell you they only need a couple of CD-ROM images, and you already have them available on an **nfs** server. You could issue the following command to mount this storage on their **/home/project55** mount point.

```
root@RHELv4u2:~# mount -t nfs 192.168.1.40:/mnt/data/iso /home/project55/
root@RHELv4u2:~# ls -lh /home/project55/
total 3.6G
drwxr-xr-x  2 1000 1000 4.0K Jan 16 17:55 RHELv4u1
drwxr-xr-x  2 1000 1000 4.0K Jan 16 14:14 RHELv4u2
drwxr-xr-x  2 1000 1000 4.0K Jan 16 14:54 RHELv4u3
drwxr-xr-x  2 1000 1000 4.0K Jan 16 11:09 RHELv4u4
-rw-r--r--  1 root root 1.6G Oct 13 15:22 sled10-vmwarews5-vm.zip
root@RHELv4u2:~#
```

# 7.7. practice : network file system

1. Create two directories with some files. Use **nfs** to share one of them as read only, the other must be writable. Have your neighbour connect to them to test.

2. Investigate the user owner of the files created by your neighbour.

3. Protect a share by ip-address or hostname, so only your neighbour can connect.

# Part II. apache and squid

# Table of Contents

# Chapter 8. apache web server

In this chapter we learn how to setup a web server with the **apache** software.

According to NetCraft (http://news.netcraft.com/archives/web_server_survey.html) about seventy percent of all web servers are running on Apache. The name is derived from **a patchy** web server, because of all the patches people wrote for the NCSA httpd server.

Later chapters will expand this web server into a LAMP stack (Linux, Apache, Mysql, Perl/PHP/Python).

# 8.1. introduction to apache

## 8.1.1. installing on Debian

This screenshot shows that there is no **apache** server installed, nor does the **/var/www** directory exist.

```
root@debian7:~# ls -l /var/www
ls: cannot access /var/www: No such file or directory
root@debian7:~# dpkg -l | grep apache
```

To install **apache** on Debian:

```
root@debian7:~# aptitude install apache2
The following NEW packages will be installed:
  apache2 apache2-mpm-worker{a} apache2-utils{a} apache2.2-bin{a} apache2.2-com\
mon{a} libapr1{a} libaprutil1{a} libaprutil1-dbd-sqlite3{a} libaprutil1-ldap{a}\
 ssl-cert{a}
0 packages upgraded, 10 newly installed, 0 to remove and 0 not upgraded.
Need to get 1,487 kB of archives. After unpacking 5,673 kB will be used.
Do you want to continue? [Y/n/?]
```

After installation, the same two commands as above will yield a different result:

```
root@debian7:~# ls -l /var/www
total 4
-rw-r--r-- 1 root root 177 Apr 29 11:55 index.html
root@debian7:~# dpkg -l | grep apache | tr -s ' '
ii apache2 2.2.22-13+deb7u1 amd64 Apache HTTP Server metapackage
ii apache2-mpm-worker 2.2.22-13+deb7u1 amd64 Apache HTTP Server - high speed th\
readed model
ii apache2-utils 2.2.22-13+deb7u1 amd64 utility programs for webservers
ii apache2.2-bin 2.2.22-13+deb7u1 amd64 Apache HTTP Server common binary files
ii apache2.2-common 2.2.22-13+deb7u1 amd64 Apache HTTP Server common files
```

## 8.1.2. installing on RHEL/CentOS

Note that Red Hat derived distributions use **httpd** as package and process name instead of **apache**.

To verify whether **apache** is installed in CentOS/RHEL:

```
[root@centos65 ~]# rpm -q httpd
package httpd is not installed
[root@centos65 ~]# ls -l /var/www
ls: cannot access /var/www: No such file or directory
```

To install apache on CentOS:

```
[root@centos65 ~]# yum install httpd
```

After running the **yum install httpd** command, the Centos 6.5 server has apache installed and the **/var/www** directory exists.

```
[root@centos65 ~]# rpm -q httpd
httpd-2.2.15-30.el6.centos.x86_64
[root@centos65 ~]# ls -l /var/www
total 16
drwxr-xr-x. 2 root root 4096 Apr  3 23:57 cgi-bin
drwxr-xr-x. 3 root root 4096 May  6 13:08 error
drwxr-xr-x. 2 root root 4096 Apr  3 23:57 html
drwxr-xr-x. 3 root root 4096 May  6 13:08 icons
[root@centos65 ~]#
```

## 8.1.3. running apache on Debian

This is how you start **apache2** on Debian.

```
root@debian7:~# service apache2 status
Apache2 is NOT running.
root@debian7:~# service apache2 start
Starting web server: apache2apache2: Could not reliably determine the server's \
fully qualified domain name, using 127.0.1.1 for ServerName
.
```

To verify, run the **service apache2 status** command again or use **ps**.

```
root@debian7:~# service apache2 status
Apache2 is running (pid 3680).
root@debian7:~# ps -C apache2
  PID TTY          TIME CMD
 3680 ?        00:00:00 apache2
 3683 ?        00:00:00 apache2
 3684 ?        00:00:00 apache2
 3685 ?        00:00:00 apache2
root@debian7:~#
```

Or use **wget** and **file** to verify that your web server serves an html document.

```
root@debian7:~# wget 127.0.0.1
--2014-05-06 13:27:02--  http://127.0.0.1/
Connecting to 127.0.0.1:80... connected.
HTTP request sent, awaiting response... 200 OK
Length: 177 [text/html]
Saving to: `index.html'

100%[=====================================================>] 177     --.-K/s   in 0s

2014-05-06 13:27:02 (15.8 MB/s) - `index.html' saved [177/177]

root@debian7:~# file index.html
index.html: HTML document, ASCII text
root@debian7:~#
```

Or verify that apache is running by opening a web browser, and browse to the ip-address of your server. An Apache test page should be shown.

You can do the following to quickly avoid the 'could not reliably determine the fqdn' message when restarting apache.

```
root@debian7:~# echo ServerName Debian7 >> /etc/apache2/apache2.conf
root@debian7:~# service apache2 restart
Restarting web server: apache2 ... waiting .
root@debian7:~#
```

## 8.1.4. running apache on CentOS

Starting the **httpd** on RHEL/CentOS is done with the **service** command.

```
[root@centos65 ~]# service httpd status
httpd is stopped
[root@centos65 ~]# service httpd start
Starting httpd: httpd: Could not reliably determine the server's fully qualifie\
d domain name, using 127.0.0.1 for ServerName
                                                        [  OK  ]
[root@centos65 ~]#
```

To verify that **apache** is running, use **ps** or issue the **service httpd status** command again.

```
[root@centos65 ~]# service httpd status
httpd (pid  2410) is running...
[root@centos65 ~]# ps -C httpd
  PID TTY          TIME CMD
 2410 ?        00:00:00 httpd
 2412 ?        00:00:00 httpd
 2413 ?        00:00:00 httpd
 2414 ?        00:00:00 httpd
 2415 ?        00:00:00 httpd
 2416 ?        00:00:00 httpd
 2417 ?        00:00:00 httpd
 2418 ?        00:00:00 httpd
 2419 ?        00:00:00 httpd
[root@centos65 ~]#
```

To prevent the 'Could not reliably determine the fqdn' message, issue the following command.

```
[root@centos65 ~]# echo ServerName Centos65 >> /etc/httpd/conf/httpd.conf
[root@centos65 ~]# service httpd restart
Stopping httpd:                                         [  OK  ]
Starting httpd:                                         [  OK  ]
[root@centos65 ~]#
```

## 8.1.5. index file on CentOS

CentOS does not provide a standard index.html or index.php file. A simple **wget** gives an error.

```
[root@centos65 ~]# wget 127.0.0.1
--2014-05-06 15:10:22--  http://127.0.0.1/
Connecting to 127.0.0.1:80... connected.
HTTP request sent, awaiting response... 403 Forbidden
2014-05-06 15:10:22 ERROR 403: Forbidden.
```

Instead when visiting the ip-address of your server in a web browser you get a **noindex.html** page. You can verify this using **wget**.

```
[root@centos65 ~]# wget http://127.0.0.1/error/noindex.html
--2014-05-06 15:16:05--  http://127.0.0.1/error/noindex.html
Connecting to 127.0.0.1:80... connected.
HTTP request sent, awaiting response... 200 OK
Length: 5039 (4.9K) [text/html]
Saving to: "noindex.html"

100%[===========================================>] 5,039        --.-K/s   in 0s

2014-05-06 15:16:05 (289 MB/s) - "noindex.html" saved [5039/5039]

[root@centos65 ~]# file noindex.html
noindex.html: HTML document text
[root@centos65 ~]#
```

Any custom **index.html** file in **/var/www/html** will immediately serve as an index for this web server.

```
[root@centos65 ~]# echo 'Welcome to my website' > /var/www/html/index.html
[root@centos65 ~]# wget http://127.0.0.1
--2014-05-06 15:19:16--  http://127.0.0.1/
Connecting to 127.0.0.1:80... connected.
HTTP request sent, awaiting response... 200 OK
Length: 22 [text/html]
Saving to: "index.html"

100%[===========================================>] 22           --.-K/s   in 0s

2014-05-06 15:19:16 (1.95 MB/s) - "index.html" saved [22/22]

[root@centos65 ~]# cat index.html
Welcome to my website
```

# 8.1.6. default website

Changing the default website of a freshly installed apache web server is easy. All you need to do is create (or change) an index.html file in the DocumentRoot directory.

To locate the DocumentRoot directory on Debian:

```
root@debian7:~# grep DocumentRoot /etc/apache2/sites-available/default
        DocumentRoot /var/www
```

This means that **/var/www/index.html** is the default web site.

```
root@debian7:~# cat /var/www/index.html
<html><body><h1>It works!</h1>
<p>This is the default web page for this server.</p>
<p>The web server software is running but no content has been added, yet.</p>
</body></html>
root@debian7:~#
```

This screenshot shows how to locate the **DocumentRoot** directory on RHEL/CentOS.

```
[root@centos65 ~]# grep ^DocumentRoot /etc/httpd/conf/httpd.conf
DocumentRoot "/var/www/html"
```

RHEL/CentOS have no default web page (only the noindex.html error page mentioned before). But an **index.html** file created in **/var/www/html/** will automatically be used as default page.

```
[root@centos65 ~]# echo '<html><head><title>Default website</title></head><body\
><p>A new web page</p></body></html>' > /var/www/html/index.html
[root@centos65 ~]# cat /var/www/html/index.html
<html><head><title>Default website</title></head><body><p>A new web page</p></b\
ody></html>
[root@centos65 ~]#
```

## 8.1.7. apache configuration

There are many similarities, but also a couple of differences when configuring **apache** on Debian or on CentOS. Both Linux families will get their own chapters with examples.

All configuration on RHEL/CentOS is done in **/etc/httpd**.

```
[root@centos65 ~]# ls -l /etc/httpd/
total 8
drwxr-xr-x. 2 root root 4096 May  6 13:08 conf
drwxr-xr-x. 2 root root 4096 May  6 13:08 conf.d
lrwxrwxrwx. 1 root root   19 May  6 13:08 logs -> ../../var/log/httpd
lrwxrwxrwx. 1 root root   29 May  6 13:08 modules -> ../../usr/lib64/httpd/modu\
les
lrwxrwxrwx. 1 root root   19 May  6 13:08 run -> ../../var/run/httpd
[root@centos65 ~]#
```

Debian (and ubuntu/mint/...) use **/etc/apache2**.

```
root@debian7:~# ls -l /etc/apache2/
total 72
-rw-r--r-- 1 root root  9659 May  6 14:23 apache2.conf
drwxr-xr-x 2 root root  4096 May  6 13:19 conf.d
-rw-r--r-- 1 root root  1465 Jan 31 18:35 envvars
-rw-r--r-- 1 root root 31063 Jul 20  2013 magic
drwxr-xr-x 2 root root  4096 May  6 13:19 mods-available
drwxr-xr-x 2 root root  4096 May  6 13:19 mods-enabled
-rw-r--r-- 1 root root   750 Jan 26 12:13 ports.conf
drwxr-xr-x 2 root root  4096 May  6 13:19 sites-available
drwxr-xr-x 2 root root  4096 May  6 13:19 sites-enabled
root@debian7:~#
```

# 8.2. port virtual hosts on Debian

## 8.2.1. default virtual host

Debian has a virtualhost configuration file for its default website in **/etc/apache2/sites-available/default**.

```
root@debian7:~# head -2 /etc/apache2/sites-available/default
<VirtualHost *:80>
        ServerAdmin webmaster@localhost
```

## 8.2.2. three extra virtual hosts

In this scenario we create three additional websites for three customers that share a clubhouse and want to jointly hire you. They are a model train club named **Choo Choo**, a chess club named **Chess Club 42** and a hackerspace named **hunter2**.

One way to put three websites on one web server, is to put each website on a different port. This screenshot shows three newly created **virtual hosts**, one for each customer.

```
root@debian7:~# vi /etc/apache2/sites-available/choochoo
root@debian7:~# cat /etc/apache2/sites-available/choochoo
<VirtualHost *:7000>
        ServerAdmin webmaster@localhost
        DocumentRoot /var/www/choochoo
</VirtualHost>
root@debian7:~# vi /etc/apache2/sites-available/chessclub42
root@debian7:~# cat /etc/apache2/sites-available/chessclub42
<VirtualHost *:8000>
        ServerAdmin webmaster@localhost
        DocumentRoot /var/www/chessclub42
</VirtualHost>
root@debian7:~# vi /etc/apache2/sites-available/hunter2
root@debian7:~# cat /etc/apache2/sites-available/hunter2
<VirtualHost *:9000>
        ServerAdmin webmaster@localhost
        DocumentRoot /var/www/hunter2
</VirtualHost>
```

Notice the different port numbers 7000, 8000 and 9000. Notice also that we specified a unique **DocumentRoot** for each website.

Are you using **Ubuntu** or **Mint**, then these configfiles need to end in **.conf**.

## 8.2.3. three extra ports

We need to enable these three ports on apache in the **ports.conf** file. Open this file with **vi** and add three lines to **listen** on three extra ports.

```
root@debian7:~# vi /etc/apache2/ports.conf
```

Verify with **grep** that the **Listen** directives are added correctly.

```
root@debian7:~# grep ^Listen /etc/apache2/ports.conf
Listen 80
Listen 7000
Listen 8000
Listen 9000
```

## 8.2.4. three extra websites

Next we need to create three **DocumentRoot** directories.

```
root@debian7:~# mkdir /var/www/choochoo
root@debian7:~# mkdir /var/www/chessclub42
root@debian7:~# mkdir /var/www/hunter2
```

And we have to put some really simple website in those directories.

```
root@debian7:~# echo 'Choo Choo model train Choo Choo' > /var/www/choochoo/inde\
x.html
root@debian7:~# echo 'Welcome to chess club 42' > /var/www/chessclub42/index.ht\
ml
root@debian7:~# echo 'HaCkInG iS fUn At HuNtEr2' > /var/www/hunter2/index.html
```

# 8.2.5. enabling extra websites

The last step is to enable the websites with the **a2ensite** command. This command will create links in **sites-enabled**.

The links are not there yet...

```
root@debian7:~# cd /etc/apache2/
root@debian7:/etc/apache2# ls sites-available/
chessclub42  choochoo  default  default-ssl  hunter2
root@debian7:/etc/apache2# ls sites-enabled/
000-default
```

So we run the **a2ensite** command for all websites.

```
root@debian7:/etc/apache2# a2ensite choochoo
Enabling site choochoo.
To activate the new configuration, you need to run:
  service apache2 reload
root@debian7:/etc/apache2# a2ensite chessclub42
Enabling site chessclub42.
To activate the new configuration, you need to run:
  service apache2 reload
root@debian7:/etc/apache2# a2ensite hunter2
Enabling site hunter2.
To activate the new configuration, you need to run:
  service apache2 reload
```

The links are created, so we can tell **apache**.

```
root@debian7:/etc/apache2# ls sites-enabled/
000-default  chessclub42  choochoo  hunter2
root@debian7:/etc/apache2# service apache2 reload
Reloading web server config: apache2.
root@debian7:/etc/apache2#
```

## 8.2.6. testing the three websites

Testing the model train club named **Choo Choo** on port 7000.

```
root@debian7:/etc/apache2# wget 127.0.0.1:7000
--2014-05-06 21:16:03--  http://127.0.0.1:7000/
Connecting to 127.0.0.1:7000... connected.
HTTP request sent, awaiting response... 200 OK
Length: 32 [text/html]
Saving to: `index.html'

100%[===============================================>] 32          --.-K/s   in 0s

2014-05-06 21:16:03 (2.92 MB/s) - `index.html' saved [32/32]

root@debian7:/etc/apache2# cat index.html
Choo Choo model train Choo Choo
```

Testing the chess club named **Chess Club 42** on port 8000.

```
root@debian7:/etc/apache2# wget 127.0.0.1:8000
--2014-05-06 21:16:20--  http://127.0.0.1:8000/
Connecting to 127.0.0.1:8000... connected.
HTTP request sent, awaiting response... 200 OK
Length: 25 [text/html]
Saving to: `index.html.1'

100%[===============================================>] 25          --.-K/s   in 0s

2014-05-06 21:16:20 (2.16 MB/s) - `index.html.1' saved [25/25]

root@debian7:/etc/apache2# cat index.html.1
Welcome to chess club 42
```

Testing the hacker club named **hunter2** on port 9000.

```
root@debian7:/etc/apache2# wget 127.0.0.1:9000
--2014-05-06 21:16:30--  http://127.0.0.1:9000/
Connecting to 127.0.0.1:9000... connected.
HTTP request sent, awaiting response... 200 OK
Length: 26 [text/html]
Saving to: `index.html.2'

100%[===============================================>] 26          --.-K/s   in 0s

2014-05-06 21:16:30 (2.01 MB/s) - `index.html.2' saved [26/26]

root@debian7:/etc/apache2# cat index.html.2
HaCkInG iS fUn At HuNtEr2
```

Cleaning up the temporary files.

```
root@debian7:/etc/apache2# rm index.html index.html.1 index.html.2
```

Try testing from another computer using the ip-address of your server.

# 8.3. named virtual hosts on Debian

## 8.3.1. named virtual hosts

The chess club and the model train club find the port numbers too hard to remember. They would prefere to have their website accessible by name.

We continue work on the same server that has three websites on three ports. We need to make sure those websites are accesible using the names **choochoo.local**, **chessclub42.local** and **hunter2.local**.

We start by creating three new virtualhosts.

```
root@debian7:/etc/apache2/sites-available# vi choochoo.local
root@debian7:/etc/apache2/sites-available# vi chessclub42.local
root@debian7:/etc/apache2/sites-available# vi hunter2.local
root@debian7:/etc/apache2/sites-available# cat choochoo.local
<VirtualHost *:80>
        ServerAdmin webmaster@localhost
        ServerName choochoo.local
        DocumentRoot /var/www/choochoo
</VirtualHost>
root@debian7:/etc/apache2/sites-available# cat chessclub42.local
<VirtualHost *:80>
        ServerAdmin webmaster@localhost
        ServerName chessclub42.local
        DocumentRoot /var/www/chessclub42
</VirtualHost>
root@debian7:/etc/apache2/sites-available# cat hunter2.local
<VirtualHost *:80>
        ServerAdmin webmaster@localhost
        ServerName hunter2.local
        DocumentRoot /var/www/hunter2
</VirtualHost>
root@debian7:/etc/apache2/sites-available#
```

Notice that they all listen on **port 80** and have an extra **ServerName** directive.

## 8.3.2. name resolution

We need some way to resolve names. This can be done with DNS, which is discussed in another chapter. For this demo it is also possible to quickly add the three names to the /etc/ hosts file.

```
root@debian7:/etc/apache2/sites-available# grep ^192 /etc/hosts
192.168.42.50 choochoo.local
192.168.42.50 chessclub42.local
192.168.42.50 hunter2.local
```

Note that you may have another ip address...

## 8.3.3. enabling virtual hosts

Next we enable them with **a2ensite**.

```
root@debian7:/etc/apache2/sites-available# a2ensite choochoo.local
Enabling site choochoo.local.
To activate the new configuration, you need to run:
  service apache2 reload
root@debian7:/etc/apache2/sites-available# a2ensite chessclub42.local
Enabling site chessclub42.local.
To activate the new configuration, you need to run:
  service apache2 reload
root@debian7:/etc/apache2/sites-available# a2ensite hunter2.local
Enabling site hunter2.local.
To activate the new configuration, you need to run:
  service apache2 reload
```

## 8.3.4. reload and verify

After a **service apache2 reload** the websites should be available by name.

```
root@debian7:/etc/apache2/sites-available# service apache2 reload
Reloading web server config: apache2.
root@debian7:/etc/apache2/sites-available# wget chessclub42.local
--2014-05-06 21:37:13--  http://chessclub42.local/
Resolving chessclub42.local (chessclub42.local)... 192.168.42.50
Connecting to chessclub42.local (chessclub42.local)|192.168.42.50|:80... conne\
cted.
HTTP request sent, awaiting response... 200 OK
Length: 25 [text/html]
Saving to: `index.html'

100%[=============================================>] 25          --.-K/s   in 0s

2014-05-06 21:37:13 (2.06 MB/s) - `index.html' saved [25/25]

root@debian7:/etc/apache2/sites-available# cat index.html
Welcome to chess club 42
```

# 8.4. password protected website on Debian

You can secure files and directories in your website with a **.htaccess** file that refers to a **.htpasswd** file. The **htpasswd** command can create a **.htpasswd** file that contains a userid and an (encrypted) password.

This screenshot creates a user and password for the hacker named **cliff** and uses the **-c** flag to create the **.htpasswd** file.

```
root@debian7:~# htpasswd -c /var/www/.htpasswd cliff
New password:
Re-type new password:
Adding password for user cliff
root@debian7:~# cat /var/www/.htpasswd
cliff:$apr1$vujll0KL$./SZ4w9q0swhX93pQ0PVp.
```

Hacker **rob** also wants access, this screenshot shows how to add a second user and password to **.htpasswd**.

```
root@debian7:~# htpasswd /var/www/.htpasswd rob
New password:
Re-type new password:
Adding password for user rob
root@debian7:~# cat /var/www/.htpasswd
cliff:$apr1$vujll0KL$./SZ4w9q0swhX93pQ0PVp.
rob:$apr1$HNln1FFt$nRlpF0H.IW11/1DRq41Qo0
```

Both Cliff and Rob chose the same password (hunter2), but that is not visible in the **.htpasswd** file because of the different salts.

Next we need to create a **.htaccess** file in the **DocumentRoot** of the website we want to protect. This screenshot shows an example.

```
root@debian7:~# cd /var/www/hunter2/
root@debian7:/var/www/hunter2# cat .htaccess
AuthUserFile /var/www/.htpasswd
AuthName "Members only!"
AuthType Basic
require valid-user
```

Note that we are protecting the website on **port 9000** that we created earlier.

And because we put the website for the Hackerspace named hunter2 in a subdirectory of the default website, we will need to adjust the **AllowOvveride** parameter in **/etc/apache2/sites-available/default** as this screenshot shows (with line numbers on Debian7, your may vary).

```
9        <Directory /var/www/>
10              Options Indexes FollowSymLinks MultiViews
11              AllowOverride Authconfig
12              Order allow,deny
13              allow from all
14       </Directory>
```

Now restart the apache2 server and test that it works!

# 8.5. port virtual hosts on CentOS

## 8.5.1. default virtual host

Unlike Debian, CentOS has no virtualHost configuration file for its default website. Instead the default configuration will throw a standard error page when no index file can be found in the default location (/var/www/html).

## 8.5.2. three extra virtual hosts

In this scenario we create three additional websites for three customers that share a clubhouse and want to jointly hire you. They are a model train club named **Choo Choo**, a chess club named **Chess Club 42** and a hackerspace named **hunter2**.

One way to put three websites on one web server, is to put each website on a different port. This screenshot shows three newly created **virtual hosts**, one for each customer.

```
[root@CentOS65 ~]# vi /etc/httpd/conf.d/choochoo.conf
[root@CentOS65 ~]# cat /etc/httpd/conf.d/choochoo.conf
<VirtualHost *:7000>
        ServerAdmin webmaster@localhost
        DocumentRoot /var/www/html/choochoo
</VirtualHost>
[root@CentOS65 ~]# vi /etc/httpd/conf.d/chessclub42.conf
[root@CentOS65 ~]# cat /etc/httpd/conf.d/chessclub42.conf
<VirtualHost *:8000>
        ServerAdmin webmaster@localhost
        DocumentRoot /var/www/html/chessclub42
</VirtualHost>
[root@CentOS65 ~]# vi /etc/httpd/conf.d/hunter2.conf
[root@CentOS65 ~]# cat /etc/httpd/conf.d/hunter2.conf
<VirtualHost *:9000>
        ServerAdmin webmaster@localhost
        DocumentRoot /var/www/html/hunter2
</VirtualHost>
```

Notice the different port numbers 7000, 8000 and 9000. Notice also that we specified a unique **DocumentRoot** for each website.

## 8.5.3. three extra ports

We need to enable these three ports on apache in the **httpd.conf** file.

```
[root@CentOS65 ~]# vi /etc/httpd/conf/httpd.conf
root@debian7:~# grep ^Listen /etc/httpd/conf/httpd.conf
Listen 80
Listen 7000
Listen 8000
Listen 9000
```

## 8.5.4. SELinux guards our ports

If we try to restart our server, we will notice the following error:

```
[root@CentOS65 ~]# service httpd restart
Stopping httpd:                                          [  OK  ]
Starting httpd:
      (13)Permission denied: make_sock: could not bind to address 0.0.0.0:7000
no listening sockets available, shutting down
                                                         [FAILED]
```

This is due to SELinux reserving ports 7000 and 8000 for other uses. We need to tell SELinux we want to use these ports for http traffic

```
[root@CentOS65 ~]# semanage port -m -t http_port_t -p tcp 7000
[root@CentOS65 ~]# semanage port -m -t http_port_t -p tcp 8000
[root@CentOS65 ~]# service httpd restart
Stopping httpd:                                          [  OK  ]
Starting httpd:                                          [  OK  ]
```

## 8.5.5. three extra websites

Next we need to create three **DocumentRoot** directories.

```
[root@CentOS65 ~]# mkdir /var/www/html/choochoo
[root@CentOS65 ~]# mkdir /var/www/html/chessclub42
[root@CentOS65 ~]# mkdir /var/www/html/hunter2
```

And we have to put some really simple website in those directories.

```
[root@CentOS65 ~]# echo 'Choo Choo model train Choo Choo' > /var/www/html/chooc\
hoo/index.html
[root@CentOS65 ~]# echo 'Welcome to chess club 42' > /var/www/html/chessclub42/\
index.html
[root@CentOS65 ~]# echo 'HaCkInG iS fUn At HuNtEr2' > /var/www/html/hunter2/ind\
ex.html
```

## 8.5.6. enabling extra websites

The only way to enable or disable configurations in RHEL/CentOS is by renaming or moving the configuration files. Any file in /etc/httpd/conf.d ending on .conf will be loaded by Apache. To disable a site we can either rename the file or move it to another directory.

The files are created, so we can tell **apache**.

```
[root@CentOS65 ~]# ls /etc/httpd/conf.d/
chessclub42.conf  choochoo.conf  hunter2.conf  README  welcome.conf
[root@CentOS65 ~]# service httpd reload
Reloading httpd:
```

# 8.5.7. testing the three websites

Testing the model train club named **Choo Choo** on port 7000.

```
[root@CentOS65 ~]# wget 127.0.0.1:7000
--2014-05-11 11:59:36--  http://127.0.0.1:7000/
Connecting to 127.0.0.1:7000... connected.
HTTP request sent, awaiting response... 200 OK
Length: 32 [text/html]
Saving to: `index.html'

100%[=============================================>] 32          --.-K/s   in 0s

2014-05-11 11:59:36 (4.47 MB/s) - `index.html' saved [32/32]

[root@CentOS65 ~]# cat index.html
Choo Choo model train Choo Choo
```

Testing the chess club named **Chess Club 42** on port 8000.

```
[root@CentOS65 ~]# wget 127.0.0.1:8000
--2014-05-11 12:01:30--  http://127.0.0.1:8000/
Connecting to 127.0.0.1:8000... connected.
HTTP request sent, awaiting response... 200 OK
Length: 25 [text/html]
Saving to: `index.html.1'

100%[=============================================>] 25          --.-K/s   in 0s

2014-05-11 12:01:30 (4.25 MB/s) - `index.html.1' saved [25/25]

root@debian7:/etc/apache2# cat index.html.1
Welcome to chess club 42
```

Testing the hacker club named **hunter2** on port 9000.

```
[root@CentOS65 ~]# wget 127.0.0.1:9000
--2014-05-11 12:02:37--  http://127.0.0.1:9000/
Connecting to 127.0.0.1:9000... connected.
HTTP request sent, awaiting response... 200 OK
Length: 26 [text/html]
Saving to: `index.html.2'

100%[=============================================>] 26          --.-K/s   in 0s

2014-05-11 12:02:37 (4.49 MB/s) - `index.html.2' saved [26/26]

root@debian7:/etc/apache2# cat index.html.2
HaCkInG iS fUn At HuNtEr2
```

Cleaning up the temporary files.

```
[root@CentOS65 ~]# rm index.html index.html.1 index.html.2
```

## 8.5.8. firewall rules

If we attempt to access the site from another machine however, we will not be able to view the website yet. The firewall is blocking incoming connections. We need to open these incoming ports first

```
[root@CentOS65 ~]# iptables -I INPUT -p tcp --dport 80 -j ACCEPT
[root@CentOS65 ~]# iptables -I INPUT -p tcp --dport 7000 -j ACCEPT
[root@CentOS65 ~]# iptables -I INPUT -p tcp --dport 8000 -j ACCEPT
[root@CentOS65 ~]# iptables -I INPUT -p tcp --dport 9000 -j ACCEPT
```

And if we want these rules to remain active after a reboot, we need to save them

```
[root@CentOS65 ~]# service iptables save
iptables: Saving firewall rules to /etc/sysconfig/iptables:[  OK  ]
```

# 8.6. named virtual hosts on CentOS

## 8.6.1. named virtual hosts

The chess club and the model train club find the port numbers too hard to remember. They would prefere to have their website accessible by name.

We continue work on the same server that has three websites on three ports. We need to make sure those websites are accesible using the names **choochoo.local**, **chessclub42.local** and **hunter2.local**.

First, we need to enable named virtual hosts in the configuration

```
[root@CentOS65 ~]# vi /etc/httpd/conf/httpd.conf
[root@CentOS65 ~]# grep ^NameVirtualHost /etc/httpd/conf/httpd.conf
NameVirtualHost *:80
[root@CentOS65 ~]#
```

Next we need to create three new virtualhosts.

```
[root@CentOS65 ~]# vi /etc/httpd/conf.d/choochoo.local.conf
[root@CentOS65 ~]# vi /etc/httpd/conf.d/chessclub42.local.conf
[root@CentOS65 ~]# vi /etc/httpd/conf.d/hunter2.local.conf
[root@CentOS65 ~]# cat /etc/httpd/conf.d/choochoo.local.conf
<VirtualHost *:80>
        ServerAdmin webmaster@localhost
        ServerName choochoo.local
        DocumentRoot /var/www/html/choochoo
</VirtualHost>
[root@CentOS65 ~]# cat /etc/httpd/conf.d/chessclub42.local.conf
<VirtualHost *:80>
        ServerAdmin webmaster@localhost
        ServerName chessclub42.local
        DocumentRoot /var/www/html/chessclub42
</VirtualHost>
[root@CentOS65 ~]# cat /etc/httpd/conf.d/hunter2.local.conf
<VirtualHost *:80>
        ServerAdmin webmaster@localhost
        ServerName hunter2.local
        DocumentRoot /var/www/html/hunter2
</VirtualHost>
[root@CentOS65 ~]#
```

Notice that they all listen on **port 80** and have an extra **ServerName** directive.

## 8.6.2. name resolution

We need some way to resolve names. This can be done with DNS, which is discussed in another chapter. For this demo it is also possible to quickly add the three names to the **/etc/hosts** file.

```
[root@CentOS65 ~]# grep ^192 /etc/hosts
192.168.1.225 choochoo.local
192.168.1.225 chessclub42.local
192.168.1.225 hunter2.local
```

Note that you may have another ip address...

## 8.6.3. reload and verify

After a **service httpd reload** the websites should be available by name.

```
[root@CentOS65 ~]# service httpd reload
Reloading httpd:
[root@CentOS65 ~]# wget chessclub42.local
--2014-05-25 16:59:14--  http://chessclub42.local/
Resolving chessclub42.local... 192.168.1.225
Connecting to chessclub42.local|192.168.1.225|:80... connected.
HTTP request sent, awaiting response... 200 OK
Length: 25 [text/html]
Saving to: âindex.htmlâ

100%[===============================================>] 25          --.-K/s   in 0s

2014-05-25 16:59:15 (1014 KB/s) - `index.html' saved [25/25]

[root@CentOS65 ~]# cat index.html
Welcome to chess club 42
```

# 8.7. password protected website on CentOS

You can secure files and directories in your website with a **.htaccess** file that refers to a **.htpasswd** file. The **htpasswd** command can create a **.htpasswd** file that contains a userid and an (encrypted) password.

This screenshot creates a user and password for the hacker named **cliff** and uses the **-c** flag to create the **.htpasswd** file.

```
[root@CentOS65 ~]# htpasswd -c /var/www/.htpasswd cliff
New password:
Re-type new password:
Adding password for user cliff
[root@CentOS65 ~]# cat /var/www/.htpasswd
cliff:QNwTrymMLBctU
```

Hacker **rob** also wants access, this screenshot shows how to add a second user and password to **.htpasswd**.

```
[root@CentOS65 ~]# htpasswd /var/www/.htpasswd rob
New password:
Re-type new password:
Adding password for user rob
[root@CentOS65 ~]# cat /var/www/.htpasswd
cliff:QNwTrymMLBctU
rob:EC2vOCcrMXDoM
[root@CentOS65 ~]#
```

Both Cliff and Rob chose the same password (hunter2), but that is not visible in the **.htpasswd** file because of the different salts.

Next we need to create a **.htaccess** file in the **DocumentRoot** of the website we want to protect. This screenshot shows an example.

```
[root@CentOS65 ~]# cat /var/www/html/hunter2/.htaccess
AuthUserFile /var/www/.htpasswd
AuthName "Members only!"
AuthType Basic
require valid-user
```

Note that we are protecting the website on **port 9000** that we created earlier.

And because we put the website for the Hackerspace named hunter2 in a subdirectory of the default website, we will need to adjust the **AllowOvveride** parameter in **/etc/httpd/conf/httpd.conf** under the **<Directory "/var/www/html">** directive as this screenshot shows.

```
[root@CentOS65 ~]# vi /etc/httpd/conf/httpd.conf

<Directory "/var/www/html">

#
# Possible values for the Options directive are "None", "All",
# or any combination of:
#   Indexes Includes FollowSymLinks SymLinksifOwnerMatch ExecCGI MultiViews
#
# Note that "MultiViews" must be named *explicitly* --- "Options All"
# doesn't give it to you.
#
# The Options directive is both complicated and important.  Please see
# http://httpd.apache.org/docs/2.2/mod/core.html#options
# for more information.
#
    Options Indexes FollowSymLinks


#
# AllowOverride controls what directives may be placed in .htaccess files.
# It can be "All", "None", or any combination of the keywords:
#   Options FileInfo AuthConfig Limit
#
    AllowOverride Authconfig


#
# Controls who can get stuff from this server.
#
    Order allow,deny
    Allow from all

</Directory>
```

Now restart the apache2 server and test that it works!

# 8.8. troubleshooting apache

When apache restarts, it will verify the syntax of files in the configuration folder **/etc/apache2** on debian or **/etc/httpd** on CentOS and it will tell you the name of the faulty file, the line number and an explanation of the error.

```
root@debian7:~# service apache2 restart
apache2: Syntax error on line 268 of /etc/apache2/apache2.conf: Syntax error o\
n line 1 of /etc/apache2/sites-enabled/chessclub42: /etc/apache2/sites-enabled\
/chessclub42:4: <VirtualHost> was not closed.\n/etc/apache2/sites-enabled/ches\
sclub42:1: <VirtualHost> was not closed.
Action 'configtest' failed.
The Apache error log may have more information.
 failed!
```

Below you see the problem... a missing / before on line 4.

```
root@debian7:~# cat /etc/apache2/sites-available/chessclub42
<VirtualHost *:8000>
        ServerAdmin webmaster@localhost
        DocumentRoot /var/www/chessclub42
<VirtualHost>
```

Let us force another error by renaming the directory of one of our websites:

```
root@debian7:~# mv /var/www/choochoo/ /var/www/chooshoo
root@debian7:~# !ser
service apache2 restart
Restarting web server: apache2Warning: DocumentRoot [/var/www/choochoo] does n\
ot exist
Warning: DocumentRoot [/var/www/choochoo] does not exist
 ... waiting Warning: DocumentRoot [/var/www/choochoo] does not exist
Warning: DocumentRoot [/var/www/choochoo] does not exist
 .
```

As you can see, apache will tell you exactly what is wrong.

You can also troubleshoot by connecting to the website via a browser and then checking the apache log files in **/var/log/apache**.

# 8.9. virtual hosts example

Below is a sample virtual host configuration. This virtual hosts overrules the default Apache **ErrorDocument** directive.

```
<VirtualHost 83.217.76.245:80>
ServerName cobbaut.be
ServerAlias www.cobbaut.be
DocumentRoot /home/paul/public_html
ErrorLog /home/paul/logs/error_log
CustomLog /home/paul/logs/access_log common
ScriptAlias /cgi-bin/ /home/paul/cgi-bin/
<Directory /home/paul/public_html>
 Options Indexes IncludesNOEXEC FollowSymLinks
 allow from all
</Directory>
ErrorDocument 404 http://www.cobbaut.be/cobbaut.php
</VirtualHost>
```

# 8.10. aliases and redirects

Apache supports aliases for directories, like this example shows.

```
Alias /paul/ "/home/paul/public_html/"
```

Similarly, content can be redirected to another website or web server.

```
Redirect permanent /foo http://www.foo.com/bar
```

# 8.11. more on .htaccess

You can do much more with **.htaccess**. One example is to use .htaccess to prevent people from certain domains to access your website. Like in this case, where a number of referer spammers are blocked from the website.

```
paul@lounge:~/cobbaut.be$ cat .htaccess
# Options +FollowSymlinks
RewriteEngine On
RewriteCond %{HTTP_REFERER} ^http://(www\.)?buy-adipex.fw.nu.*$ [OR]
RewriteCond %{HTTP_REFERER} ^http://(www\.)?buy-levitra.asso.ws.*$ [NC,OR]
RewriteCond %{HTTP_REFERER} ^http://(www\.)?buy-tramadol.fw.nu.*$ [NC,OR]
RewriteCond %{HTTP_REFERER} ^http://(www\.)?buy-viagra.lookin.at.*$ [NC,OR]
...
RewriteCond %{HTTP_REFERER} ^http://(www\.)?www.healthinsurancehelp.net.*$ [NC]
RewriteRule .* - [F,L]
paul@lounge:~/cobbaut.be$
```

# 8.12. traffic

Apache keeps a log of all visitors. The **webalizer** is often used to parse this log into nice html statistics.

# 8.13. self signed cert on Debian

Below is a very quick guide on setting up Apache2 on Debian 7 with a self-signed certificate.

Chances are these packages are already installed.

```
root@debian7:~# aptitude install apache2 openssl
No packages will be installed, upgraded, or removed.
0 packages upgraded, 0 newly installed, 0 to remove and 0 not upgraded.
Need to get 0 B of archives. After unpacking 0 B will be used.
```

Create a directory to store the certs, and use **openssl** to create a self signed cert that is valid for 999 days.

```
root@debian7:~# mkdir /etc/ssl/localcerts
root@debian7:~# openssl req -new -x509 -days 999 -nodes -out /etc/ssl/local\
certs/apache.pem -keyout /etc/ssl/localcerts/apache.key
Generating a 2048 bit RSA private key
...
...
writing new private key to '/etc/ssl/localcerts/apache.key'
-----
You are about to be asked to enter information that will be incorporated
into your certificate request.
What you are about to enter is what is called a Distinguished Name or a DN.
There are quite a few fields but you can leave some blank
For some fields there will be a default value,
If you enter '.', the field will be left blank.
-----
Country Name (2 letter code) [AU]:BE
State or Province Name (full name) [Some-State]:Antwerp
Locality Name (eg, city) []:Antwerp
Organization Name (eg, company) [Internet Widgits Pty Ltd]:linux-training.be
Organizational Unit Name (eg, section) []:
Common Name (e.g. server FQDN or YOUR name) []:Paul
Email Address []:
```

A little security never hurt anyone.

```
root@debian7:~# ls -l /etc/ssl/localcerts/
total 8
-rw-r--r-- 1 root root 1704 Sep 16 18:24 apache.key
-rw-r--r-- 1 root root 1302 Sep 16 18:24 apache.pem
root@debian7:~# chmod 600 /etc/ssl/localcerts/*
root@debian7:~# ls -l /etc/ssl/localcerts/
total 8
-rw------- 1 root root 1704 Sep 16 18:24 apache.key
-rw------- 1 root root 1302 Sep 16 18:24 apache.pem
```

Enable the **apache ssl mod**.

```
root@debian7:~# a2enmod ssl
Enabling module ssl.
See /usr/share/doc/apache2.2-common/README.Debian.gz on how to configure SSL\
 and create self-signed certificates.
To activate the new configuration, you need to run:
  service apache2 restart
```

Create the website configuration.

```
root@debian7:~# vi /etc/apache2/sites-available/choochoos
```

```
root@debian7:~# cat /etc/apache2/sites-available/choochoos
<VirtualHost *:7000>
        ServerAdmin webmaster@localhost
        DocumentRoot /var/www/choochoos
        SSLEngine On
        SSLCertificateFile /etc/ssl/localcerts/apache.pem
        SSLCertificateKeyFile /etc/ssl/localcerts/apache.key
</VirtualHost>
root@debian7:~#
```

And create the website itself.

```
root@debian7:/var/www/choochoos# vi index.html
root@debian7:/var/www/choochoos# cat index.html
Choo Choo HTTPS secured model train Choo Choo
```

Enable the website and restart (or reload) apache2.

```
root@debian7:/var/www/choochoos# a2ensite choochoos
Enabling site choochoos.
To activate the new configuration, you need to run:
  service apache2 reload
root@debian7:/var/www/choochoos# service apache2 restart
Restarting web server: apache2 ... waiting .
```

Chances are your browser will warn you about the self signed certificate.

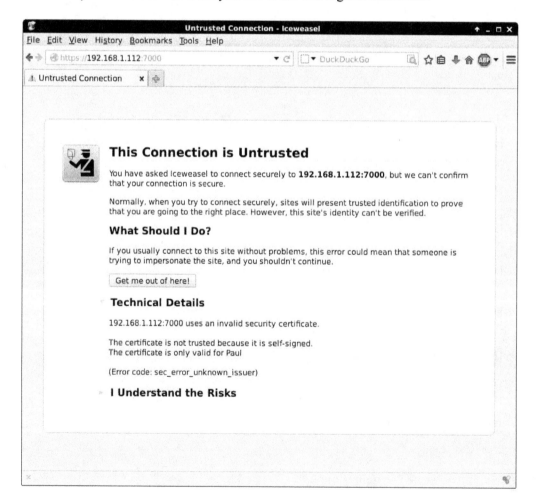

# 8.14. self signed cert on RHEL/CentOS

Below is a quick way to create a self signed cert for https on RHEL/CentOS. You may need these packages:

```
[root@paulserver ~]# yum install httpd openssl mod_ssl
Loaded plugins: fastestmirror
Loading mirror speeds from cached hostfile
 * base: ftp.belnet.be
 * extras: ftp.belnet.be
 * updates: mirrors.vooservers.com
base                                                    | 3.7 kB     00:00
Setting up Install Process
Package httpd-2.2.15-31.el6.centos.x86_64 already installed and latest version
Package openssl-1.0.1e-16.el6_5.15.x86_64 already installed and latest version
Package 1:mod_ssl-2.2.15-31.el6.centos.x86_64 already ins... and latest version
Nothing to do
```

## We use **openssl** to create the certificate.

```
[root@paulserver ~]# mkdir certs
[root@paulserver ~]# cd certs
[root@paulserver certs]# openssl genrsa -out ca.key 2048
Generating RSA private key, 2048 bit long modulus
.........+++
...............................................+++
e is 65537 (0x10001)
[root@paulserver certs]# openssl req -new -key ca.key -out ca.csr
You are about to be asked to enter information that will be incorporated
into your certificate request.
What you are about to enter is what is called a Distinguished Name or a DN.
There are quite a few fields but you can leave some blank
For some fields there will be a default value,
If you enter '.', the field will be left blank.
-----
Country Name (2 letter code) [XX]:BE
State or Province Name (full name) []:antwerp
Locality Name (eg, city) [Default City]:antwerp
Organization Name (eg, company) [Default Company Ltd]:antwerp
Organizational Unit Name (eg, section) []:
Common Name (eg, your name or your server's hostname) []:paulserver
Email Address []:

Please enter the following 'extra' attributes
to be sent with your certificate request
A challenge password []:
An optional company name []:
[root@paulserver certs]# openssl x509 -req -days 365 -in ca.csr -signkey ca.ke\
y -out ca.crt
Signature ok
subject=/C=BE/ST=antwerp/L=antwerp/O=antwerp/CN=paulserver
Getting Private key
```

We copy the keys to the right location (You may be missing SELinux info here).

```
[root@paulserver certs]# cp ca.crt /etc/pki/tls/certs/
[root@paulserver certs]# cp ca.key ca.csr /etc/pki/tls/private/
```

We add the location of our keys to this file, and also add the **NameVirtualHost *:443** directive.

```
[root@paulserver certs]# vi /etc/httpd/conf.d/ssl.conf
```

```
[root@paulserver certs]# grep ^SSLCerti /etc/httpd/conf.d/ssl.conf
SSLCertificateFile /etc/pki/tls/certs/ca.crt
SSLCertificateKeyFile /etc/pki/tls/private/ca.key
```

Create a website configuration.

```
[root@paulserver certs]# vi /etc/httpd/conf.d/choochoos.conf
[root@paulserver certs]# cat /etc/httpd/conf.d/choochoos.conf
<VirtualHost *:443>
        SSLEngine on
        SSLCertificateFile /etc/pki/tls/certs/ca.crt
        SSLCertificateKeyFile /etc/pki/tls/private/ca.key
        DocumentRoot /var/www/choochoos
        ServerName paulserver
</VirtualHost>
[root@paulserver certs]#
```

Create a simple website and restart apache.

```
[root@paulserver certs]# mkdir /var/www/choochoos
[root@paulserver certs]# echo HTTPS model train choochoos > /var/www/choochoos/\
index.html
[root@paulserver httpd]# service httpd restart
Stopping httpd:                                           [  OK  ]
Starting httpd:                                           [  OK  ]
```

And your browser will probably warn you that this certificate is self signed.

104

# 8.15. practice: apache

1. Verify that Apache is installed and running.

2. Browse to the Apache HTML manual.

3. Create three virtual hosts that listen on ports 8472, 31337 and 1201. Test that it all works.

4. Create three named virtual hosts startrek.local, starwars.local and stargate.local. Test that it all works.

5. Create a virtual hosts that listens on another ip-address.

6. Protect one of your websites with a user/password combo.

# Chapter 9. introduction to squid

## 9.1. about proxy servers

### 9.1.1. usage

A **proxy server** is a server that caches the internet. Clients connect to the proxy server with a request for an internet server. The proxy server will connect to the internet server on behalf of the client. The proxy server will also cache the pages retrieved from the internet server. A proxy server may provide pages from his cache to a client, instead of connecting to the internet server to retrieve the (same) pages.

A proxy server has two main advantages. It improves web surfing speed when returning cached data to clients, and it reduces the required bandwidth (cost) to the internet.

Smaller organizations sometimes put the proxy server on the same physical computer that serves as a NAT to the internet. In larger organizations, the proxy server is one of many servers in the DMZ.

When web traffic passes via a proxy server, it is common practice to configure the proxy with extra settings for access control. Access control in a proxy server can mean user account access, but also website(url), ip-address or dns restrictions.

### 9.1.2. open proxy servers

You can find lists of open proxy servers on the internet that enable you to surf anonymously. This works when the proxy server connects on your behalf to a website, without logging your ip-address. But be careful, these (listed) open proxy servers could be created in order to eavesdrop upon their users.

### 9.1.3. squid

This module is an introduction to the **squid** proxy server (http://www.squid-cache.org). We will first configure squid as a normal proxy server.

## 9.2. installing squid

This screenshot shows how to install squid on Debian with **aptitude**. Use **yum** if you are on Red Hat/CentOS.

```
root@debian7:~# aptitude install squid
The following NEW packages will be installed:
  squid squid-common{a} squid-langpack{a}
0 packages upgraded, 3 newly installed, 0 to remove and 0 not upgraded.
Need to get 1,513 kB of archives. After unpacking 4,540 kB will be used.
Do you want to continue? [Y/n/?]
...output truncated...
Setting up squid-langpack (20120616-1) ...
Setting up squid-common (2.7.STABLE9-4.1) ...
Setting up squid (2.7.STABLE9-4.1) ...
Creating squid spool directory structure
2014/08/01 15:19:31| Creating Swap Directories
Restarting Squid HTTP proxy: squid.
```

**squid**'s main configuration file is **/etc/squid/squid.conf**. The file explains every parameter in great detail.

```
root@debian7:~# wc -l /etc/squid/squid.conf
4948 /etc/squid/squid.conf
```

## 9.3. port 3128

By default the **squid proxy server** will lsiten to **port 3128**.

```
root@debian7:~# grep ^http_port /etc/squid/squid.conf
http_port 3128
root@debian7:~#
```

## 9.4. starting and stopping

You can manage **squid** with the standard **service** command as shown in this screenshot.

```
root@debian7:~# service squid start
Starting Squid HTTP proxy: squid.
root@debian7:~# service squid restart
Restarting Squid HTTP proxy: squid.
root@debian7:~# service squid status
squid is running.
root@debian7:~# service squid stop
Stopping Squid HTTP proxy: squid.
root@debian7:~#
```

# 9.5. client proxy settings

To enable a proxy server in **Firefox** or **Iceweasel** go to **Edit Preferences** and configure as shown in this screenshot (replace 192.168.1.60 with the ip address of your proxy server).

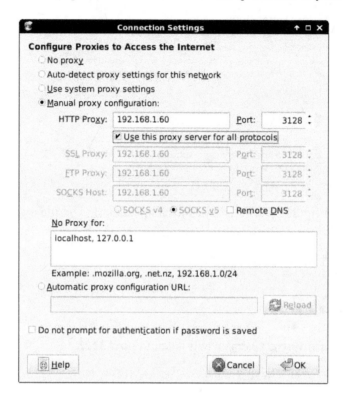

Test that your internet works with the proxy enabled. Also test that after a **service squid stop** command on your proxy server that you get a message similar to this schreenshot.

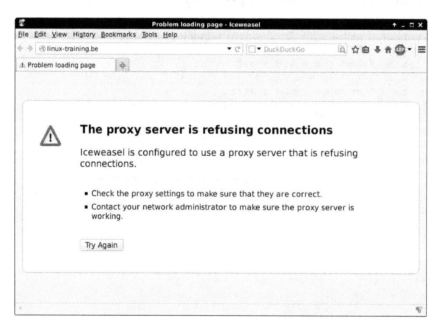

To enable a proxy server with Google Chrome (or Debian Chromium) start the program from the command line like this:

```
paul@debian7:~$ chromium --proxy-server='192.168.1.60:3128'
```

Disabling the proxy with **service squid stop** should result in an error message similar to this screenshot.

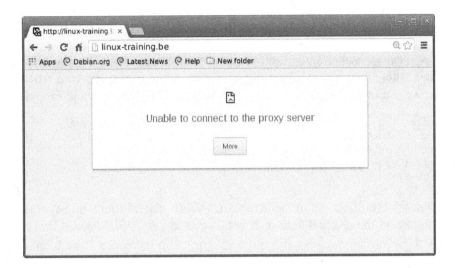

# 9.6. upside down images

A proxy server sits inbetween your browser and the internet. So besides caching of internet data (the original function of a proxy server) and besides firewall like restrictions based on www content, a proxy server is in the perfect position to alter the webpages that you visit.

You could for instance change the advertising on a webpage (or remove certain advertisers), or like we do in this example; change all images so they are upside down.

The server needs command line tools to manipulate images and a perl script that uses these tools (and **wget** to download the images locally and serve them with **apache2**). In this example we use **imagemagick** (which provides tools like **convert** and **mogrify**).

```
root@debian7:~# aptitude install imagemagick wget perl apache2
...output truncated...
root@debian7:~# dpkg -S $(readlink -f $(which mogrify))
imagemagick: /usr/bin/mogrify.im6
root@debian7:~#
```

The perl script that is shown in the screenshot below can be found on several websites, yet I have not found the original author. It is however a very simple script that uses **wget** and **mogrify** to download images (.jpg .gif and .png), flip them and store them in **/var/www/ images**.

```perl
root@debian7:~# cat /usr/local/bin/flip.pl
#!/usr/bin/perl
$|=1;
$count = 0;
$pid = $$;
while (<>) {
 chomp $_;
 if ($_ =~ /(.*\.jpg)/i) {
  $url = $1;
  system("/usr/bin/wget", "-q", "-O","/var/www/images/$pid-$count.jpg", "$url");
  system("/usr/bin/mogrify", "-flip","/var/www/images/$pid-$count.jpg");
  print "http://127.0.0.1/images/$pid-$count.jpg\n";
 }
 elsif ($_ =~ /(.*\.gif)/i) {
  $url = $1;
  system("/usr/bin/wget", "-q", "-O","/var/www/images/$pid-$count.gif", "$url");
  system("/usr/bin/mogrify", "-flip","/var/www/images/$pid-$count.gif");
  print "http://127.0.0.1/images/$pid-$count.gif\n";
 }
 elsif ($_ =~ /(.*\.png)/i) {
  $url = $1;
  system("/usr/bin/wget", "-q", "-O","/var/www/images/$pid-$count.png", "$url");
  system("/usr/bin/mogrify", "-flip","/var/www/images/$pid-$count.png");
  print "http://127.0.0.1/images/$pid-$count.png\n";
 }
 else {
        print "$_\n";;
 }
 $count++;
}
```

Change (or enable) also the following line in **/etc/squid/suiqd.conf**.

```
http_access allow localnet
http_port 3128 transparent
```

```
url_rwwrite_program /usr/local/bin/flip.pl
```

The directory this script uses is **/var/www/images** and should be accessible by both the **squid server** (which uses the user named **proxy** and by the **apache2** webserver (which uses the user **www-data**. The screenshot below shows how to create this directory, set the permissions and make the users a member of the other groups.

```
root@debian7:~# mkdir /var/www/images
root@debian7:~# chown www-data:www-data /var/www/images
root@debian7:~# chmod 755 /var/www/images
root@debian7:~# usermod -aG www-data proxy
root@debian7:~# usermod -aG proxy www-data
```

Test that it works after restarting **squid** and **apache2**.

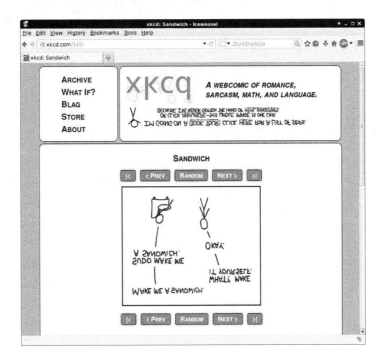

# 9.7. /var/log/squid

The standard log file location for squid is **/var/log/squid**.

```
[root@RHEL4 ~]# grep "/var/log" /etc/squid/squid.conf
# cache_access_log /var/log/squid/access.log
# cache_log /var/log/squid/cache.log
# cache_store_log /var/log/squid/store.log
```

# 9.8. access control

The default squid setup only allows localhost access. To enable access for a private network range, look for the "INSERT YOUR OWN RULE(S) HERE..." sentence in squid.conf and add two lines similar to the screenshot below.

```
# INSERT YOUR OWN RULE(S) HERE TO ALLOW ACCESS FROM YOUR CLIENTS

acl company_network src 192.168.1.0/24
http_access allow company_network
```

# 9.9. testing squid

First, make sure that the server running squid has access to the internet.

```
[root@RHEL4 ~]# wget -q http://linux-training.be/index.html
[root@RHEL4 ~]# ls -l index.html
-rw-r--r-- 1 root root 2269 Sep 18 13:18 index.html
[root@RHEL4 ~]#
```

Then configure a browser on a client to use the proxy server, or you could set the HTTP_PROXY (sometimes http_proxy) variable to point command line programs to the proxy.

```
[root@fedora ~]# export HTTP_PROXY=http://192.168.1.39:8080
[root@ubuntu ~]# export http_proxy=http://192.168.1.39:8080
```

Testing a client machine can then be done with wget (wget -q is used to simplify the screenshot).

```
[root@RHEL5 ~]# > /etc/resolv.conf
[root@RHEL5 ~]# wget -q http://www.linux-training.be/index.html
[root@RHEL5 ~]# ls -l index.html
-rw-r--r-- 1 root root 2269 Sep 18  2008 index.html
[root@RHEL5 ~]#
```

# 9.10. name resolution

You need name resolution working on the **squid** server, but you don't need name resolution on the clients.

```
[paul@RHEL5 ~]$ wget http://grep.be
--14:35:44--  http://grep.be
Resolving grep.be... failed: Temporary failure in name resolution.
[paul@RHEL5 ~]$ export http_proxy=http://192.168.1.39:8080
[paul@RHEL5 ~]$ wget http://grep.be
--14:35:49--  http://grep.be/
```

```
Connecting to 192.168.1.39:8080... connected.
Proxy request sent, awaiting response... 200 OK
Length: 5390 (5.3K) [text/html]
Saving to: `index.html.1'

100%[================================>] 5,390        --.-K/s    in 0.1s

14:38:29 (54.8 KB/s) - `index.html' saved [5390/5390]

[paul@RHEL5 ~]$
```

# Part III. dns server

# Table of Contents

# Chapter 10. introduction to DNS

**dns** is a fundamental part of every large computer network. **dns** is used by many network services to translate names into network addresses and to locate services on the network (by name).

Whenever you visit a web site, send an e-mail, log on to Active Directory, play Minecraft, chat, or use VoIP, there will be one or (many) more queries to **dns** services.

Should **dns** fail at your organization, then the whole network will grind to a halt (unless you hardcoded the network addresses).

You will notice that even the largest of organizations benefit greatly from having one **dns** infrastructure. Thus **dns** requires all business units to work together.

Even at home, most home modems and routers have builtin **dns** functionality.

This module will explain what **dns** actually is and how to set it up using **Linux** and **bind9**.

# 10.1. about dns

## 10.1.1. name to ip address resolution

The **domain name system** or **dns** is a service on a tcp/ip network that enables clients to translate names into ip addresses. Actually **dns** is much more than that, but let's keep it simple for now.

When you use a browser to go to a website, then you type the name of that website in the url bar. But for your computer to actually communicate with the web server hosting said website, your computer needs the ip address of that web server. That is where **dns** comes in.

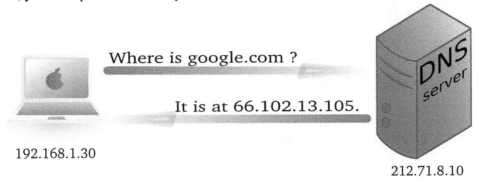

In wireshark you can use the **dns** filter to see this traffic.

| No. - | Time | Source | Destination | Protocol | Info |
|-------|------|--------|-------------|----------|------|
| 4560 | 11.467767 | 192.168.1.30 | 212.71.8.10 | DNS | Standard query A google.com |
| 4569 | 11.487774 | 212.71.8.10 | 192.168.1.30 | DNS | Standard query response A 66.102.13.105 |

Filter: dns    Expression... | Clear | Apply

## 10.1.2. history

In the Seventies, only a few hundred computers were connected to the internet. To resolve names, computers had a flat file that contained a table to resolve hostnames to ip addresses. This local file was downloaded from **hosts.txt** on an ftp server in Stanford.

In 1984 **Paul Mockapetris** created **dns**, a distributed treelike hierarchical database that will be explained in detail in these chapters.

Today, **dns** or **domain name system** is a worldwide distributed hierarchical database controlled by **ICANN**. Its primary function is to resolve names to ip addresses, and to point to internet servers providing **smtp** or **ldap** services.

The old **hosts.txt** file is still active today on most computer systems under the name **/etc/hosts** (or C:/Windows/System32/Drivers/etc/hosts). We will discuss this file later, as it can influence name resolution.

# 10.1.3. forward and reverse lookup queries

The question a client asks a dns server is called a **query**. When a client queries for an ip address, this is called a **forward lookup query** (as seen in the previous drawing).

The reverse, a query for the name of a host, is called a **reverse lookup query**.

Below a picture of a **reverse lookup query**.

Who is 178.63.30.100 ?

It is antares.ginsys.net.

192.168.1.30

212.71.8.10

Here is a screenshot of a **reverse lookup query** in **nslookup**.

```
root@debian7:~# nslookup
> set type=PTR
> 188.93.155.87
Server:         192.168.1.42
Address:        192.168.1.42#53

Non-authoritative answer:
87.155.93.188.in-addr.arpa      name = antares.ginsys.net.
```

This is what a reverse lookup looks like when sniffing with **tcpdump**.

```
root@debian7:~# tcpdump udp port 53
tcpdump: verbose output suppressed, use -v or -vv for full protocol decode
listening on eth0, link-type EN10MB (Ethernet), capture size 65535 bytes
11:01:29.357685 IP 192.168.1.103.42041 > 192.168.1.42.domain: 14763+ PT\
R? 87.155.93.188.in-addr.arpa. (44)
11:01:29.640093 IP 192.168.1.42.domain > 192.168.1.103.42041: 14763 1/0\
/0 PTR antares.ginsys.net. (76)
```

And here is what it looks like in **wireshark** (note this is an older screenshot).

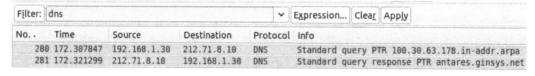

# 10.1.4. /etc/resolv.conf

A client computer needs to know the ip address of the **dns server** to be able to send queries to it. This is either provided by a **dhcp server** or manually entered.

Linux clients keep this information in the **/etc/resolv.conf** file.

```
root@debian7:~# cat /etc/resolv.conf
domain linux-training.be
search linux-training.be
nameserver 192.168.1.42
root@debian7:~#
```

You can manually change the ip address in this file to use another **dns** server. For example Google provides a public name server at **8.8.8.8** and **8.8.4.4**.

```
root@debian7:~# cat /etc/resolv.conf
nameserver 8.8.8.8
root@debian7:~#
```

Please note that on **dhcp clients** this value can be overwritten when the **dhcp lease** is renewed.

# 10.2. dns namespace

## 10.2.1. hierarchy

The **dns namespace** is hierarchical tree structure, with the **root servers** (aka dot-servers) at the top. The **root servers** are usually represented by a dot.

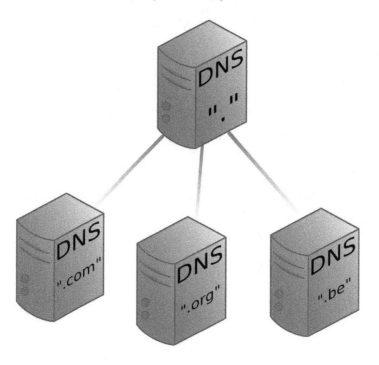

Below the **root-servers** are the **Top Level Domains** or **tld**'s.

There are more **tld**'s than shown in the picture. Currently about 200 countries have a **tld**. And there are several general **tld**'s like .com, .edu, .org, .gov, .net, .mil, .int and more recently also .aero, .info, .museum, ...

## 10.2.2. root servers

There are thirteen **root servers** on the internet, they are named **A** to **M**. Journalists often refer to these servers as **the master servers of the internet**, because if these servers go down, then nobody can (use names to) connect to websites.

The root servers are not thirteen physical machines, they are many more. For example the **F** root server consists of 46 physical machines that all behave as one (using anycast).

```
http://root-servers.org
http://f.root-servers.org
http://en.wikipedia.org/wiki/Root_nameserver.
```

## 10.2.3. root hints

Every **dns server software** will come with a list of **root hints** to locate the **root servers**.

This screenshot shows a small portion of the root hints file that comes with **bind 9.8.4**.

```
root@debian7:~# grep -w 'A ' /etc/bind/db.root
A.ROOT-SERVERS.NET.        3600000        A        198.41.0.4
B.ROOT-SERVERS.NET.        3600000        A        192.228.79.201
C.ROOT-SERVERS.NET.        3600000        A        192.33.4.12
D.ROOT-SERVERS.NET.        3600000        A        199.7.91.13
E.ROOT-SERVERS.NET.        3600000        A        192.203.230.10
F.ROOT-SERVERS.NET.        3600000        A        192.5.5.241
G.ROOT-SERVERS.NET.        3600000        A        192.112.36.4
H.ROOT-SERVERS.NET.        3600000        A        128.63.2.53
I.ROOT-SERVERS.NET.        3600000        A        192.36.148.17
J.ROOT-SERVERS.NET.        3600000        A        192.58.128.30
K.ROOT-SERVERS.NET.        3600000        A        193.0.14.129
L.ROOT-SERVERS.NET.        3600000        A        199.7.83.42
M.ROOT-SERVERS.NET.        3600000        A        202.12.27.33
root@debian7:~#
```

## 10.2.4. domains

One level below the **top level domains** are the **domains**. Domains can have subdomains (also called child domains).

This picture shows **dns domains** like google.com, chess.com, linux-training.be (there are millions more).

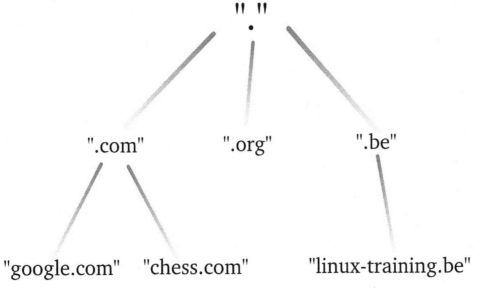

DNS domains are registered at the **tld** servers, the **tld** servers are registered at the **dot servers**.

## 10.2.5. top level domains

Below the root level are the **top level domains** or **tld's**. Originally there were only seven defined:

**Table 10.1. the first top level domains**

| year | TLD | purpose |
|------|------|---------|
| 1985 | .arpa | Reverse lookup via in-addr.arpa |
| 1985 | .com | Commercial Organizations |
| 1985 | .edu | US Educational Institutions |
| 1985 | .gov | US Government Institutions |
| 1985 | .mil | US Military |
| 1985 | .net | Internet Service Providers, Internet Infrastructure |
| 1985 | .org | Non profit Organizations |
| 1988 | .int | International Treaties like nato.int |

Country **tld**'s were defined for individual countries, like **.uk** in 1985 for Great Britain (yes really), **.be** for Belgium in 1988 and **.fr** for France in 1986. See RFC 1591 for more info.

In 1998 seven new general purpose **tld**'s where chosen, they became active in the 21st century.

**Table 10.2. new general purpose tld's**

| year | TLD | purpose |
|------|------|---------|
| 2002 | .aero | aviation related |
| 2001 | .biz | businesses |
| 2001 | .coop | for co-operatives |
| 2001 | .info | informative internet resources |
| 2001 | .museum | for museums |
| 2001 | .name | for all kinds of names, pseudonyms and labels... |
| 2004 | .pro | for professionals |

Many people were surprised by the choices, claiming not much use for them and wanting a separate **.xxx** domain (introduced in 2011) for adult content, and **.kidz** a save haven for children. In the meantime more useless **tld**'s were create like **.travel** (for travel agents) and **.tel** (for internet communications) and **.jobs** (for jobs sites).

In 2012 **ICANN** released a list of 2000 new **tld**'s that would gradually become available.

## 10.2.6. fully qualified domain name

The **fully qualified domain name** or **fqdn** is the combination of the **hostname** of a machine appended with its **domain name**.

If for example a system is called **gwen** and it is in the domain **linux-training.be**, then the fqdn of this system is **gwen.linux-training.be**.

On Linux systems you can use the **hostname** and **dnsdomainname** commands to verify this information.

```
root@gwen:~# hostname
gwen
root@gwen:~# dnsdomainname
linux-training.be
root@gwen:~# hostname --fqdn
gwen.linux-training.be
root@gwen:~# cat /etc/debian_version
6.0.10
```

## 10.2.7. dns zones

A **zone** (aka a **zone of authority**) is a portion of the DNS tree that covers one domain name or child domain name. The picture below represents zones as blue ovals. Some zones will contain delegate authority over a child domain to another zone.

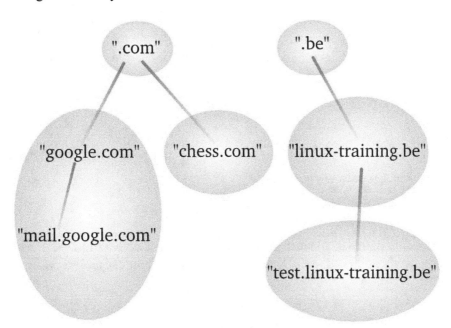

A **dns server** can be **authoritative** over 0, 1 or more **dns zones**. We will see more details later on the relation between a **dns server** and a **dns zone**.

A **dns zone** consists of **records**, also called **resource records**. We will list some of those **resource records** on the next page.

# 10.2.8. dns records

## A record

The **A record**, which is also called a **host record** contains the ipv4-address of a computer. When a DNS client queries a DNS server for an A record, then the DNS server will resolve the hostname in the query to an ip address. An **AAAA record** is similar but contains an ipv6 address instead of ipv4.

## PTR record

A **PTR record** is the reverse of an A record. It contains the name of a computer and can be used to resolve an ip address to a hostname.

## NS record

A **NS record** or **nameserver record** is a record that points to a DNS name server (in this zone). You can list all your name servers for your DNS zone in distinct NS records.

## glue A record

An A record that maps the name of an NS record to an ip address is said to be a **glue record**.

## SOA record

The SOA record of a zone contains meta information about the zone itself. The contents of the SOA record is explained in detail in the section about zone transfers. There is exactly one SOA record for each zone.

## CNAME record

A **CNAME record** maps a hostname to a hostname, creating effectively an alias for an existing hostname. The name of the mail server is often aliased to **mail** or **smtp**, and the name of a web server to **www**.

## MX record

The **MX** record points to an **smtp server**. When you send an email to another domain, then your mail server will need the MX record of the target domain's mail server.

# 10.3. caching only servers

A **dns server** that is set up without **authority** over a **zone**, but that is connected to other name servers and caches the queries is called a **caching only name server**. Caching only name servers do not have a **zone database** with resource records. Instead they connect to other name servers and cache that information.

There are two kinds of caching only name servers. Those with a **forwarder**, and those that use the **root servers**.

# 10.3.1. caching only server without forwarder

A caching only server without forwarder will have to get information elsewhere. When it receives a query from a client, then it will consult one of the **root servers**. The **root server** will refer it to a **tld** server, which will refer it to another **dns** server. That last server might know the answer to the query, or may refer to yet another server. In the end, our hard working **dns** server will find an answer and report this back to the client.

In the picture below, the clients asks for the ip address of linux-training.be. Our caching only server will contact the root server, and be refered to the .be server. It will then contact the .be server and be refered to one of the name servers of Openminds. One of these name servers (in this cas ns1.openminds.be) will answer the query with the ip address of linux-training.be. When our caching only server reports this to the client, then the client can connect to this website.

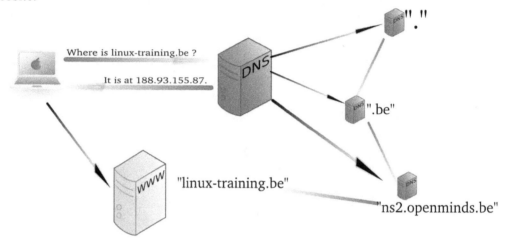

Sniffing with **tcpdump** will give you this (the first 20 characters of each line are cut).

```
192.168.1.103.41251 > M.ROOT-SERVERS.NET.domain: 37279% [1au] A? linux-tr\
aining.be. (46)
M.ROOT-SERVERS.NET.domain > 192.168.1.103.41251: 37279- 0/11/13 (740)
192.168.1.103.65268 > d.ns.dns.be.domain: 38555% [1au] A? linux-training.\
be. (46)
d.ns.dns.be.domain > 192.168.1.103.65268: 38555- 0/7/5 (737)
192.168.1.103.7514 > ns2.openminds.be.domain: 60888% [1au] A? linux-train\
ing.be. (46)
ns2.openminds.be.domain > 192.168.1.103.7514: 60888*- 1/0/1 A 188.93.155.\
87 (62)
```

## 10.3.2. caching only server with forwarder

A **caching only server** with a **forwarder** is a DNS server that will get all its information from the **forwarder**. The **forwarder** must be a **dns server** for example the **dns server** of an **internet service provider**.

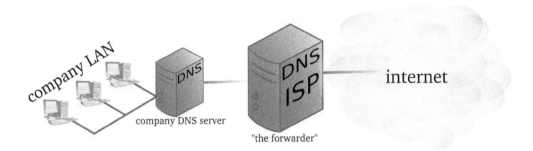

company DNS server

"the forwarder"

This picture shows a **dns server** on the company LAN that has set the **dns server** from their **isp** as a **forwarder**. If the ip address of the **isp dns server** is 212.71.8.10, then the following lines would occur in the **named.conf** file of the company **dns server**:

```
forwarders {
  212.71.8.10;
 };
```

You can also configure your **dns server** to work with **conditional forwarder(s)**. The definition of a conditional forwarder looks like this.

```
zone "someotherdomain.local" {
        type forward;
        forward only;
        forwarders { 10.104.42.1; };
};
```

## 10.3.3. iterative or recursive query

A **recursive query** is a DNS query where the client that is submitting the query expects a complete answer (Like the fat red arrow above going from the Macbook to the DNS server). An **iterative query** is a DNS query where the client does not expect a complete answer (the three black arrows originating from the DNS server in the picture above). Iterative queries usually take place between name servers. The root name servers do not respond to recursive queries.

# 10.4. authoritative dns servers

A DNS server that is controlling a zone, is said to be the **authoritative** DNS server for that zone. Remember that a **zone** is a collection of **resource records**.

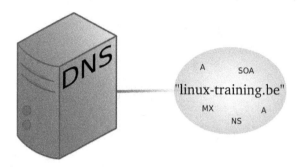

# 10.5. primary and secondary

When you set up the first **authoritative** dns server for a zone, then this is called the **primary dns server**. This server will have a readable and writable copy of the **zone database**. For reasons of fault tolerance, performance or load balancing you may decide to set up another **dns server** with authority over that zone. This is called a **secondary** dns server.

# 10.6. zone transfers

The slave server receives a copy of the zone database from the master server using a **zone transfer**. Zone transfers are requested by the slave servers at regular intervals. Those intervals are defined in the **soa record**.

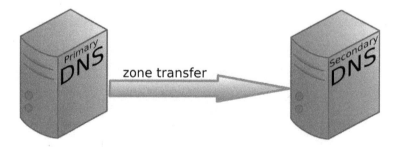

You can force a refresh from a zone with **rndc**. The example below force a transfer of the **fred.local** zone, and shows the log from **/var/log/syslog**.

```
root@debian7:/etc/bind# rndc refresh fred.local
```

```
root@debian7:/etc/bind# grep fred /var/log/syslog | tail -7 | cut -c38-
zone fred.local/IN: sending notifies (serial 1)
received control channel command 'refresh fred.local'
zone fred.local/IN: Transfer started.
transfer of 'fred.local/IN' from 10.104.109.1#53: connected using 10.104.33.30#57367
zone fred.local/IN: transferred serial 2
transfer of 'fred.local/IN' from 10.104.109.1#53: Transfer completed: 1 messages, 10 records,
zone fred.local/IN: sending notifies (serial 2)
root@debian7:/etc/bind#
```

# 10.7. master and slave

When adding a **secondary dns server** to a zone, then you will configure this server as a **slave server** to the **primary server**. The primary server then becomes the **master server** of the slave server.

Often the **primary dns server** is the **master** server of all slaves. Sometimes a **slave server** is **master server** for a second line slave server. In the picture below ns1 is the primary dns server and ns2, ns3 and ns4 are secondaries. The master for slaves ns2 and ns3 is ns1, but the master for ns4 is ns2.

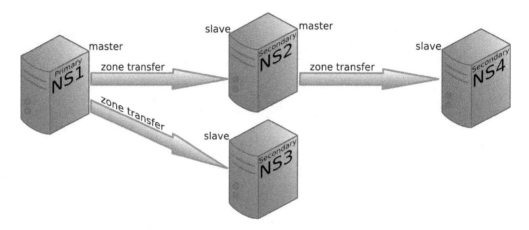

# 10.8. SOA record

The **soa record** contains a **refresh** value. If this is set to 30 minutes, then the slave server will request a copy of the zone file every 30 minutes. There is also a **retry** value. The retry value is used when the master server did not reply to the last zone transfer request. The value for **expiry time** says how long the slave server will answer to queries, without receiving a zone update.

Below an example of how to use nslookup to query the **soa record** of a zone (linux-training.be).

```
root@debian6:~# nslookup
> set type=SOA
> server ns1.openminds.be
> linux-training.be
Server:         ns1.openminds.be
Address:        195.47.215.14#53

linux-training.be
        origin = ns1.openminds.be
        mail addr = hostmaster.openminds.be
        serial = 2321001133
        refresh = 14400
        retry = 3600
        expire = 604800
        minimum = 3600
```

Zone transfers only occur when the zone database was updated (meaning when one or more resource records were added, removed or changed on the master server). The slave server will compare the **serial number** of its own copy of the SOA record with the serial number of its master's SOA record. When both serial numbers are the same, then no update is needed (because no records were added, removed or deleted). When the slave has a lower serial number than its master, then a zone transfer is requested.

Below a zone transfer captured in wireshark.

| | Time | Source | Destination | Protocol | Info |
|---|---|---|---|---|---|
| 1 | 0.000000 | 192.168.1.37 | 192.168.1.35 | DNS | Standard query SOA cobbaut.paul |
| 2 | 0.008502 | 192.168.1.35 | 192.168.1.37 | DNS | Standard query response SOA ns.cobbaut.paul |
| 3 | 0.014672 | 192.168.1.37 | 192.168.1.35 | TCP | 33713 > domain [SYN] Seq=0 Win=5840 Len=0 MS |
| 4 | 0.015215 | 192.168.1.35 | 192.168.1.37 | TCP | domain > 33713 [SYN, ACK] Seq=0 Ack=1 Win=57 |
| 5 | 0.015307 | 192.168.1.37 | 192.168.1.35 | TCP | 33713 > domain [ACK] Seq=1 Ack=1 Win=5856 Le |
| 6 | 0.015954 | 192.168.1.37 | 192.168.1.35 | TCP | [TCP segment of a reassembled PDU] |
| 7 | 0.018359 | 192.168.1.35 | 192.168.1.37 | TCP | domain > 33713 [ACK] Seq=1 Ack=3 Win=5792 Le |
| 8 | 0.018411 | 192.168.1.37 | 192.168.1.35 | DNS | Standard query IXFR cobbaut.paul |
| 9 | 0.018823 | 192.168.1.35 | 192.168.1.37 | TCP | domain > 33713 [ACK] Seq=1 Ack=77 Win=5792 L |
| 10 | 0.019784 | 192.168.1.35 | 192.168.1.37 | DNS | Standard query response SOA ns.cobbaut.paul |
| 11 | 0.019821 | 192.168.1.37 | 192.168.1.35 | TCP | 33713 > domain [ACK] Seq=77 Ack=295 Win=6912 |
| 12 | 0.020618 | 192.168.1.37 | 192.168.1.35 | TCP | 33713 > domain [FIN, ACK] Seq=77 Ack=295 Wir |
| 13 | 0.021011 | 192.168.1.35 | 192.168.1.37 | TCP | domain > 33713 [FIN, ACK] Seq=295 Ack=78 Win |
| 14 | 0.021040 | 192.168.1.37 | 192.168.1.35 | TCP | 33713 > domain [ACK] Seq=78 Ack=296 Win=691 |

# 10.9. full or incremental zone transfers

When a zone tranfer occurs, this can be either a full zone transfer or an incremental zone transfer. The decision depends on the size of the transfer that is needed to completely update the zone on the slave server. An incremental zone transfer is prefered when the total size of changes is smaller than the size of the zone database. Full zone transfers use the **axfr** protocol, incremental zone transfer use the **ixfr** protocol.

# 10.10. DNS cache

DNS is a caching protocol.

When a client queries its local DNS server, and the local DNS server is not authoritative for the query, then this server will go looking for an authoritative name server in the DNS tree. The local name server will first query a root server, then a **tld** server and then a domain server. When the local name server resolves the query, then it will relay this information to the client that submitted the query, and it will also keep a copy of these queries in its cache. So when a(nother) client submits the same query to this name server, then it will retrieve this information form its cache.

For example, a client queries for the A record on www.linux-training.be to its local server. This is the first query ever received by this local server. The local server checks that it is not authoritative for the linux-training.be domain, nor for the **.be tld**, and it is also not a root server. So the local server will use the root hints to send an **iterative** query to a root server.

The root server will reply with a reference to the server that is authoritative for the .be domain (root DNS servers do not resolve fqdn's, and root servers do not respond to recursive queries).

The local server will then sent an iterative query to the authoritative server for the **.be tld**. This server will respond with a reference to the name server that is authoritative for the linux-training.be domain.

The local server will then sent the query for www.linux-training.be to the authoritative server (or one of its slave servers) for the linux-training.be domain. When the local server receives the ip address for www.linux-training.be, then it will provide this information to the client that submitted this query.

Besides caching the A record for www.linux-training.be, the local server will also cache the NS and A record for the linux-training.be name server and the .be name server.

# 10.11. forward lookup zone example

The way to set up zones in **/etc/bind/named.conf.local** is to create a zone entry with a reference to another file (this other file contains the **zone database**).

Here is an example of such an entry in **/etc/bind/named.conf.local**:

```
root@debian7:~# cat /etc/bind/named.conf.local
//
// Do any local configuration here
//

// Consider adding the 1918 zones here, if they are not used in your
// organization
//include "/etc/bind/zones.rfc1918";

zone "paul.local" IN {
        type master;
        file "/etc/bind/db.paul.local";
        allow-update { none; };
};
root@debian7:~#
```

To create the zone file, the easy method is to copy an existing zone file (this is easier than writing from scratch).

```
root@debian7:/etc/bind# cp db.empty db.paul.local
root@debian7:/etc/bind# vi db.paul.local
```

Here is an example of a zone file.

```
root@debian7:/etc/bind# cat db.paul.local
; zone for classroom teaching
$TTL    86400
@       IN      SOA     debianpaul.paul.local. root.paul.local (
                        2014100100      ; Serial
                        1h              ; Refresh
                        1h              ; Retry
                        2h              ; Expire
                        86400 )         ; Negative Cache TTL
;
; name servers
;
        IN      NS      ns1
        IN      NS      debianpaul
        IN      NS      debian7
;
; servers
;
debianpaul      IN      A       10.104.33.30
debian7         IN      A       10.104.33.30
ns1             IN      A       10.104.33.30
;www            IN      A       10.104.33.30
```

# 10.12. example: caching only DNS server

1. installing DNS software on Debian

```
root@debian7:~# aptitude update && aptitude upgrade
...
root@debian7:~# aptitude install bind9
...
root@debian7:~# dpkg -l | grep bind9 | tr -s ' '
ii bind9 1:9.8.4.dfsg.P1-6+nmu2+deb7u2 amd64 Internet Domain Name Server
ii bind9-host 1:9.8.4.dfsg.P1-6+nmu2+deb7u2 amd64 Version of 'host' bundled...
ii bind9utils 1:9.8.4.dfsg.P1-6+nmu2+deb7u2 amd64 Utilities for BIND
ii libbind9-80 1:9.8.4.dfsg.P1-6+nmu2+deb7u2 amd64 BIND9 Shared Library use...
root@debian7:~#
```

2. Discover the default configuration files. Can you define the purpose of each file ?

```
root@debian7:~# ls -l /etc/bind
total 52
-rw-r--r-- 1 root root 2389 Sep  5 20:25 bind.keys
-rw-r--r-- 1 root root  237 Sep  5 20:25 db.0
-rw-r--r-- 1 root root  271 Sep  5 20:25 db.127
-rw-r--r-- 1 root root  237 Sep  5 20:25 db.255
-rw-r--r-- 1 root root  353 Sep  5 20:25 db.empty
-rw-r--r-- 1 root root  270 Sep  5 20:25 db.local
-rw-r--r-- 1 root root 3048 Sep  5 20:25 db.root
-rw-r--r-- 1 root bind  463 Sep  5 20:25 named.conf
-rw-r--r-- 1 root bind  490 Sep  5 20:25 named.conf.default-zones
-rw-r--r-- 1 root bind  374 Oct  1 20:01 named.conf.local
-rw-r--r-- 1 root bind  913 Oct  1 13:24 named.conf.options
-rw-r----- 1 bind bind   77 Oct  1 11:14 rndc.key
-rw-r--r-- 1 root root 1317 Sep  5 20:25 zones.rfc191
```

3. Setup caching only dns server. This is normally the default setup. A caching-only name server will look up names for you and cache them. Many tutorials will tell you to add a **forwarder**, but we first try without this!

Hey this seems to work without a **forwarder**. Using a sniffer you can find out what really happens. Your freshly install dns server is not using a cache, and it is not using your local dns server (from /etc/resolv.conf). So where is this information coming from ? And what can you learn from sniffing this dns traffic ?

4. Explain in detail what happens when you enable a caching only dns server without forwarder. This wireshark screenshot can help, but you learn more by sniffing the traffic yourself.

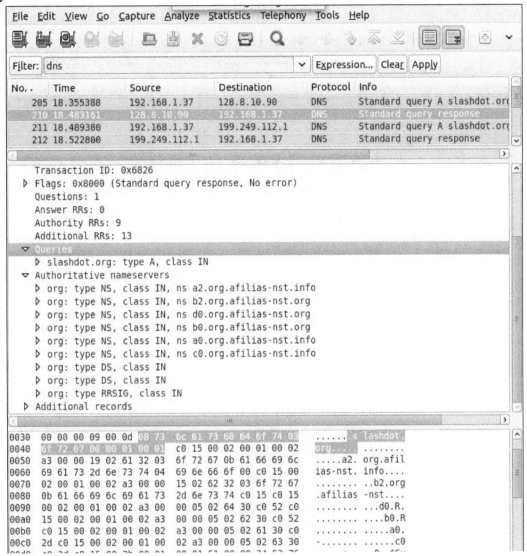

You should see traffic to a **root name server** whenever you try a new **tld** for the first time. Remember that **dns** is a caching protocol, which means that repeating a query will generate a lot less traffic since your **dns server** will still have the answer in its memory.

# 10.13. example: caching only with forwarder

5. Add the public Google **dns server** as a **forwarder**. The ip address of this server is **8.8.8.8** .

Before the change:

```
root@debian7:~# grep -A2 'forwarders {' /etc/bind/named.conf.options
        // forwarders {
        //      0.0.0.0;
        // };
```

changing:

```
root@debian7:~# vi /etc/bind/named.conf.options
```

After the change:

```
root@debian7:~# grep -A2 'forwarders {' /etc/bind/named.conf.options
        forwarders {
                8.8.8.8;
        };
```

Restart the server:

```
root@debian7:~# service bind9 restart
Stopping domain name service...: bind9.
Starting domain name service...: bind9.
```

6. Explain the purpose of adding the **forwarder**. What is our **dns server** doing when it receives a query ?

```
root@debian7:~# nslookup
> server
Default server: 10.104.33.30
Address: 10.104.33.30#53
> linux-training.be
Server:         10.104.33.30
Address:        10.104.33.30#53

Non-authoritative answer:
Name:   linux-training.be
Address: 188.93.155.87
>
```

This is the output of **tcpdump udp port 53** while executing the above query for **linux-training.be** in **nslookup**.

```
root@debian7:~# tcpdump udp port 53
tcpdump: verbose output suppressed, use -v or -vv for full protocol decode
listening on eth0, link-type EN10MB (Ethernet), capture size 65535 bytes
```

You should find the following two lines in the output of **tcpdump**:

```
10.104.33.30.19381 > google-public-dns-a.google.com.domain: 18237+% [1au] A? \
linux-training.be. (46)
google-public-dns-a.google.com.domain > 10.104.33.30.19381: 18237 1/0/1 A 188\
.93.155.87 (62)
```

Below is an (old) wireshark screenshot that can help, you should see something similar (but with different ip addresses).

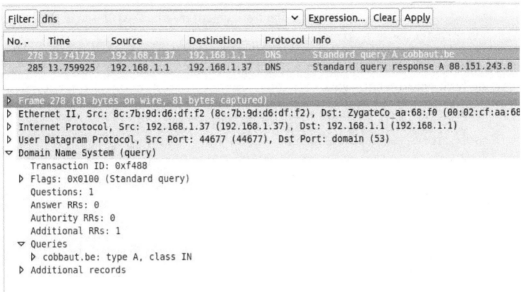

7. What happens when you query for the same domain name more than once ?

8. Why does it say "non-authoritative answer" ? When is a dns server authoritative ?

9. You can also use **dig** instead of **nslookup**.

```
root@debian7:~# dig @10.104.33.30 linux-training.be +short
188.93.155.87
root@debian7:~#
```

10. How can we avoid having to set the server in dig or nslookup ?

Change this:

```
root@debian7:~# cat /etc/resolv.conf
nameserver 10.46.101.1
root@debian7:~#
```

into this:

```
root@debian7:~# cat /etc/resolv.conf
nameserver 10.104.33.30
root@debian7:~#
```

11. When you use **dig** for the first time for a domain, where is the answer coming from ? And the second time ? How can you tell ?

# 10.14. example: primary authoritative server

1. Instead of only cachng the information from other servers, we will now make our server authoritative for our own domain.

2. I choose the top level domain **.local** and the domain **paul.local** and put the information in **/etc/bind/named.conf.local**.

```
root@debian7:~# cat /etc/bind/named.conf.local
//
// Do any local configuration here
//

// Consider adding the 1918 zones here, if they are not used in your
// organization
//include "/etc/bind/zones.rfc1918";

zone "paul.local" IN {
        type master;
        file "/etc/bind/db.paul.local";
        allow-update { none; };
};
```

3. Also add a **zone database file**, similar to this one (add some A records for testing). Set the **Refresh** and **Retry** values not too high so you can sniff this traffic (this example makes the slave server contact the master every hour).

```
root@debian7:~# cat /etc/bind/db.paul.local
; zone for classroom teaching
$TTL    86400
@       IN      SOA     debianpaul.paul.local. root.paul.local (
                        2014100101      ; Serial
                        1h              ; Refresh
                        1h              ; Retry
                        2h              ; Expire
                        900 )           ; Negative Cache TTL
;
; name servers
;
        IN      NS      ns1
        IN      NS      debianpaul
        IN      NS      debian7
;
; servers
;
debianpaul      IN      A       10.104.33.30
debian7         IN      A       10.104.33.30
ns1             IN      A       10.104.33.30
;www            IN      A       10.104.33.30
root@debian7:~#
```

Note that the **www** record is commented out, so it will not resolve.

# 10.14.1. using your own DNS server

If you are confident that your **dns server** works, then set it as default and only dns server in **/etc/resolv.conf**.

```
root@debian7:~# cat /etc/resolv.conf
nameserver 10.104.33.30
root@debian7:~#
```

In case you also use **dhclient**, you will need to add your dns server to **/etc/dhcp/dhclient.conf**.

```
root@debian7:~# diff /etc/dhcp/dhclient.conf /etc/dhcp/dhclient.conf.original
21c21
< prepend domain-name-servers 10.104.33.30;
---
> #prepend domain-name-servers 127.0.0.1;
23,24c23
< #      domain-name, domain-name-servers, domain-search, host-name,
<        domain-name, domain-search, host-name,
---
>        domain-name, domain-name-servers, domain-search, host-name,
root@debian7:~#
```

The above screenshot shows that 10.104.33.30 is now a default option that the **dhcp client** should no longer request from the **dhcp server**.

Adjust **/etc/hosts** to reflect your **domain name** and verify with **hostname** and **dnsdomainname**.

```
root@debian7:~# grep debian7 /etc/hosts
127.0.1.1 debian7.paul.local debian7
root@debian7:~# hostname
debian7
root@debian7:~# hostname --fqdn
debian7.paul.local
root@debian7:~# dnsdomainname
paul.local
```

## 10.14.2. using your own domain

Consider the following screenshot:

```
root@debian7b:~# cat /etc/resolv.conf
nameserver 10.104.33.30
root@debian7b:~# ping -c1 www
ping: unknown host www
root@debian7b:~# vi /etc/resolv.conf
root@debian7b:~# cat /etc/resolv.conf
nameserver 10.104.33.30
domain paul.local
root@debian7b:~# ping -c1 www
PING www.paul.local (10.104.33.31) 56(84) bytes of data.
64 bytes from 10.104.33.31: icmp_req=1 ttl=64 time=0.021 ms

--- www.paul.local ping statistics ---
1 packets transmitted, 1 received, 0% packet loss, time 0ms
rtt min/avg/max/mdev = 0.021/0.021/0.021/0.000 ms
root@debian7b:~#
```

Adding the **domain paul.local** directive to **/etc/resolv.conf** allows omitting the domain when using hostnames.

You can accomplish this feature automatically by adjusting **dhclient.conf**.

```
root@debian7:~# grep paul.local /etc/dhcp/dhclient.conf
prepend domain-name "paul.local";
prepend domain-search "paul.local";
root@debian7:~#
```

## 4. Restart the DNS server and check your zone in the error log.

```
root@debian7:~# service bind9 restart
Stopping domain name service...: bind9.
Starting domain name service...: bind9.
root@debian7:~# grep paul.local /var/log/syslog
Oct  6 09:22:18 debian7 named[2707]: zone paul.local/IN: loaded seria\
l 2014100101
Oct  6 09:22:18 debian7 named[2707]: zone paul.local/IN: sending noti\
fies (serial 2014100101)
```

## 5. Use **dig** or **nslookup** (or even **ping**) to test your A records.

```
root@debian7:~# ping -c1 ns1.paul.local
PING ns1.paul.local (10.104.33.30) 56(84) bytes of data.
64 bytes from 10.104.33.30: icmp_req=1 ttl=64 time=0.006 ms

--- ns1.paul.local ping statistics ---
1 packets transmitted, 1 received, 0% packet loss, time 0ms
rtt min/avg/max/mdev = 0.006/0.006/0.006/0.000 ms
root@debian7:~# ping -c1 www.paul.local
ping: unknown host www.paul.local
```

## Note that the **www** record was commented out, so it should fail.

```
root@debian7:~# dig debian7.paul.local

; <<>> DiG 9.8.4-rpz2+rl005.12-P1 <<>> debian7.paul.local
;; global options: +cmd
;; Got answer:
;; ->>HEADER<<- opcode: QUERY, status: NOERROR, id: 50491
;; flags: qr aa rd ra; QUERY: 1, ANSWER: 1, AUTHORITY: 3, ADDITIONAL: 2

;; QUESTION SECTION:
;debian7.paul.local.            IN      A

;; ANSWER SECTION:
debian7.paul.local.     86400   IN      A       10.104.33.30

;; AUTHORITY SECTION:
paul.local.             86400   IN      NS      ns1.paul.local.
paul.local.             86400   IN      NS      debian7.paul.local.
paul.local.             86400   IN      NS      debianpaul.paul.local.

;; ADDITIONAL SECTION:
ns1.paul.local.         86400   IN      A       10.104.33.30
debianpaul.paul.local.  86400   IN      A       10.104.33.30

;; Query time: 4 msec
;; SERVER: 10.104.33.30#53(10.104.33.30)
;; WHEN: Mon Oct  6 09:35:25 2014
;; MSG SIZE  rcvd: 141

root@debian7:~#
```

## 6. Our primary server appears to be up and running. Note the information here:

```
server os  : Debian 7
ip address : 10.104.33.30
domain name: paul.local
server name: ns1.paul.local
```

# 10.15. example: a DNS slave server

1. A slave server transfers zone information over the network from a master server (a slave can also be a master). A primary server maintains zone records in its local file system. As an exercise, and to verify the work of all students, set up a slave server of all the master servers in the classroom.

2. Before configuring the slave server, we may have to allow transfers from our zone to this server. Remember that this is not very secure since transfers are in clear text and limited to an ip address. This example follows our demo from above.

Imagine a student named **Jesse** having completed the setup as shown before, with the domain name **jesse.local** and the ip address 10.104.15.20. The goal is to have a slave server of paul.local on Jesse's computer and a slave zone of jesse.local on my computer.

Below is an example of an **allow-transfer** statement. Careful, maybe the default allows transfer to any.

```
root@debian7:/etc/bind# cat named.conf.local
//
// Do any local configuration here
//

// Consider adding the 1918 zones here, if they are not used in your
// organization
//include "/etc/bind/zones.rfc1918";

zone "paul.local" IN {
        type master;
        file "/etc/bind/db.paul.local";
        allow-update { none; };
        allow-transfer { 10.104.15.20; };
};
```

3. With the configuration below I can make my server a slave for the **jesse.local** zone.

```
root@debian7:/etc/bind# tail -6 named.conf.local
zone "jesse.local" IN {
        type slave;
        file "/var/cache/named/db.jesse.local";
        masters { 10.104.15.20; };
};

root@debian7:/etc/bind# mkdir /var/cache/named/
root@debian7:/etc/bind# chown bind:bind /var/cache/named/
root@debian7:/etc/bind# ls -ld /var/cache/named/
drwxr-xr-x 2 bind bind 4096 Oct  1 20:01 /var/cache/named/
```

Note that we put the **slave zones** in **/var/cache/named** and not in **/etc/bind**.

4. Restarting bind on the slave server should transfer the zone database file. Verify this in /**var/log/syslog**. (time and date are truncated from the screenshot, and Jesse did not use the current date in the serial number...)

```
root@debian7:/etc/bind# grep jesse /var/log/syslog
named[2731]: zone jesse.local/IN: Transfer started.
named[2731]: transfer of 'jesse.local/IN' from 10.104.15.20#53: connected u\
sing 10.104.33.30#44719
named[2731]: zone jesse.local/IN: transferred serial 20110516
named[2731]: transfer of 'jesse.local/IN' from 10.104.15.20#53: Transfer co\
mpleted: 1 messages, 8 records, 239 bytes, 0.001 secs (239000 bytes/sec)
```

And the contents of the **slave zone**:

```
root@debian7:/etc/bind# cat /var/cache/named/db.jesse.local
$ORIGIN .
$TTL 604800     ; 1 week
jesse.local             IN SOA  ns.jesse.local. root.jesse.local.jesse.local. (
                                20110516    ; serial
                                300         ; refresh (5 minutes)
                                200         ; retry (3 minutes 20 seconds)
                                2419200     ; expire (4 weeks)
                                604800      ; minimum (1 week)
                                )
                        NS      ns.jesse.local.
$ORIGIN jesse.local.
anya                    A       10.104.15.1
mac                     A       10.104.15.30
ns                      A       10.104.15.20
ubu1010srv              A       10.104.15.20
www                     A       10.104.15.25
root@debian7:/etc/bind#
```

# 10.16. practice: dns

1. Install **bind9** and verify with a sniffer how it works.

2. Add a **forwarder** and verify that it works.

3. Create a **primary forward lookup zone** named yourname.local with at least two NS records and four A records.

4. Use **dig** and **nslookup** to verify your NS and A records.

5. Create a **slave** of your primary zone (on another server) and verify the **zone transfer**.

6. Set up two primary zones on two servers and implement a **conditional forwarder** (you can use the two servers from before).

# 10.17. solution: dns

1. Install **bind9** and verify with a sniffer how it works.

You should see queries to the root name servers with **tcpdump** or **wireshark**.

2. Add a **forwarder** and verify that it works.

The forwarder van be added in named.conf.options as seen in the theory.

3. Create a **primary forward lookup zone** named yourname.local with at least two NS records and four A records.

This is literally explained in the theory.

4. Use **dig** and **nslookup** to verify your NS and A records.

This is literally explained in the theory.

5. Create a **slave** of your primary zone (on another server) and verify the **zone transfer**.

This is literally explained in the theory.

6. Set up two primary zones on two servers and implement a **conditional forwarder** (you can use the two servers from before).

A conditional forwarder is set in named.conf.local as a zone.
(see the theory on forwarder)

# Chapter 11. advanced DNS

This chapter expands your DNS server with topics like **round robin dns** for load balancing servers, **dns delegation** to delegate child domains to another team and **split horizon dns** so you can provide local service locations to clients.

There is more to **dns**, content will be added **rsn**.

# 11.1. example: DNS round robin

When you create multiple A records for the same name, then **bind** will do a **round robin** of the order in which the records are returned. This allows the use of DNS as a load balancer between hosts, since clients will usually take the first ip-address offered.

Consider this example from the **/etc/bind/db.paul.local** zone configuration file. There are two A records for **www** pointing to two distinct ip addresses.

```
root@debian7:~# grep www /etc/bind/db.paul.local
www            IN      A        10.104.33.30
www            IN      A        10.104.33.31
```

Below a screenshot of **nslookup** querying a load balanced A record. Notice the order of ip addresses returned.

```
root@debian7:~# nslookup www.paul.local 10.104.33.30
Server:         10.104.33.30
Address:        10.104.33.30#53

Name:   www.paul.local
Address: 10.104.33.31
Name:   www.paul.local
Address: 10.104.33.30

root@debian7:~# nslookup www.paul.local 10.104.33.30
Server:         10.104.33.30
Address:        10.104.33.30#53

Name:   www.paul.local
Address: 10.104.33.30
Name:   www.paul.local
Address: 10.104.33.31
```

Try to set up a website on two web servers (with a small difference so you can distinguish the websites) and test the **round robin**.

## 11.2. DNS delegation

You can **delegate** a child domain to another DNS server. The child domain then becomes a new zone, with authority at the new dns server.

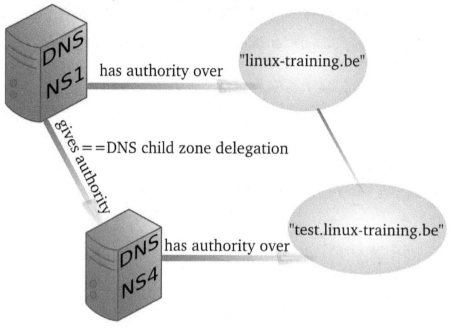

When **delegation** is properly set up, then clients that query your parent zone will also be able to resolve the delegated child zones.

# 11.3. example: DNS delegation

We have another **Linux server** named **debian7b** and we want to make it responsible for the child domain **test42.paul.local**.

*Note the name of the servers in the screenshots are either **debian7** (hosting the parent domain) or **debian7b** (hosting the child domain).*

We start by adjusting the **/etc/bind/named.comf.local** file (on the server hosting the parent domain) to make sure that no forwarder will be used when resolving authoritative names.

```
root@debian7:~# grep -A4 paul.local /etc/bind/named.conf.local
zone "paul.local" IN {
        type master;
        file "/etc/bind/db.paul.local";
        allow-update { none; };
        allow-transfer { 10.104.15.20; };
        forwarders { };
};
root@debian7:~#
```

Technically, you could also set **allow-transfer** to **{ any; };** while troubleshooting and then refine it later, but this is not needed for delegation.

Then we add the delegation to our zone database:

```
root@debian7:~# tail -3 /etc/bind/db.paul.local
$ORIGIN test42.paul.local.
@       IN      NS      ns2.test42.paul.local.
ns2     IN      A       10.104.33.31     ; the glue record
root@debian7:~#
```

Don't forget to restart **bind** and verify **/var/log/syslog**.

```
root@debian7:~# service bind9 restart
Stopping domain name service...: bind9.
Starting domain name service...: bind9.
root@debian7:~# grep paul.local /var/log/syslog | cut -c28- | tail -2
named[3202]: zone paul.local/IN: loaded serial 2014100801
named[3202]: zone paul.local/IN: sending notifies (serial 2014100801)
root@debian7:~#
```

*Note that on your terminal you can type **tail -40 /var/log/syslog** because the only reason I use **grep**, **cut** and **tail -2** is to limit the size of the screenshots in this book.*

Next we create a zone database file on the second server, as seen in this screenshot:

```
root@debian7b:~# cat /etc/bind/db.test42.paul.local
; child zone for classroom teaching
$TTL    86400
$ORIGIN test42.paul.local.
@       IN      SOA     ns2.test42.paul.local. root.test42.paul.local. (
                        2014100802      ; Serial
                        1h              ; Refresh
                        1h              ; Retry
                        2h              ; Expire
                        900 )           ; Negative Cache TTL
;
; name servers
;
        IN      NS      ns2.test42.paul.local.
        IN      NS      debian7b.test42.paul.local.
;
; servers
;
ns2             IN      A       10.104.33.31
debian7b        IN      A       10.104.33.31
testsrv         IN      A       10.104.33.31
root@debian7b:~#
```

The second server also needs a zone definition in **named.conf.local**, followed by a restart of **bind**.

```
root@debian7b:~# cat /etc/bind/named.conf.local
//
// Do any local configuration here
//

// Consider adding the 1918 zones here, if they are not used in your
// organization
//include "/etc/bind/zones.rfc1918";

zone "test42.paul.local" IN {
        type master;
        file "/etc/bind/db.test42.paul.local";
        allow-update { none; };
        allow-transfer { any; };
};
root@debian7b:~#
```

Testing on the parent server:

```
root@debian7:~# dig ns1.paul.local +short
10.104.33.30
root@debian7:~# dig ns2.test42.paul.local +short
10.104.33.31
root@debian7:~# dig debian7b.test42.paul.local +short
10.104.33.31
```

# 11.4. example: split-horizon dns

Suppose you want to answer dns queries depending on who is asking. For example when someone from the 10.104.15.0/24 network (managed by Jesse) asks for the A record www.paul.local, then dns answers with 10.104.33.30. But when someone from the 10.104.42.0/24 network (managed by Keith) asks for the same A record of www.paul.local, he will get 10.104.33.31 as an answer.

A **split-horizon** setup can be used to redirect people to **local** copies of certain services.

In this example we want to decide on specific answers for two networks (Jesse's and Keith's) and prevent them from using our dns server for **recursion**, while maintaining the capability to resolve the internet and our paul.local zone from our own network.

We start by creating three **view** clauses in **named.conf.local**.

```
root@debian7:/etc/bind# cat named.conf.local
view "paul" {
match-clients { 10.104.33.0; localhost; };
include "/etc/bind/named.conf.default-zones";
zone "paul.local" IN {
        type master;
        file "/etc/bind/db.paul.local";
        allow-update { none; };
        };
};      // end view internal

view "jesse" {
match-clients { 10.104.15/24; };
zone "paul.local" IN {
        type master;
        file "/etc/bind/db.paul.local.jesse";
        allow-update { none; };
        };
};      // end view jesse

view "keith" {
match-clients { 10.104.42/24; };
zone "paul.local" IN {
        type master;
        file "/etc/bind/db.paul.local.keith";
        allow-update { none; };
        };
};      // end view keith
```

Note that we included the **default-zones** in the internal zone. It is mandatory to put all zones inside views when using a view.

The zone files are identical copies, except for the **www** record. You can see that the **round robin** is still active for internal users, computers from 10.104.15.0/24 (Jesse) will always receive 10.104.33.30 while computers from 10.104.42.0/24 (Keith) will receive 10.104.33.31.

```
root@debian7:/etc/bind# grep www db.paul.local db.paul.local.[jk]*
db.paul.local:www               IN      A       10.104.33.30
db.paul.local:www               IN      A       10.104.33.31
db.paul.local.jesse:www         IN      A       10.104.33.30
db.paul.local.keith:www         IN      A       10.104.33.31
```

# 11.5. old dns topics

All the dns things below this paragraph are old and in urgent need of review.

## 11.5.1. old example: reverse DNS

1. We can add ip to name resolution to our dns-server using a reverse dns zone.

2. Start by adding a .arpa zone to /etc/bind/named.conf.local like this (we set notify to no to avoid sending of notify messages to other name servers):

```
root@ubu1010srv:/etc/bind# grep -A4 arpa named.conf.local
zone "1.168.192.in-addr.arpa" {
 type master;
 notify no;
 file "/etc/bind/db.192";
};
```

3. Also create a zone database file for this reverse lookup zone.

```
root@ubu1010srv:/etc/bind# cat db.192
;
; BIND reverse data file for 192.168.1.0/24 network
;
$TTL 604800
@ IN SOA ns.cobbaut.paul root.cobbaut.paul. (
   20110516 ; Serial
    604800  ; Refresh
     86400  ; Retry
   2419200  ; Expire
    604800 ) ; Negative Cache TTL
;
@ IN NS ns.
37 IN PTR ns.cobbaut.paul.
1 IN PTR anya.cobbaut.paul.
30 IN PTR mac.cobbaut.paul.
root@ubu1010srv:/etc/bind#
```

4. Test with nslookup or dig:

```
root@ubu1010srv:/etc/bind# dig 1.168.192.in-addr.arpa AXFR
```

## 11.5.2. old DNS load balancing

Not as above. When you have more than one DNS server authoritative for a zone, you can spread queries amongst all server. One way to do this is by creating NS records for all servers that participate in the load balancing of external queries.

You could also configure different name servers on internal clients.

## 11.5.3. old DNS notify

The original design of DNS in rfc 1034 and rfc 1035 implemented a **refresh** time in the **SOA** record to configure a time loop for slaves to query their master server. This can result in a lot of useless pull requests, or in a significant lag between updates.

For this reason **dns notify (rfc 1996)** was designed. The server will now notify slaves whenever there is an update. By default this feature is activated in **bind**.

Notify can be disabled as in this screenshot.

```
zone "1.168.192.in-addr.arpa" {
        type master;
        notify no;
        file "/etc/bind/db.192";
};
```

## 11.5.4. old testing IXFR and AXFR

Full zone transfers (AXFR) are initiated when you restart the bind server, or when you manually update the zone database file directly. With **nsupdate** you can update a zone database and initiate an incremental zone transfer.

You need DDNS allowed for **nsupdate** to work.

```
root@ubu1010srv:/etc/bind# nsupdate
> server 127.0.0.1
> update add mac14.linux-training.be 86400 A 192.168.1.23
> send
update failed: REFUSED
```

## 11.5.5. old DDNS integration with DHCP

Some organizations like to have all their client computers in DNS. This can be cumbersome to maintain. Luckily **rfc 2136** describes integration of DHCP servers with a DNS server. Whenever DHCP acknowledges a client ip configuration, it can notify DNS with this clients ip-address and name. This is called **dynamic updates** or DDNS.

## 11.5.6. old reverse is forward in-addr.arpa

Reverse lookup is actually iomplemented as a forward lookup in the **in-addr.arpa** domain. This domain has 256 child domains (from 0.in-addr.arpa to 255.in-addr.arpa), with each child domain having again 256 child domains. And this twice more to a structure of over four billion (2 to the power 32) domains.

## 11.5.7. old ipv6

With rfc 3596 came ipv6 extensions for DNS. There is the AAAA record for ipv6 hosts on the network, and there is the **ip6.int** domain for reverse lookup (having 16 child domains from 0.ip6.int to f.ip6.int, each of those having again 16 child domains...and this 16 times.

## 11.5.8. old DNS security: file corruption

To mitigate file corruption on the **zone files** and the **bind configuration** files protect them with Unix permissions and take regular backups.

## 11.5.9. old DNS security: zone transfers

Limit zone transfers to certain ip addresses instead of to **any**. Nevermind that ip-addresses can be spoofed, still use this.

## 11.5.10. old DNS security: zone transfers, ip spoofing

You could setup DNSSEC (which is not the easiest to maintain) and with rfc 2845(tsig?) and with rfc 2930(tkey, but this is open to brute force), or you could disable all zone transfers and use a script with ssh to copy them manually.

## 11.5.11. old DNS security: queries

Allow recursion only from the local network, and iterative queries from outside only when necessary. This can be configured on master and slave servers.

```
view "internal" {
match-clients { 192.168.42/24; };
recursion yes;
...

};

view "external" {
match-clients { any; };
recursion no;
...

};
```

Or allow only queries from the local network.

```
options {
        allow-query { 192.168.42.0/24; localhost; };
};

zone "cobbaut.paul" {
        allow-query { any; };
};
```

Or only allow recursive queries from internal clients.

```
options {
        allow-recursion { 192.168.42.0/24; localhost; };
```

```
};
```

## 11.5.12. old DNS security: chrooted bind

Most Linux distributions allow an easy setup of bind in a **chrooted** environment.

## 11.5.13. old DNS security: DNSSEC

DNSSEC uses public/private keys to secure communications, this is described in rfc's 4033, 4034 and 4035.

## 11.5.14. old DNS security: root

Do not run bind as root. Do not run any application daemon as root.

# Part IV. dhcp server

# Table of Contents

# Chapter 12. introduction to dhcp

Dynamic Host Configuration Protocol (or short **dhcp**) is a standard tcp/ip protocol that distributes ip configurations to clients. **dhcp** is defined in **rfc 2131** (before that it was defined as an update to **bootp** in rfc 1531/1541.

The alternative to **dhcp** is manually entering the ip configuration on each client computer.

# 12.1. four broadcasts

**dhcp** works with layer 2 broadcasts. A dhcp client that starts, will send a **dhcp discover** on the network. All **dhcp servers** (that have a lease available) will respond with a **dhcp offer**. The client will choose one of those offers and will send a **dhcp request** containing the chosen offer. The **dhcp server** usually responds with a **dhcp ack**(knowledge).

In wireshark it looks like this.

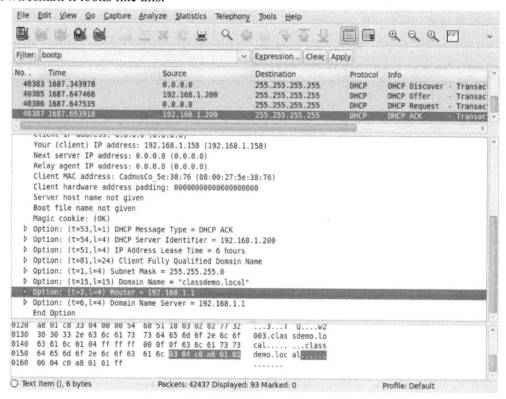

When this procedure is finished, then the client is allowed to use that ip-configuration until the end of its lease time.

# 12.2. picturing dhcp

Here we have a small network with two **dhcp servers** named DHCP-SRV1 and DHCP-SRV2 and two clients (SunWS1 and Mac42). All computers are connected by a hub or switch (pictured in the middle). All four computers have a cable to the hub (cables not pictured).

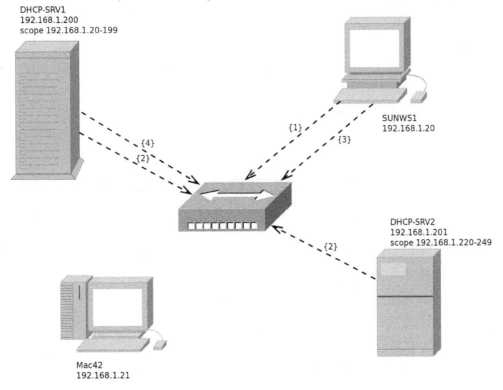

1. The client SunWS1 sends a **dhcp discover** on the network. All computers receive this broadcast.

2. Both **dhcp servers** answer with a **dhcp offer**. DHCP-SRV1 is a **dedicated dhcp server** and is faster in sending a **dhcp offer** than DHCP-SRV2 (who happens to also be a file server).

3. The client chooses the offer from DHCP-SRV1 and sends a **dhcp request** on the network.

4. DHCP-SRV1 answers with a **dhcp ack** (short for acknowledge).

All four broadcasts (or five when you count both offers) can be layer 2 ethernet broadcast to mac address **ff:ff:ff:ff:ff:ff** and a layer 3 ip broadcast to 255.255.255.255.

The same story can be read in **rfc 2131**.

## 12.3. installing a dhcp server

dhcp server for Debian/Mint

```
debian5:~# aptitude install dhcp3-server
Reading package lists... Done
Building dependency tree
Reading state information... Done
Reading extended state information
Initializing package states... Done
Reading task descriptions... Done
The following NEW packages will be installed:
  dhcp3-server
```

You get a configuration file with many examples.

```
debian5:~# ls -l /etc/dhcp3/dhcpd.conf
-rw-r--r-- 1 root root 3551 2011-04-10 21:23 /etc/dhcp3/dhcpd.conf
```

## 12.4. dhcp server for RHEL/CentOS

Installing is easy with **yum**.

```
[root@rhel71 ~]# yum install dhcp
Loaded plugins: product-id, subscription-manager
Resolving Dependencies
--> Running transaction check
---> Package dhcp.x86_64 12:4.2.5-36.el7 will be installed
--> Finished Dependency Resolution

Dependencies Resolved

================================================================================
 Package      Arch        Version            Repository             Size
================================================================================
Installing:
 dhcp         x86_64      12:4.2.5-36.el7    rhel-7-server-rpms     510 k

Transaction Summary
================================================================================
Install  1 Package

Total download size: 510 k
Installed size: 1.4 M
Is this ok [y/d/N]: y
Downloading packages:
dhcp-4.2.5-36.el7.x86_64.rpm                            | 510 kB   00:01
Running transaction check
Running transaction test
Transaction test succeeded
Running transaction
  Installing : 12:dhcp-4.2.5-36.el7.x86_64                          1/1
  Verifying  : 12:dhcp-4.2.5-36.el7.x86_64                          1/1

Installed:
  dhcp.x86_64 12:4.2.5-36.el7

Complete!
[root@rhel71 ~]#
```

After installing we get a **/etc/dhcp/dhcpd.conf** that points us to an example file named **dhcpd.conf.sample**.

```
[root@rhel71 ~]# cat /etc/dhcp/dhcpd.conf
#
# DHCP Server Configuration file.
#   see /usr/share/doc/dhcp*/dhcpd.conf.example
#   see dhcpd.conf(5) man page
#
[root@rhel71 ~]#
```

So we copy the sample and adjust it for our real situation. We name the copy **/etc/dhcp/ dhcpd.conf**.

```
[root@rhel71 ~]# cp /usr/share/doc/dhcp-4.2.5/dhcpd.conf.example /etc/dhcp/dhcp\
d.conf
[root@rhel71 ~]# vi /etc/dhcp/dhcpd.conf
[root@rhel71 ~]# cat /etc/dhcp/dhcpd.conf
option domain-name "linux-training.be";
option domain-name-servers 10.42.42.42;
default-lease-time 600;
max-lease-time 7200;
log-facility local7;

subnet 10.42.0.0 netmask 255.255.0.0 {
  range 10.42.200.11 10.42.200.120;
  option routers 10.42.200.1;
}
[root@rhel71 ~]#
```

The 'routers' option is valid for the subnet alone, whereas the 'domain-name' option is global (for all subnets).

Time to start the server. Remember to use **systemctl start dhcpd** on RHEL7/CentOS7 and **service dhcpd start** on previous versions of RHEL/CentOS.

```
[root@rhel71 ~]# systemctl start dhcpd
[root@rhel71 ~]#
```

# 12.5. client reservations

You can reserve an ip configuration for a client using the mac address.

```
host pc42 {
hardware ethernet 11:22:33:44:55:66;
fixed-address 192.168.42.42;
}
```

You can add individual options to this reservation.

```
host pc42 {
hardware ethernet 11:22:33:44:55:66;
fixed-address 192.168.42.42;
option domain-name "linux-training.be";
option routers 192.168.42.1;
}
```

# 12.6. example config files

Below you see several sections of **/etc/dhcp/dhcpd.conf** on a **Debian 6** server.

```
# NetSec Antwerp Network
```

```
subnet 192.168.1.0 netmask 255.255.255.0 {
 range 192.168.1.20 192.168.1.199;
 option domain-name-servers ns1.netsec.local;
 option domain-name "netsec.local";
 option routers 192.168.1.1;
 option broadcast-address 192.168.1.255;
 default-lease-time 7200;
 max-lease-time 7200;
}
```

Above the general configuration for the network, with a pool of 180 addresses.

Below two client reservations:

```
#
# laptops
#

host mac {
  hardware ethernet 00:26:bb:xx:xx:xx;
  fixed-address mac.netsec.local;
}

host vmac {
  hardware ethernet 8c:7b:9d:xx:xx:xx;
  fixed-address vmac.netsec.local;
}
```

# 12.7. older example config files

For dhcpd.conf on Fedora with dynamic updates for a DNS domain.

```
[root@fedora14 ~]# cat /etc/dhcp/dhcpd.conf
authoritative;
include "/etc/rndc.key";

log-facility local6;

server-identifier    fedora14;
ddns-domainname  "office.linux-training.be";
ddns-update-style interim;
ddns-updates  on;
update-static-leases on;

option domain-name "office.linux-training.be";
option domain-name-servers 192.168.42.100;
option ip-forwarding off;

default-lease-time 1800;
max-lease-time  3600;

zone office.linux-training.be {
 primary 192.168.42.100;
}

subnet 192.168.4.0 netmask 255.255.255.0 {
 range 192.168.4.24 192.168.4.40;
}
```

Allowing any updates in the zone database (part of the named.conf configuration)

```
zone "office.linux-training.be" {
```

```
type master;
file "/var/named/db.office.linux-training.be";
allow-transfer { any; };
allow-update { any; };
};
```

### Allowing secure key updates in the zone database (part of the named.conf configuration)

```
zone "office.linux-training.be" {
type master;
file "/var/named/db.office.linux-training.be";
allow-transfer { any; };
allow-update { key mykey; };
};
```

### Sample key file contents:

```
[root@fedora14 ~]# cat /etc/rndc.key
key "rndc-key" {
algorithm hmac-md5;
secret "4Ykd58uIeUr3Ve6ad1qTfQ==";
};
```

Generate your own keys with **dnssec-keygen**.

How to include a key in a config file:

```
include "/etc/bind/rndc.key";
```

Also make sure that **bind** can write to your db.zone file (using chmod/chown). For Ubuntu this can be in /etc/bind, for Fedora in /var/named.

# 12.8. advanced dhcp

## 12.8.1. 80/20 rule

DHCP servers should not be a single point of failure. Let us discuss redundant dhcp server setups.

## 12.8.2. relay agent

To avoid having to place a dhcp server on every segment, we can use **dhcp relay agents**.

## 12.8.3. rogue dhcp servers

Rogue dhcp servers are a problem without a solution. For example accidental connection of a (believed to be simple) hub/switch to a network with an internal dhcp server.

## 12.8.4. dhcp and ddns

DHCP can dynamically update DNS when it configures a client computer. DDNS can be used with or without secure keys.

When set up properly records can be added automaticall to the zone file:

```
root@fedora14~# tail -2 /var/named/db.office.linux-training.be
ubu1010srv        A     192.168.42.151
                  TXT   "00dfbb15e144a273c3cf2d6ae933885782"
```

# 12.9. Practice: dhcp

1. Make sure you have a unique fixed ip address for your DNS and DHCP server (easier on the same machine).

2. Install DHCP and browse the explanation in the default configuration file /etc/dhcp/ dhcpd.conf or /etc/dhcp3/dhcpd.conf.

3. Decide on a valid scope and activate it.

4. Test with a client that your DHCP server works.

5. Use wireshark to capture the four broadcasts when a client receives an ip (for the first time).

6. Use wireshark to capture a DHCPNAK and a DHCPrelease.

7. Reserve a configuration for a particular client (using mac address).

8. Configure your DHCP/DNS server(s) with a proper hostname and domainname (/etc/ hosts, /etc/hostname, /etc/sysconfig/network on Fedora/RHEL, /etc/resolv.conf ...). You may need to disable NetworkManager on *buntu-desktops.

9. Make sure your DNS server still works, and is master over (at least) one domain.

There are several ways to do steps 10-11-12. Google is your friend in exploring DDNS with keys, with key-files or without keys.

10. Configure your DNS server to allow dynamic updates from your DHCP server.

11. Configure your DHCP server to send dynamic updates to your DNS server.

12. Test the working of Dynamic DNS.

# Part V. iptables firewall

# Table of Contents

# Chapter 13. introduction to routers

What follows is a very brief introduction to using Linux as a router.

# 13.1. router or firewall

A **router** is a device that connects two networks. A **firewall** is a device that besides acting as a **router**, also contains (and implements) rules to determine whether packets are allowed to travel from one network to another. A firewall can be configured to block access based on networks, hosts, protocols and ports. Firewalls can also change the contents of packets while forwarding them.

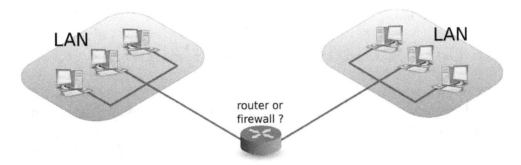

# 13.2. packet forwarding

**Packet forwarding** means allowing packets to go from one network to another. When a multihomed host is connected to two different networks, and it allows packets to travel from one network to another through its two network interfaces, it is said to have enabled **packet forwarding**.

# 13.3. packet filtering

**Packet filtering** is very similar to packet forwarding, but every packet is individually tested against rules that decide on allowing or dropping the packet. The rules are stored by iptables.

# 13.4. stateful

A **stateful** firewall is an advancement over stateless firewalls that inspect every individual packet. A stateful firewall will keep a table of active connections, and is knowledgeable enough to recognise when new connections are part of an active session. Linux iptables is a stateful firewall.

## 13.5. nat (network address translation)

A **nat** device is a router that is also changing the source and/or target ip-address in packets. It is typically used to connect multiple computers in a private address range (rfc 1918) with the (public) internet. A **nat** can hide private addresses from the internet.

It is important to understand that people and vendors do not always use the right term when referring to a certain type of **nat**. Be sure you talk about the same thing. We can distuinguish several types of **nat**.

## 13.6. pat (port address translation)

**nat** often includes **pat**. A **pat** device is a router that is also changing the source and/or target tcp/udp port in packets. **pat** is Cisco terminology and is used by **snat, dnat, masquerading** and **port forwarding** in Linux. RFC 3022 calls it **NAPT** and defines the **nat/pat** combo as "traditional nat". A device sold to you as a nat-device will probably do **nat** and **pat**.

## 13.7. snat (source nat)

A **snat** device is changing the source ip-address when a packet passes our **nat**. **snat** configuration with iptables includes a fixed target source address.

## 13.8. masquerading

**Masquerading** is a form of **snat** that will hide the (private) source ip-addresses of your private network using a public ip-address. Masquerading is common on dynamic internet interfaces (broadband modem/routers). Masquerade configuration with iptables uses a dynamic target source address.

## 13.9. dnat (destination nat)

A **dnat** device is changing the destination ip-address when a packet passes our **nat**.

## 13.10. port forwarding

When static **dnat** is set up in a way that allows outside connections to enter our private network, then we call it **port forwarding**.

# 13.11. /proc/sys/net/ipv4/ip_forward

Whether a host is forwarding packets is defined in **/proc/sys/net/ipv4/ip_forward**. The following screenshot shows how to enable packet forwarding on Linux.

```
root@router~# echo 1 > /proc/sys/net/ipv4/ip_forward
```

The next command shows how to disable packet forwarding.

```
root@router~# echo 0 > /proc/sys/net/ipv4/ip_forward
```

Use cat to check if packet forwarding is enabled.

```
root@router~# cat /proc/sys/net/ipv4/ip_forward
```

# 13.12. /etc/sysctl.conf

By default, most Linux computers are not configured for automatic packet forwarding. To enable packet forwarding whenever the system starts, change the **net.ipv4.ip_forward** variable in **/etc/sysctl.conf** to the value 1.

```
root@router~# grep ip_forward /etc/sysctl.conf
net.ipv4.ip_forward = 0
```

# 13.13. sysctl

For more information, take a look at the man page of **sysctl**.

```
root@debian6~# man sysctl
root@debian6~# sysctl -a 2>/dev/null | grep ip_forward
net.ipv4.ip_forward = 0
```

# 13.14. practice: packet forwarding

0. You have the option to select (or create) an internal network when adding a network card in **VirtualBox** or **VMWare**. Use this option to create two internal networks. I named them **leftnet** and **rightnet**, but you can choose any other name.

1. Set up two Linux machines, one on **leftnet**, the other on **rightnet**. Make sure they both get an ip-address in the correct subnet. These two machines will be 'left' and 'right' from the 'router'.

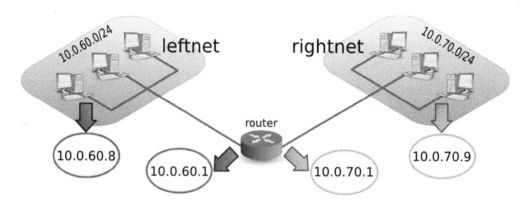

2. Set up a third Linux computer with three network cards, one on **leftnet**, the other on **rightnet**. This computer will be the 'router'. Complete the table below with the relevant names, ip-addresses and **mac-addresses**.

**Table 13.1. Packet Forwarding Exercise**

|      | leftnet computer | the router |  | rightnet computer |
|------|------------------|------------|--|-------------------|
| MAC  |                  |            |  |                   |
| IP   |                  |            |  |                   |

3. How can you verify whether the **router** will allow packet forwarding by default or not ? Test that you can **ping** from the **router** to the two other machines, and from those two machines to the **router**. Use **arp -a** to make sure you are connected with the correct **mac addresses**.

4. **Ping** from the leftnet computer to the rightnet computer. Enable and/or disable packet forwarding on the **router** and verify what happens to the ping between the two networks. If you do not succeed in pinging between the two networks (on different subnets), then use a sniffer like **wireshark** or **tcpdump** to discover the problem.

5. Use **wireshark** or **tcpdump** -xx to answer the following questions. Does the source MAC change when a packet passes through the filter ? And the destination MAC ? What about source and destination IP-addresses ?

6. Remember the third network card on the router ? Connect this card to a LAN with internet connection. On many LAN's the command **dhclient eth0** just works (replace **eth0** with the correct interface).

```
root@router~# dhclient eth0
```

You now have a setup similar to this picture. What needs to be done to give internet access to **leftnet** and **rightnet**.

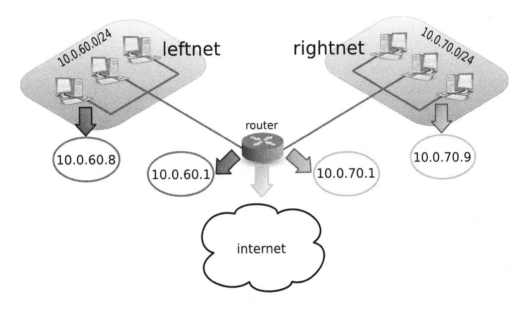

# 13.15. solution: packet forwarding

**Network**

Adapter 1:  Intel PRO/1000 MT Desktop (Bridged Adapter, en1: AirPort)
Adapter 2:  Intel PRO/1000 MT Desktop (Internal Network, 'leftnet')
Adapter 3:  Intel PRO/1000 MT Desktop (Internal Network, 'rightnet')

1. Set up two Linux machines, one on **leftnet**, the other on **rightnet**. Make sure they both get an ip-address in the correct subnet. These two machines will be 'left' and 'right' from the 'router'.

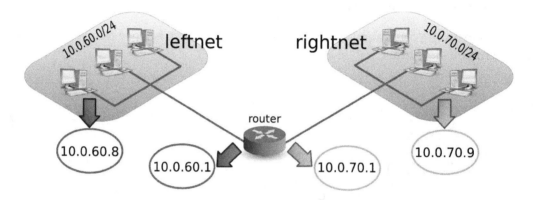

The ip configuration on your computers should be similar to the following two screenshots. Both machines must be in a different subnet (here 192.168.60.0/24 and 192.168.70.0/24). I created a little script on both machines to configure the interfaces.

```
root@left~# cat leftnet.sh
pkill dhclient
ifconfig eth0 192.168.60.8 netmask 255.255.255.0

root@right~# cat rightnet.sh
pkill dhclient
ifconfig eth0 192.168.70.9 netmask 255.255.255.0
```

2. Set up a third Linux computer with three network cards, one on **leftnet**, the other on **rightnet**. This computer will be the 'router'. Complete the table below with the relevant names, ip-addresses and mac-addresses.

```
root@router~# cat router.sh
ifconfig eth1 192.168.60.1 netmask 255.255.255.0
ifconfig eth2 192.168.70.1 netmask 255.255.255.0
#echo 1 > /proc/sys/net/ipv4/ip_forward
```

Your setup may use different ip and mac addresses than the ones in the table below.

**Table 13.2. Packet Forwarding Solution**

| leftnet computer | the router | | rightnet computer |
|---|---|---|---|
| 08:00:27:f6:ab:b9 | 08:00:27:43:1f:5a | 08:00:27:be:4a:6b | 08:00:27:14:8b:17 |
| 192.168.60.8 | 192.168.60.1 | 192.168.70.1 | 192.168.70.9 |

3. How can you verify whether the **router** will allow packet forwarding by default or not ? Test that you can ping from the **router** to the two other machines, and from those two machines to the **router**. Use **arp -a** to make sure you are connected with the correct **mac addresses**.

This can be done with **"grep ip_forward /etc/sysctl.conf"** (1 is enabled, 0 is disabled) or with **sysctl -a | grep ip_for**.

```
root@router~# grep ip_for /etc/sysctl.conf
net.ipv4.ip_forward = 0
```

4. Ping from the leftnet computer to the rightnet computer. Enable and/or disable packet forwarding on the **router** and verify what happens to the ping between the two networks. If you do not succeed in pinging between the two networks (on different subnets), then use a sniffer like wireshark or tcpdump to discover the problem.

Did you forget to add a **default gateway** to the LAN machines ? Use **route add default gw 'ip-address'**.

```
root@left~# route add default gw 192.168.60.1
```

```
root@right~# route add default gw 192.168.70.1
```

You should be able to ping when packet forwarding is enabled (and both default gateways are properly configured). The ping will not work when packet forwarding is disabled or when gateways are not configured correctly.

5. Use wireshark or tcpdump -xx to answer the following questions. Does the source MAC change when a packet passes through the filter ? And the destination MAC ? What about source and destination IP-addresses ?

Both MAC addresses are changed when passing the router. Use **tcpdump -xx** like this:

```
root@router~# tcpdump -xx -i eth1
```

```
root@router~# tcpdump -xx -i eth2
```

6. Remember the third network card on the router ? Connect this card to a LAN with internet connection. On many LAN's the command **dhclient eth0** just works (replace **eth0** with the correct interface.

```
root@router~# dhclient eth0
```

You now have a setup similar to this picture. What needs to be done to give internet access to **leftnet** and **rightnet**.

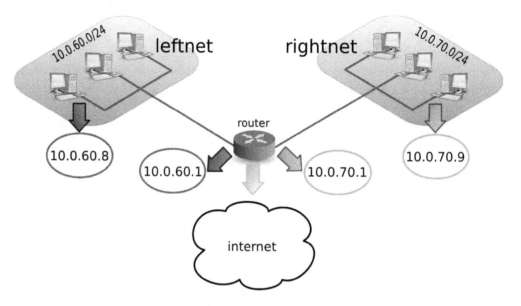

The clients on **leftnet** and **rightnet** need a working **dns server**. We use one of Google's dns servers here.

```
echo nameserver 8.8.8.8 > /etc/resolv.conf
```

# Chapter 14. iptables firewall

This chapter introduces some simple firewall rules and how to configure them with **iptables**.

**iptables** is an application that allows a user to configure the firewall functionality built into the **Linux** kernel.

# 14.1. iptables tables

By default there are three **tables** in the kernel that contain sets of rules.

The **filter table** is used for packet filtering.

```
root@debian6~# iptables -t filter -L
Chain INPUT (policy ACCEPT)
target       prot opt source               destination

Chain FORWARD (policy ACCEPT)
target       prot opt source               destination

Chain OUTPUT (policy ACCEPT)
target       prot opt source               destination
```

The **nat table** is used for address translation.

```
root@debian6~# iptables -t nat -L
Chain PREROUTING (policy ACCEPT)
target       prot opt source               destination

Chain POSTROUTING (policy ACCEPT)
target       prot opt source               destination

Chain OUTPUT (policy ACCEPT)
target       prot opt source               destination
```

The **mangle table** can be used for special-purpose processing of packets.

Series of rules in each table are called a **chain**. We will discuss chains and the nat table later in this chapter.

# 14.2. starting and stopping iptables

The following screenshot shows how to stop and start **iptables** on Red Hat/Fedora/CentOS and compatible distributions.

```
[root@centos6 ~]# service iptables stop
[root@centos6 ~]# service iptables start
iptables: Applying firewall rules                              [ ok ]
[root@centos6 ~]#
```

Debian and *buntu distributions do not have this script, but allow for an uninstall.

```
root@debian6~# aptitude purge iptables
```

# 14.3. the filter table

## 14.3.1. about packet filtering

**Packet filtering** is a bit more than **packet forwarding**. While **packet forwarding** uses only a routing table to make decisions, **packet filtering** also uses a list of rules. The kernel will inspect packets and decide based on these rules what to do with each packet.

## 14.3.2. filter table

The filter table in **iptables** has three chains (sets of rules). The INPUT chain is used for any packet coming into the system. The OUTPUT chain is for any packet leaving the system. And the FORWARD chain is for packets that are forwarded (routed) through the system.

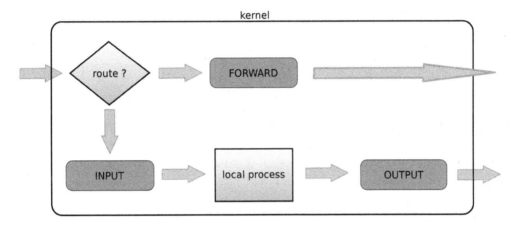

The screenshot below shows how to list the filter table and all its rules.

```
[root@RHEL5 ~]# iptables -t filter -nL
Chain INPUT (policy ACCEPT)
target     prot opt source               destination

Chain FORWARD (policy ACCEPT)
target     prot opt source               destination

Chain OUTPUT (policy ACCEPT)
target     prot opt source               destination
[root@RHEL5 ~]#
```

As you can see, all three chains in the filter table are set to ACCEPT everything. ACCEPT is the default behaviour.

### 14.3.3. setting default rules

The default for the default rule is indeed to ACCEPT everything. This is not the most secure firewall.

A more secure setup would be to DROP everything. A package that is **dropped** will not continue in any chain, and no warning or error will be sent anywhere.

The below commands lock down a computer. Do not execute these commands inside a remote ssh shell.

```
root@debianpaul~# iptables -P INPUT DROP
root@debianpaul~# iptables -P OUTPUT DROP
root@debianpaul~# iptables -P FORWARD DROP
root@debianpaul~# iptables -L
Chain INPUT (policy DROP)
target      prot opt source            destination

Chain FORWARD (policy DROP)
target      prot opt source            destination

Chain OUTPUT (policy DROP)
target      prot opt source            destination
```

### 14.3.4. changing policy rules

To start, let's set the default policy for all three chains to drop everything. Note that you might lose your connection when typing this over ssh ;-).

```
[root@RHEL5 ~]# iptables -P INPUT DROP
[root@RHEL5 ~]# iptables -P FORWARD DROP
[root@RHEL5 ~]# iptables -P OUTPUT DROP
```

Next, we allow the server to use its own loopback device (this allows the server to access its services running on localhost). We first append a rule to the INPUT chain to allow (ACCEPT) traffic from the lo (loopback) interface, then we do the same to allow packets to leave the system through the loopback interface.

```
[root@RHEL5 ~]# iptables -A INPUT -i lo -j ACCEPT
[root@RHEL5 ~]# iptables -A OUTPUT -o lo -j ACCEPT
```

Looking at the filter table again (omitting -t filter because it is the default table).

```
[root@RHEL5 ~]# iptables -nL
Chain INPUT (policy DROP)
target      prot opt source            destination
ACCEPT      all  --  0.0.0.0/0         0.0.0.0/0

Chain FORWARD (policy DROP)
target      prot opt source            destination

Chain OUTPUT (policy DROP)
target      prot opt source            destination
ACCEPT      all  --  0.0.0.0/0         0.0.0.0/0
```

## 14.3.5. Allowing ssh over eth0

This example show how to add two rules to allow ssh access to your system from outside.

```
[root@RHEL5 ~]# iptables -A INPUT -i eth0 -p tcp --dport 22 -j ACCEPT
[root@RHEL5 ~]# iptables -A OUTPUT -o eth0 -p tcp --sport 22 -j ACCEPT
```

The filter table will look something like this screenshot (note that -v is added for more verbose output).

```
[root@RHEL5 ~]# iptables -nvL
Chain INPUT (policy DROP 7 packets, 609 bytes)
 pkts bytes target prot opt in      out     source          destination
    0     0 ACCEPT all  --  lo      *       0.0.0.0/0       0.0.0.0/0
    0     0 ACCEPT tcp  --  eth0    *       0.0.0.0/0       0.0.0.0/0  tcp dpt:22

Chain FORWARD (policy DROP 0 packets, 0 bytes)
 pkts bytes target prot opt in      out     source          destination

Chain OUTPUT (policy DROP 3 packets, 228 bytes)
 pkts bytes target prot opt in      out     source          destination
    0     0 ACCEPT all  --  *       lo      0.0.0.0/0       0.0.0.0/0
    0     0 ACCEPT tcp  --  *       eth0    0.0.0.0/0       0.0.0.0/0  tcp spt:22
[root@RHEL5 ~]#
```

## 14.3.6. Allowing access from a subnet

This example shows how to allow access from any computer in the 10.1.1.0/24 network, but only through eth1. There is no port (application) limitation here.

```
[root@RHEL5 ~]# iptables -A INPUT -i eth1 -s 10.1.1.0/24 -p tcp -j ACCEPT
[root@RHEL5 ~]# iptables -A OUTPUT -o eth1 -d 10.1.1.0/24 -p tcp -j ACCEPT
```

Together with the previous examples, the policy is expanding.

```
[root@RHEL5 ~]# iptables -nvL
Chain INPUT (policy DROP 7 packets, 609 bytes)
 pkts bytes target prot opt in      out     source          destination
    0     0 ACCEPT all  --  lo      *       0.0.0.0/0       0.0.0.0/0
    0     0 ACCEPT tcp  --  eth0    *       0.0.0.0/0       0.0.0.0/0  tcp dpt:22
    0     0 ACCEPT tcp  --  eth1    *       10.1.1.0/24 0.0.0.0/0

Chain FORWARD (policy DROP 0 packets, 0 bytes)
 pkts bytes target prot opt in      out     source          destination

Chain OUTPUT (policy DROP 3 packets, 228 bytes)
 pkts bytes target prot opt in      out     source          destination
    0     0 ACCEPT all  --  *       lo      0.0.0.0/0       0.0.0.0/0
    0     0 ACCEPT tcp  --  *       eth0    0.0.0.0/0       0.0.0.0/0  tcp spt:22
    0     0 ACCEPT tcp  --  *       eth1    0.0.0.0/0       10.1.1.0/24
```

## 14.3.7. iptables save

Use **iptables save** to automatically implement these rules when the firewall is (re)started.

```
[root@RHEL5 ~]# /etc/init.d/iptables save
Saving firewall rules to /etc/sysconfig/iptables:          [  OK  ]
[root@RHEL5 ~]#
```

## 14.3.8. scripting example

You can write a simple script for these rules. Below is an example script that implements the firewall rules that you saw before in this chapter.

```
#!/bin/bash
# first cleanup everything
iptables -t filter -F
iptables -t filter -X
iptables -t nat -F
iptables -t nat -X

# default drop
iptables -P INPUT DROP
iptables -P FORWARD DROP
iptables -P OUTPUT DROP

# allow loopback device
iptables -A INPUT -i lo -j ACCEPT
iptables -A OUTPUT -o lo -j ACCEPT

# allow ssh over eth0 from outside to system
iptables -A INPUT -i eth0 -p tcp --dport 22 -j ACCEPT
iptables -A OUTPUT -o eth0 -p tcp --sport 22 -j ACCEPT

# allow any traffic from 10.1.1.0/24 to system
iptables -A INPUT -i eth1 -s 10.1.1.0/24 -p tcp -j ACCEPT
iptables -A OUTPUT -o eth1 -d 10.1.1.0/24 -p tcp -j ACCEPT
```

# 14.3.9. Allowing ICMP(ping)

When you enable iptables, you will get an **'Operation not permitted'** message when trying to ping other hosts.

```
[root@RHEL5 ~# ping 192.168.187.130
PING 192.168.187.130 (192.168.187.130) 56(84) bytes of data.
ping: sendmsg: Operation not permitted
ping: sendmsg: Operation not permitted
```

The screenshot below shows you how to setup iptables to allow a ping from or to your machine.

```
[root@RHEL5 ~]# iptables -A INPUT -p icmp --icmp-type any -j ACCEPT
[root@RHEL5 ~]# iptables -A OUTPUT -p icmp --icmp-type any -j ACCEPT
```

The previous two lines do not allow other computers to route ping messages through your router, because it only handles INPUT and OUTPUT. For routing of ping, you will need to enable it on the FORWARD chain. The following command enables routing of icmp messages between networks.

```
[root@RHEL5 ~]# iptables -A FORWARD -p icmp --icmp-type any -j ACCEPT
```

# 14.4. practice: packet filtering

1. Make sure you can ssh to your router-system when iptables is active.

2. Make sure you can ping to your router-system when iptables is active.

3. Define one of your networks as 'internal' and the other as 'external'. Configure the router to allow visits to a website (http) to go from the internal network to the external network (but not in the other direction).

4. Make sure the internal network can ssh to the external, but not the other way around.

# 14.5. solution: packet filtering

A possible solution, where leftnet is the internal and rightnet is the external network.

```
#!/bin/bash

# first cleanup everything
iptables -t filter -F
iptables -t filter -X
iptables -t nat -F
iptables -t nat -X

# default drop
iptables -P INPUT DROP
iptables -P FORWARD DROP
iptables -P OUTPUT DROP

# allow loopback device
iptables -A INPUT -i lo -j ACCEPT
iptables -A OUTPUT -o lo -j ACCEPT

# question 1: allow ssh over eth0
iptables -A INPUT -i eth0 -p tcp --dport 22 -j ACCEPT
iptables -A OUTPUT -o eth0 -p tcp --sport 22 -j ACCEPT

# question 2: Allow icmp(ping) anywhere
iptables -A INPUT -p icmp --icmp-type any -j ACCEPT
iptables -A FORWARD -p icmp --icmp-type any -j ACCEPT
iptables -A OUTPUT -p icmp --icmp-type any -j ACCEPT

# question 3: allow http from internal(leftnet) to external(rightnet)
iptables -A FORWARD -i eth1 -o eth2 -p tcp --dport 80 -j ACCEPT
iptables -A FORWARD -i eth2 -o eth1 -p tcp --sport 80 -j ACCEPT

# question 4: allow ssh from internal(leftnet) to external(rightnet)
iptables -A FORWARD -i eth1 -o eth2 -p tcp --dport 22 -j ACCEPT
iptables -A FORWARD -i eth2 -o eth1 -p tcp --sport 22 -j ACCEPT

# allow http from external(rightnet) to internal(leftnet)
# iptables -A FORWARD -i eth2 -o eth1 -p tcp --dport 80 -j ACCEPT
# iptables -A FORWARD -i eth1 -o eth2 -p tcp --sport 80 -j ACCEPT

# allow rpcinfo over eth0 from outside to system
# iptables -A INPUT -i eth2 -p tcp --dport 111 -j ACCEPT
# iptables -A OUTPUT -o eth2 -p tcp --sport 111 -j ACCEPT
```

# 14.6. network address translation

## 14.6.1. about NAT

A NAT device is a router that is also changing the source and/or target ip-address in packets. It is typically used to connect multiple computers in a private address range with the (public) internet. A NAT can hide private addresses from the internet.

NAT was developed to mitigate the use of real ip addresses, to allow private address ranges to reach the internet and back, and to not disclose details about internal networks to the outside.

The nat table in iptables adds two new chains. PREROUTING allows altering of packets before they reach the INPUT chain. POSTROUTING allows altering packets after they exit the OUTPUT chain.

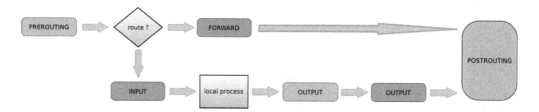

Use **iptables -t nat -nvL** to look at the NAT table. The screenshot below shows an empty NAT table.

```
[root@RHEL5 ~]# iptables -t nat -nL
Chain PREROUTING (policy ACCEPT)
target     prot opt source               destination

Chain POSTROUTING (policy ACCEPT)
target     prot opt source               destination

Chain OUTPUT (policy ACCEPT)
target     prot opt source               destination
[root@RHEL5 ~]#
```

## 14.6.2. SNAT (Source NAT)

The goal of source nat is to change the source address inside a packet before it leaves the system (e.g. to the internet). The destination will return the packet to the NAT-device. This means our NAT-device will need to keep a table in memory of all the packets it changed, so it can deliver the packet to the original source (e.g. in the private network).

Because SNAT is about packets leaving the system, it uses the POSTROUTING chain.

Here is an example SNAT rule. The rule says that packets coming from 10.1.1.0/24 network and exiting via eth1 will get the source ip-address set to 11.12.13.14. (Note that this is a one line command!)

```
iptables -t nat -A POSTROUTING -o eth1 -s 10.1.1.0/24 -j SNAT \
--to-source 11.12.13.14
```

Of course there must exist a proper iptables filter setup to allow the packet to traverse from one network to the other.

## 14.6.3. SNAT example setup

This example script uses a typical nat setup. The internal (eth0) network has access via SNAT to external (eth1) webservers (port 80).

```
#!/bin/bash
#
# iptables script for simple classic nat websurfing
# eth0 is internal network, eth1 is internet
#
echo 0 > /proc/sys/net/ipv4/ip_forward
iptables -P INPUT ACCEPT
iptables -P OUTPUT ACCEPT
iptables -P FORWARD DROP
iptables -A FORWARD -i eth0 -o eth1 -s 10.1.1.0/24 -p tcp \
--dport 80 -j ACCEPT
iptables -A FORWARD -i eth1 -o eth0 -d 10.1.1.0/24 -p tcp \
--sport 80 -j ACCEPT
iptables -t nat -A POSTROUTING -o eth1 -s 10.1.1.0/24 -j SNAT \
--to-source 11.12.13.14
echo 1 > /proc/sys/net/ipv4/ip_forward
```

## 14.6.4. IP masquerading

IP masquerading is very similar to SNAT, but is meant for dynamic interfaces. Typical example are broadband 'router/modems' connected to the internet and receiving a different ip-address from the isp, each time they are cold-booted.

The only change needed to convert the SNAT script to a masquerading is one line.

```
iptables -t nat -A POSTROUTING -o eth1 -s 10.1.1.0/24 -j MASQUERADE
```

## 14.6.5. DNAT (Destination NAT)

DNAT is typically used to allow packets from the internet to be redirected to an internal server (in your DMZ) and in a private address range that is inaccessible directly form the internet.

This example script allows internet users to reach your internal (192.168.1.99) server via ssh (port 22).

```
#!/bin/bash
#
# iptables script for DNAT
# eth0 is internal network, eth1 is internet
#
echo 0 > /proc/sys/net/ipv4/ip_forward
iptables -P INPUT ACCEPT
iptables -P OUTPUT ACCEPT
iptables -P FORWARD DROP
iptables -A FORWARD -i eth0 -o eth1 -s 10.1.1.0/24 -j ACCEPT
iptables -A FORWARD -i eth1 -o eth0 -p tcp --dport 22 -j ACCEPT
iptables -t nat -A PREROUTING -i eth1 -p tcp --dport 22 \
-j DNAT --to-destination 10.1.1.99
echo 1 > /proc/sys/net/ipv4/ip_forward
```

# Part VI. Introduction to Samba

# Table of Contents

# Chapter 15. introduction to samba

This introduction to the Samba server simply explains how to install Samba 3 and briefly mentions the SMB protocol.

# 15.1. verify installed version

## 15.1.1. .rpm based distributions

To see the version of samba installed on Red Hat, Fedora or CentOS use **rpm -q samba**.

```
[root@RHEL52 ~]# rpm -q samba
samba-3.0.28-1.el5_2.1
```

The screenshot above shows that RHEL5 has **Samba** version 3.0 installed. The last number in the Samba version counts the number of updates or patches.

Below the same command on a more recent version of CentOS with Samba version 3.5 installed.

```
[root@centos6 ~]# rpm -q samba
samba-3.5.10-116.el6_2.i686
```

## 15.1.2. .deb based distributions

Use **dpkg -l** or **aptitide show** on Debian or Ubuntu. Both Debian 7.0 (Wheezy) and Ubuntu 12.04 (Precise) use version 3.6.3 of the Samba server.

```
root@debian7~# aptitude show samba | grep Version
Version: 2:3.6.3-1
```

Ubuntu 12.04 is currently at Samba version 3.6.3.

```
root@ubu1204:~# dpkg -l samba | tail -1
ii samba 2:3.6.3-2ubuntu2.1 SMB/CIFS file, print, and login server for Unix
```

# 15.2. installing samba

## 15.2.1. .rpm based distributions

Samba is installed by default on Red Hat Enterprise Linux. If Samba is not yet installed, then you can use the graphical menu (Applications -- System Settings -- Add/Remove Applications) and select "Windows File Server" in the Server section. The non-graphical way is to use **rpm** or **yum**.

When you downloaded the .rpm file, you can install Samba like this.

```
[paul@RHEL52 ~]$ rpm -i samba-3.0.28-1.el5_2.1.rpm
```

When you have a subscription to RHN (Red Hat Network), then **yum** is an easy tool to use. This **yum** command works by default on Fedora and CentOS.

```
[root@centos6 ~]# yum install samba
```

## 15.2.2. .deb based distributions

Ubuntu and Debian users can use the **aptitude** program (or use a graphical tool like Synaptic).

```
root@debian7~# aptitude install samba
The following NEW packages will be installed:
  samba samba-common{a} samba-common-bin{a} tdb-tools{a}
0 packages upgraded, 4 newly installed, 0 to remove and 1 not upgraded.
Need to get 15.1 MB of archives. After unpacking 42.9 MB will be used.
Do you want to continue? [Y/n/?]
...
```

# 15.3. documentation

## 15.3.1. samba howto

Samba comes with excellent documentation in html and pdf format (and also as a free download from samba.org and it is for sale as a printed book).

The documentation is a separate package, so install it if you want it on the server itself.

```
[root@centos6 ~]# yum install samba-doc
...
[root@centos6 ~]# ls -l /usr/share/doc/samba-doc-3.5.10/
total 10916
drwxr-xr-x. 6 root root    4096 May  6 15:50 htmldocs
-rw-r--r--. 1 root root 4605496 Jun 14  2011 Samba3-ByExample.pdf
-rw-r--r--. 1 root root  608260 Jun 14  2011 Samba3-Developers-Guide.pdf
-rw-r--r--. 1 root root 5954602 Jun 14  2011 Samba3-HOWTO.pdf
```

This action is very similar on Ubuntu and Debian except that the pdf files are in a separate package named **samba-doc-pdf**.

```
root@ubu1204:~# aptitude install samba-doc-pdf
The following NEW packages will be installed:
  samba-doc-pdf
...
```

## 15.3.2. samba by example

Besides the howto, there is also an excellent book called **Samba By Example** (again available as printed edition in shops, and as a free pdf and html).

# 15.4. starting and stopping samba

You can start the daemons by invoking **/etc/init.d/smb start** (some systems use **/etc/init.d/ samba**) on any linux.

```
root@laika:~# /etc/init.d/samba stop
 * Stopping Samba daemons                                     [ OK ]
root@laika:~# /etc/init.d/samba start
 * Starting Samba daemons                                     [ OK ]
root@laika:~# /etc/init.d/samba restart
 * Stopping Samba daemons                                     [ OK ]
 * Starting Samba daemons                                     [ OK ]
root@laika:~# /etc/init.d/samba status
 * SMBD is running                                            [ OK ]
```

Red Hat derived systems are happy with **service smb start**.

```
[root@RHEL4b ~]# /etc/init.d/smb start
Starting SMB services:                                      [  OK  ]
Starting NMB services:                                      [  OK  ]
[root@RHEL4b ~]# service smb restart
Shutting down SMB services:                                 [  OK  ]
Shutting down NMB services:                                 [  OK  ]
Starting SMB services:                                      [  OK  ]
Starting NMB services:                                      [  OK  ]
[root@RHEL4b ~]#
```

# 15.5. samba daemons

Samba 3 consists of three daemons, they are named **nmbd**, **smbd** and **winbindd**.

## 15.5.1. nmbd

The **nmbd** daemon takes care of all the names and naming. It registers and resolves names, and handles browsing. According to the Samba documentation, it should be the first daemon to start.

```
[root@RHEL52 ~]# ps -C nmbd
  PID TTY          TIME CMD
 5681 ?        00:00:00 nmbd
```

## 15.5.2. smbd

The **smbd** daemon manages file transfers and authentication.

```
[root@RHEL52 ~]# ps -C smbd
  PID TTY          TIME CMD
 5678 ?        00:00:00 smbd
 5683 ?        00:00:00 smbd
```

## 15.5.3. winbindd

The **winbind daemon** (winbindd) is only started to handle Microsoft Windows domain membership.

Note that **winbindd** is started by the **/etc/init.d/winbind** script (two dd's for the daemon and only one d for the script).

```
[root@RHEL52 ~]# /etc/init.d/winbind start
Starting Winbind services:                              [  OK  ]
[root@RHEL52 ~]# ps -C winbindd
  PID TTY          TIME CMD
 5752 ?        00:00:00 winbindd
 5754 ?        00:00:00 winbindd
```

On Debian and Ubuntu, the winbindd daemon is installed via a separate package called **winbind**.

# 15.6. the SMB protocol

## 15.6.1. brief history

Development of this protocol was started by **IBM** in the early eighties. By the end of the eighties, most develpment was done by **Microsoft**. SMB is an application level protocol designed to run on top of NetBIOS/NetBEUI, but can also be run on top of tcp/ip.

In 1996 Microsoft was asked to document the protocol. They submitted CIFS (Common Internet File System) as an internet draft, but it never got final rfc status.

In 2004 the European Union decided Microsoft should document the protocol to enable other developers to write compatible software. December 20th 2007 Microsoft came to an agreement. The Samba team now has access to SMB/CIFS, Windows for Workgroups and Active Directory documentation.

## 15.6.2. broadcasting protocol

SMB uses the NetBIOS **service location protocol**, which is a broadcasting protocol. This means that NetBIOS names have to be unique on the network (even when you have different IP-addresses). Having duplicate names on an SMB network can seriously harm communications.

## 15.6.3. NetBIOS names

NetBIOS names are similar to **hostnames**, but are always uppercase and only 15 characters in length. Microsoft Windows computers and Samba servers will broadcast this name on the network.

## 15.6.4. network bandwidth

Having many broadcasting SMB/CIFS computers on your network can cause bandwidth issues. A solution can be the use of a **NetBIOS name server** (NBNS) like **WINS** (Windows Internet Naming Service).

# 15.7. practice: introduction to samba

0. !! Make sure you know your student number, anything *ANYTHING* you name must include your student number!

1. Verify that you can logon to a Linux/Unix computer. Write down the name and ip address of this computer.

2. Do the same for all the other (virtual) machines available to you.

3. Verify networking by pinging the computer, edit the appropriate hosts files so you can use names. Test the names by pinging them.

4. Make sure Samba is installed, write down the version of Samba.

5. Open the Official Samba-3 howto pdf file that is installed on your computer. How many A4 pages is this file ? Then look at the same pdf on samba.org, it is updated regularly.

6. Stop the Samba server.

# Chapter 16. getting started with samba

# 16.1. /etc/samba/smb.conf

## 16.1.1. smbd -b

Samba configuration is done in the **smb.conf** file. The file can be edited manually, or you can use a web based interface like webmin or swat to manage it. The file is usually located in /etc/samba. You can find the exact location with **smbd -b**.

```
[root@RHEL4b ~]# smbd -b | grep CONFIGFILE
CONFIGFILE: /etc/samba/smb.conf
```

## 16.1.2. the default smb.conf

The default smb.conf file contains a lot of examples with explanations.

```
[paul@RHEL4b ~]$ ls -l /etc/samba/smb.conf
-rw-r--r--  1 root root 10836 May 30 23:08 /etc/samba/smb.conf
```

Also on Ubuntu and Debian, smb.conf is packed with samples and explanations.

```
paul@laika:~$ ls -l /etc/samba/smb.conf
-rw-r--r-- 1 root root 10515 2007-05-24 00:21 /etc/samba/smb.conf
```

## 16.1.3. minimal smb.conf

Below is an example of a very minimalistic **smb.conf**. It allows samba to start, and to be visible to other computers (Microsoft shows computers in Network Neighborhood or My Network Places).

```
[paul@RHEL4b ~]$ cat /etc/samba/smb.conf
[global]
workgroup = WORKGROUP
[firstshare]
path = /srv/samba/public
```

## 16.1.4. net view

Below is a screenshot of the **net view** command on Microsoft Windows Server 2003 sp2. It shows how a Red Hat Enterprise Linux 5.3 and a Ubuntu 9.04 Samba server, both with a minimalistic smb.conf, are visible to Microsoft computers nearby.

```
C:\Documents and Settings\Administrator>net view
Server Name            Remark
-------------------------------------------------------------------
\\LAIKA                Samba 3.3.2
\\RHEL53               Samba 3.0.33-3.7.el5
\\W2003
The command completed successfully.
```

## 16.1.5. long lines in smb.conf

Some parameters in smb.conf can get a long list of values behind them. You can continue a line (for clarity) on the next by ending the line with a backslash.

```
valid users = Serena, Venus, Lindsay \
```

```
              Kim, Justine, Sabine \
              Amelie, Marie, Suzanne
```

## 16.1.6. curious smb.conf

Curious but true: smb.conf accepts synonyms like **create mode** and **create mask**, and (sometimes) minor spelling errors like **browsable** and **browseable**. And on occasion you can even switch words, the **guest only** parameter is identical to **only guest**. And **writable = yes** is the same as **readonly = no**.

## 16.1.7. man smb.conf

You can access a lot of documentation when typing **man smb.conf**.

```
[root@RHEL4b samba]# apropos samba
cupsaddsmb       (8)  - export printers to samba for windows clients
lmhosts          (5)  - The Samba NetBIOS hosts file
net              (8)  - Tool for administration of Samba and remote CIFS servers
pdbedit          (8)  - manage the SAM database (Database of Samba Users)
samba            (7)  - A Windows SMB/CIFS fileserver for UNIX
smb.conf [smb]   (5)  - The configuration file for the Samba suite
smbpasswd        (5)  - The Samba encrypted password file
smbstatus        (1)  - report on current Samba connections
swat             (8)  - Samba Web Administration Tool
tdbbackup        (8)  - tool for backing up and ... of samba .tdb files
[root@RHEL4b samba]#
```

# 16.2. /usr/bin/testparm

## 16.2.1. syntax check smb.conf

To verify the syntax of the smb.conf file, you can use **testparm**.

```
[paul@RHEL4b ~]$ testparm
Load smb config files from /etc/samba/smb.conf
Processing section "[firstshare]"
Loaded services file OK.
Server role: ROLE_STANDALONE
Press enter to see a dump of your service definitions
```

## 16.2.2. testparm -v

An interesting option is **testparm -v**, which will output all the global options with their default value.

```
[root@RHEL52 ~]# testparm -v | head
Load smb config files from /etc/samba/smb.conf
Processing section "[pub0]"
Processing section "[global$]"
Loaded services file OK.
Server role: ROLE_STANDALONE
Press enter to see a dump of your service definitions

[global]
 dos charset = CP850
 unix charset = UTF-8
 display charset = LOCALE
 workgroup = WORKGROUP
```

```
realm =
netbios name = TEACHER0
netbios aliases =
netbios scope =
server string = Samba 3.0.28-1.el5_2.1
...
```

There were about 350 default values for smb.conf parameters in Samba 3.0.x. This number grew to almost 400 in Samba 3.5.x.

## 16.2.3. testparm -s

The samba daemons are constantly (once every 60 seconds) checking the smb.conf file, so it is good practice to keep this file small. But it is also good practice to document your samba configuration, and to explicitly set options that have the same default values. The **testparm -s** option allows you to do both. It will output the smallest possible samba configuration file, while retaining all your settings. The idea is to have your samba configuration in another file (like smb.conf.full) and let testparm parse this for you. The screenshot below shows you how. First the smb.conf.full file with the explicitly set option workgroup to WORKGROUP.

```
[root@RHEL4b samba]# cat smb.conf.full
[global]
workgroup = WORKGROUP

# This is a demo of a documented smb.conf
# These two lines are removed by testparm -s

server string = Public Test Server

[firstshare]
path = /srv/samba/public
```

Next, we execute testparm with the -s option, and redirect stdout to the real **smb.conf** file.

```
[root@RHEL4b samba]# testparm -s smb.conf.full > smb.conf
Load smb config files from smb.conf.full
Processing section "[firstshare]"
Loaded services file OK.
```

And below is the end result. The two comment lines and the default option are no longer there.

```
[root@RHEL4b samba]# cat smb.conf
# Global parameters
[global]
server string = Public Test Server

[firstshare]
path = /srv/samba/public
[root@RHEL4b samba]#
```

# 16.3. /usr/bin/smbclient

## 16.3.1. smbclient looking at Samba

With **smbclient** you can see browsing and share information from your smb server. It will display all your shares, your workgroup, and the name of the Master Browser. The -N switch is added to avoid having to enter an empty password. The -L switch is followed by the name of the host to check.

```
[root@RHEL4b init.d]# smbclient -NL rhel4b
Anonymous login successful
Domain=[WORKGROUP] OS=[Unix] Server=[Samba 3.0.10-1.4E.9]

Sharename       Type        Comment
---------       ----        -------
firstshare      Disk
IPC$            IPC         IPC Service (Public Test Server)
ADMIN$          IPC         IPC Service (Public Test Server)
Anonymous login successful
Domain=[WORKGROUP] OS=[Unix] Server=[Samba 3.0.10-1.4E.9]

Server                  Comment
---------               -------
RHEL4B                  Public Test Server
WINXP

Workgroup               Master
---------               -------
WORKGROUP               WINXP
```

## 16.3.2. smbclient anonymous

The screenshot below uses **smbclient** to display information about a remote smb server (in this case a computer with Ubuntu 11.10).

```
root@ubu1110:/etc/samba# testparm smbclient -NL 127.0.0.1
Anonymous login successful
Domain=[LINUXTR] OS=[Unix] Server=[Samba 3.5.11]

 Sharename       Type        Comment
 ---------       ----        -------
 share1          Disk
 IPC$            IPC         IPC Service (Samba 3.5.11)
Anonymous login successful
Domain=[LINUXTR] OS=[Unix] Server=[Samba 3.5.11]

 Server                  Comment
 ---------               -------

 Workgroup               Master
 ---------               -------
 LINUXTR                 DEBIAN6
 WORKGROUP               UBU1110
```

## 16.3.3. smbclient with credentials

Windows versions after xp sp2 and 2003 sp1 do not accept guest access (the NT_STATUS_ACCESS_DENIED error). This example shows how to provide credentials with **smbclient**.

```
[paul@RHEL53 ~]$ smbclient -L w2003 -U administrator%stargate
Domain=[W2003] OS=[Windows Server 2003 3790 Service Pack 2] Server=...

 Sharename       Type        Comment
 ---------       ----        -------
 C$              Disk        Default share
```

```
IPC$          IPC       Remote IPC
ADMIN$        Disk      Remote Admin
...
```

# 16.4. /usr/bin/smbtree

Another useful tool to troubleshoot Samba or simply to browse the SMB network is **smbtree**. In its simplest form, smbtree will do an anonymous browsing on the local subnet. displaying all SMB computers and (if authorized) their shares.

Let's take a look at two screenshots of smbtree in action (with blank password). The first one is taken immediately after booting four different computers (one MS Windows 2000, one MS Windows xp, one MS Windows 2003 and one RHEL 4 with Samba 3.0.10).

```
[paul@RHEL4b ~]$ smbtree
Password:
WORKGROUP
PEGASUS
 \\WINXP
 \\RHEL4B                          Pegasus Domain Member Server
Error connecting to 127.0.0.1 (Connection refused)
cli_full_connection: failed to connect to RHEL4B<20> (127.0.0.1)
 \\HM2003
[paul@RHEL4b ~]$
```

The information displayed in the previous screenshot looks incomplete. The browsing elections are still ongoing, the browse list is not yet distributed to all clients by the (to be elected) browser master. The next screenshot was taken about one minute later. And it shows even less.

```
[paul@RHEL4b ~]$ smbtree
Password:
WORKGROUP
 \\W2000
[paul@RHEL4b ~]$
```

So we wait a while, and then run **smbtree** again, this time it looks a lot nicer.

```
[paul@RHEL4b ~]$ smbtree
Password:
WORKGROUP
 \\W2000
PEGASUS
 \\WINXP
 \\RHEL4B                          Pegasus Domain Member Server
  \\RHEL4B\ADMIN$                  IPC Service (Pegasus Domain Member Server)
  \\RHEL4B\IPC$                    IPC Service (Pegasus Domain Member Server)
  \\RHEL4B\domaindata              Active Directory users only
 \\HM2003
[paul@RHEL4b ~]$ smbtree --version
Version 3.0.10-1.4E.9
[paul@RHEL4b ~]$
```

I added the version number of **smbtree** in the previous screenshot, to show you the difference when using the latest version of smbtree (below a screenshot taken from Ubuntu Feisty Fawn). The latest version shows a more complete overview of machines and shares.

```
paul@laika:~$ smbtree --version
Version 3.0.24
```

```
paul@laika:~$ smbtree
Password:
WORKGROUP
 \\W2000
  \\W2000\firstshare
  \\W2000\C$              Default share
  \\W2000\ADMIN$          Remote Admin
  \\W2000\IPC$            Remote IPC
PEGASUS
 \\WINXP
cli_rpc_pipe_open: cli_nt_create failed on pipe \srvsvc to machine WINXP.
Error was NT_STATUS_ACCESS_DENIED
  \\RHEL4B                        Pegasus Domain Member Server
   \\RHEL4B\ADMIN$          IPC Service (Pegasus Domain Member Server)
   \\RHEL4B\IPC$            IPC Service (Pegasus Domain Member Server)
   \\RHEL4B\domaindata      Active Directory users only
  \\HM2003
cli_rpc_pipe_open: cli_nt_create failed on pipe \srvsvc to machine HM2003.
Error was NT_STATUS_ACCESS_DENIED
paul@laika:~$
```

The previous screenshot also provides useful errors on why we cannot see shared info on computers winxp and w2003. Let us try the old **smbtree** version on our RHEL server, but this time with Administrator credentials (which are the same on all computers).

```
[paul@RHEL4b ~]$ smbtree -UAdministrator%Stargate1
WORKGROUP
 \\W2000
PEGASUS
 \\WINXP
   \\WINXP\C$               Default share
   \\WINXP\ADMIN$           Remote Admin
   \\WINXP\share55
   \\WINXP\IPC$             Remote IPC
  \\RHEL4B                  Pegasus Domain Member Server
   \\RHEL4B\ADMIN$          IPC Service (Pegasus Domain Member Server)
   \\RHEL4B\IPC$            IPC Service (Pegasus Domain Member Server)
   \\RHEL4B\domaindata      Active Directory users only
  \\HM2003
   \\HM2003\NETLOGON        Logon server share
   \\HM2003\SYSVOL          Logon server share
   \\HM2003\WSUSTemp        A network share used by Local Publishing ...
   \\HM2003\ADMIN$          Remote Admin
   \\HM2003\tools
   \\HM2003\IPC$            Remote IPC
   \\HM2003\WsusContent     A network share to be used by Local ...
   \\HM2003\C$              Default share
[paul@RHEL4b ~]$
```

As you can see, this gives a very nice overview of all SMB computers and their shares.

# 16.5. server string

The comment seen by the **net view** and the **smbclient** commands is the default value for the **server string** option. Simply adding this value to the global section in **smb.conf** and restarting samba will change the option.

```
[root@RHEL53 samba]# testparm -s 2>/dev/null | grep server
 server string = Red Hat Server in Paris
```

After a short while, the changed option is visible on the Microsoft computers.

```
C:\Documents and Settings\Administrator>net view
Server Name             Remark

------------------------------------------------------------------------
\\LAIKA                  Ubuntu 9.04 server in Antwerp
\\RHEL53                 Red Hat Server in Paris
\\W2003
```

# 16.6. Samba Web Administration Tool (SWAT)

Samba comes with a web based tool to manage your samba configuration file. **SWAT** is accessible with a web browser on port 901 of the host system. To enable the tool, first find out whether your system is using the **inetd** or the **xinetd** superdaemon.

```
[root@RHEL4b samba]# ps fax | grep inet
 15026 pts/0     S+      0:00                        \_ grep inet
  2771 ?         Ss      0:00 xinetd -stayalive -pidfile /var/run/xinetd.pid
[root@RHEL4b samba]#
```

Then edit the **inetd.conf** or change the disable = yes line in **/etc/xinetd.d/swat** to disable = no.

```
[root@RHEL4b samba]# cat /etc/xinetd.d/swat
# default: off
# description: SWAT is the Samba Web Admin Tool. Use swat \
#              to configure your Samba server. To use SWAT, \
#              connect to port 901 with your favorite web browser.
service swat
{
 port            = 901
 socket_type     = stream
 wait            = no
 only_from       = 127.0.0.1
 user            = root
 server          = /usr/sbin/swat
 log_on_failure  += USERID
 disable         = no
}
[root@RHEL4b samba]# /etc/init.d/xinetd restart
Stopping xinetd:                                        [  OK  ]
Starting xinetd:                                        [  OK  ]
[root@RHEL4b samba]#
```

Change the **only from** value to enable swat from remote computers. This examples shows how to provide swat access to all computers in a /24 subnet.

```
[root@RHEL53 xinetd.d]# grep only /etc/xinetd.d/swat
 only_from    = 192.168.1.0/24
```

Be careful when using SWAT, it erases all your manually edited comments in smb.conf.

# 16.7. practice: getting started with samba

1. Take a backup copy of the original smb.conf, name it smb.conf.orig

2. Enable SWAT and take a look at it.

3. Stop the Samba server.

4. Create a minimalistic smb.conf.minimal and test it with testparm.

5. Use tesparm -s to create /etc/samba/smb.conf from your smb.conf.minimal .

6. Start Samba with your minimal smb.conf.

7. Verify with smbclient that your Samba server works.

8. Verify that another (Microsoft) computer can see your Samba server.

9. Browse the network with net view, smbtree and with Windows Explorer.

10. Change the "Server String" parameter in smb.conf. How long does it take before you see the change (net view, smbclient, My Network Places,...) ?

11. Will restarting Samba after a change to smb.conf speed up the change ?

12. Which computer is the master browser master in your workgroup ? What is the master browser ?

13. If time permits (or if you are waiting for other students to finish this practice), then install a sniffer (wireshark) and watch the browser elections.

# 16.8. solution: getting started with samba

1. Take a backup copy of the original smb.conf, name it smb.conf.orig

```
cd /etc/samba ; cp smb.conf smb.conf.orig
```

2. Enable SWAT and take a look at it.

```
on Debian/Ubuntu: vi /etc/inetd.conf (remove # before swat)
```

```
on RHEL/Fedora: vi /etc/xinetd.d/swat (set disable to no)
```

3. Stop the Samba server.

```
/etc/init.d/smb stop (Red Hat)
```

```
/etc/init.d/samba stop (Debian)
```

4. Create a minimalistic smb.conf.minimal and test it with testparm.

```
cd /etc/samba ; mkdir my_smb_confs ; cd my_smb_confs
```

```
vi smb.conf.minimal
```

```
testparm smb.conf.minimal
```

5. Use tesparm -s to create /etc/samba/smb.conf from your smb.conf.minimal .

```
testparm -s smb.conf.minimal > ../smb.conf
```

6. Start Samba with your minimal smb.conf.

```
/etc/init.d/smb restart (Red Hat)
```

```
/etc/init.d/samba restart (Debian)
```

7. Verify with smbclient that your Samba server works.

```
smbclient -NL 127.0.0.1
```

8. Verify that another computer can see your Samba server.

```
smbclient -NL 'ip-address' (on a Linux)
```

9. Browse the network with net view, smbtree and with Windows Explorer.

```
on Linux: smbtree
```

```
on Windows: net view (and WindowsKey + e)
```

10. Change the "Server String" parameter in smb.conf. How long does it take before you see the change (net view, smbclient, My Network Places,...) ?

```
vi /etc/samba/smb.conf
```

```
(should take only seconds when restarting samba)
```

11. Will restarting Samba after a change to smb.conf speed up the change ?

```
yes
```

12. Which computer is the master browser master in your workgroup ? What is the master browser ?

```
The computer that won the elections.

This machine will make the list of computers in the network
```

13. If time permits (or if you are waiting for other students to finish this practice), then install a sniffer (wireshark) and watch the browser elections.

```
On ubuntu: sudo aptitude install wireshark

then: sudo wireshark, select interface
```

# Chapter 17. a read only file server

# 17.1. Setting up a directory to share

Let's start with setting up a very simple read only file server with Samba. Everyone (even anonymous guests) will receive read access.

The first step is to create a directory and put some test files in it.

```
[root@RHEL52 ~]# mkdir -p /srv/samba/readonly
[root@RHEL52 ~]# cd /srv/samba/readonly/
[root@RHEL52 readonly]# echo "It is cold today." > winter.txt
[root@RHEL52 readonly]# echo "It is hot today." > summer.txt
[root@RHEL52 readonly]# ls -l
total 8
-rw-r--r-- 1 root root 17 Jan 21 05:49 summer.txt
-rw-r--r-- 1 root root 18 Jan 21 05:49 winter.txt
[root@RHEL52 readonly]#
```

# 17.2. configure the share

## 17.2.1. smb.conf [global] section

In this example the samba server is a member of WORKGROUP (the default workgroup). We also set a descriptive server string, this string is visible to users browsing the network with net view, windows explorer or smbclient.

```
[root@RHEL52 samba]# head -5 smb.conf
[global]
 workgroup = WORKGROUP
 server string = Public Anonymous File Server
 netbios name = TEACHER0
 security = share
```

You might have noticed the line with **security = share**. This line sets the default security mode for our samba server. Setting the security mode to **share** will allow clients (smbclient, any windows, another Samba server, ...) to provide a password for each share. This is one way of using the SMB/CIFS protocol. The other way (called **user mode**) will allow the client to provide a username/password combination, before the server knows which share the client wants to access.

## 17.2.2. smb.conf [share] section

The share is called pubread and the path is set to our newly created directory. Everyone is allowed access (**guest ok = yes**) and security is set to read only.

```
[pubread]
path = /srv/samba/readonly
comment = files to read
read only = yes
guest ok = yes
```

Here is a very similar configuration on Ubuntu 11.10.

```
root@ubu1110:~# cat /etc/samba/smb.conf
[global]
workgroup = LINUXTR
netbios name = UBU1110
security = share
[roshare1]
path = /srv/samba/readonly
read only = yes
guest ok = yes
```

It doesn't really matter which Linux distribution you use. Below the same config on Debian 6, as good as identical.

```
root@debian6:~# cat /etc/samba/smb.conf
[global]
workgroup = LINUXTR
netbios name = DEBIAN6
security = share
[roshare1]
path = /srv/samba/readonly
read only = yes
guest ok = yes
```

# 17.3. restart the server

After testing with **testparm**, restart the samba server (so you don't have to wait).

```
[root@RHEL4b readonly]# service smb restart
Shutting down SMB services:                          [  OK  ]
Shutting down NMB services:                          [  OK  ]
Starting SMB services:                               [  OK  ]
Starting NMB services:                               [  OK  ]
```

# 17.4. verify the share

## 17.4.1. verify with smbclient

You can now verify the existence of the share with **smbclient**. Our **pubread** is listed as the fourth share.

```
[root@RHEL52 samba]# smbclient -NL 127.0.0.1
Domain=[WORKGROUP] OS=[Unix] Server=[Samba 3.0.33-3.7.el5]

        Sharename       Type        Comment
        ---------       ----        -------
        IPC$            IPC         IPC Service (Public Anonymous File Server)
        global$         Disk
        pub0            Disk
        pubread         Disk        files to read
Domain=[WORKGROUP] OS=[Unix] Server=[Samba 3.0.33-3.7.el5]

        Server          Comment
        ---------       -------
        TEACHER0        Samba 3.0.33-3.7.el5
        W2003EE

        Workgroup       Master
        ---------       -------
        WORKGROUP       W2003EE
```

## 17.4.2. verify on windows

The final test is to go to a Microsoft windows computer and read a file on the Samba server. First we use the **net use** command to mount the pubread share on the driveletter k.

```
C:\>net use K: \\teacher0\pubread
The command completed successfully.
```

Then we test looking at the contents of the share, and reading the files.

```
C:\>dir k:
 Volume in drive K is pubread
 Volume Serial Number is 0C82-11F2

 Directory of K:\

21/01/2009  05:49    <DIR>          .
21/01/2009  05:49    <DIR>          ..
21/01/2009  05:49                17 summer.txt
21/01/2009  05:49                18 winter.txt
               2 File(s)             35 bytes
               2 Dir(s)  13.496.242.176 bytes free
```

Just to be on the safe side, let us try writing.

```
K:\>echo very cold > winter.txt
Access is denied.

K:\>
```

Or you can use windows explorer...

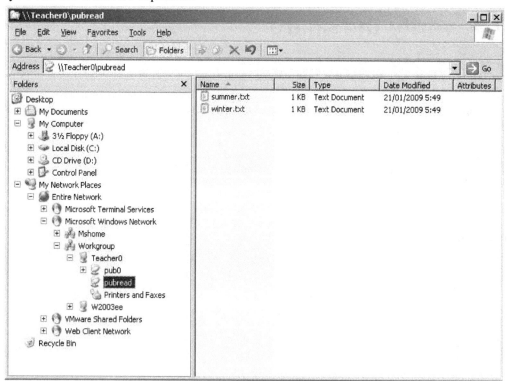

# 17.5. a note on netcat

The Windows command line screenshot is made in a Linux console, using **netcat** as a pipe to a Windows command shell.

The way this works, is by enabling netcat to listen on the windows computer to a certain port, executing cmd.exe when a connection is received. Netcat is similar to cat, in the way that cat does nothing, only netcat does nothing over the network.

To enable this connection, type the following on the windows computer (after downloading netcat for windows).

```
nc -l -p 23 -t -e cmd.exe
```

And then connect to this machine with netcat from any Linux computer. You end up with a cmd.exe prompt inside your Linux shell.

```
paul@laika:~$ nc 192.168.1.38 23
Microsoft Windows [Version 5.2.3790]
(C) Copyright 1985-2003 Microsoft Corp.

C:\>net use k: /delete
net use k: /delete
k: was deleted successfully.
```

# 17.6. practice: read only file server

1. Create a directory in a good location (FHS) to share files for everyone to read.

2. Make sure the directory is owned properly and is world accessible.

3. Put a textfile in this directory.

4. Share the directory with Samba.

5. Verify from your own and from another computer (smbclient, net use, ...) that the share is accessible for reading.

6. Make a backup copy of your smb.conf, name it smb.conf.ReadOnlyFileServer.

# 17.7. solution: read only file server

1. Create a directory in a good location (FHS) to share files for everyone to read.

```
choose one of these...

mkdir -p /srv/samba/readonly

mkdir -p /home/samba/readonly

/home/paul/readonly is wrong!!

/etc/samba/readonly is wrong!!

/readonly is wrong!!
```

2. Make sure the directory is owned properly and is world accessible.

```
chown root:root /srv/samba/readonly

chmod 755 /srv/samba/readonly
```

3. Put a textfile in this directory.

```
echo Hello World > hello.txt
```

4. Share the directory with Samba.

```
You smb.conf.readonly could look like this:
[global]
 workgroup = WORKGROUP
 server string = Read Only File Server
 netbios name = STUDENTx
 security = share

[readonlyX]
 path = /srv/samba/readonly
 comment = read only file share
 read only = yes
 guest ok = yes


test with testparm before going in production!
```

5. Verify from your own and from another computer (smbclient, net use, ...) that the share is accessible for reading.

```
On Linux: smbclient -NL 127.0.0.1

On Windows Explorer: browse to My Network Places

On Windows cmd.exe: net use L: //studentx/readonly
```

6. Make a backup copy of your smb.conf, name it smb.conf.ReadOnlyFileServer.

```
cp smb.conf smb.conf.ReadOnlyFileServer
```

# Chapter 18. a writable file server

# 18.1. set up a directory to share

In this second example, we will create a share where everyone can create files and write to files. Again, we start by creating a directory

```
[root@RHEL52 samba]# mkdir -p /srv/samba/writable
[root@RHEL52 samba]# chmod 777 /srv/samba/writable/
```

# 18.2. share section in smb.conf

There are two parameters to make a share writable. We can use **read only** or **writable**. This example shows how to use **writable** to give write access to a share.

```
writable = yes
```

And this is an example of using the **read only** parameter to give write access to a share.

```
read only = no
```

# 18.3. configure the share

Then we simply add a share to our file server by editing **smb.conf**. Below the check with testparm. (We could have changed the description of the server...)

```
[root@RHEL52 samba]# testparm
Load smb config files from /etc/samba/smb.conf
Processing section "[pubwrite]"
Processing section "[pubread]"
Loaded services file OK.
Server role: ROLE_STANDALONE
Press enter to see a dump of your service definitions

[global]
 netbios name = TEACHER0
 server string = Public Anonymous File Server
 security = SHARE

[pubwrite]
 comment = files to write
 path = /srv/samba/writable
 read only = No
 guest ok = Yes

[pubread]
 comment = files to read
 path = /srv/samba/readonly
 guest ok = Yes
```

# 18.4. test connection with windows

We can now test the connection on a windows 2003 computer. We use the **net use** for this.

```
C:\>net use L: \\teacher0\pubwrite
net use L: \\teacher0\pubwrite
The command completed successfully.
```

## 18.5. test writing with windows

We mounted the **pubwrite** share on the L: drive in windows. Below we test that we can write to this share.

```
L:\>echo hoi > hoi.txt

L:\>dir
 Volume in drive L is pubwrite
 Volume Serial Number is 0C82-272A

 Directory of L:\

21/01/2009  06:11    <DIR>          .
21/01/2009  06:11    <DIR>          ..
21/01/2009  06:16                 6 hoi.txt
               1 File(s)              6 bytes
               2 Dir(s)   13.496.238.080 bytes free
```

## 18.6. How is this possible ?

Linux (or any Unix) always needs a user account to gain access to a system. The windows computer did not provide the samba server with a user account or a password. Instead, the Linux owner of the files created through this writable share is the Linux guest account (usually named nobody).

```
[root@RHEL52 samba]# ls -l /srv/samba/writable/
total 4
-rwxr--r-- 1 nobody nobody 6 Jan 21 06:16 hoi.txt
```

So this is not the cleanest solution. We will need to improve this.

# 18.7. practice: writable file server

1. Create a directory and share it with Samba.

2. Make sure everyone can read and write files, test writing with smbclient and from a Microsoft computer.

3. Verify the ownership of files created by (various) users.

# 18.8. solution: writable file server

1. Create a directory and share it with Samba.

```
mkdir /srv/samba/writable
```

```
chmod 777 /srv/samba/writable
```

```
the share section in smb.conf can look like this:
```

```
[pubwrite]
 path = /srv/samba/writable
 comment = files to write
 read only = no
 guest ok = yes
```

2. Make sure everyone can read and write files, test writing with smbclient and from a Microsoft computer.

```
to test writing with smbclient:
```

```
echo one > count.txt
echo two >> count.txt
echo three >> count.txt
smbclient //localhost/pubwrite
Password:
smb: \> put count.txt
```

3. Verify the ownership of files created by (various) users.

```
ls -l /srv/samba/writable
```

# Chapter 19. samba first user account

# 19.1. creating a samba user

We will create a user for our samba file server and make this user the owner of the directory and all of its files. This anonymous user gets a clear description, but does not get a login shell.

```
[root@RHEL52 samba]# useradd -s /bin/false sambanobody
[root@RHEL52 samba]# usermod -c "Anonymous Samba Access" sambanobody
[root@RHEL52 samba]# passwd sambanobody
Changing password for user sambanobody.
New UNIX password:
Retype new UNIX password:
passwd: all authentication tokens updated successfully.
```

# 19.2. ownership of files

We can use this user as owner of files and directories, instead of using the root account. This approach is clear and more secure.

```
[root@RHEL52 samba]# chown -R sambanobody:sambanobody /srv/samba/
[root@RHEL52 samba]# ls -al /srv/samba/writable/
total 12
drwxrwxrwx 2 sambanobody sambanobody 4096 Jan 21 06:11 .
drwxr-xr-x 6 sambanobody sambanobody 4096 Jan 21 06:11 ..
-rwxr--r-- 1 sambanobody sambanobody    6 Jan 21 06:16 hoi.txt
```

# 19.3. /usr/bin/smbpasswd

The sambanobody user account that we created in the previous examples is not yet used by samba. It just owns the files and directories that we created for our shares. The goal of this section is to force ownership of files created through the samba share to belong to our sambanobody user. Remember, our server is still accessible to everyone, nobody needs to know this user account or password. We just want a clean Linux server.

To accomplish this, we first have to tell Samba about this user. We can do this by adding the account to **smbpasswd**.

```
[root@RHEL52 samba]# smbpasswd -a sambanobody
New SMB password:
Retype new SMB password:
Added user sambanobody.
```

# 19.4. /etc/samba/smbpasswd

To find out where Samba keeps this information (for now), use **smbd -b**. The PRIVATE_DIR variable will show you where the smbpasswd database is located.

```
[root@RHEL52 samba]# smbd -b | grep PRIVATE
   PRIVATE_DIR: /etc/samba
[root@RHEL52 samba]# ls -l smbpasswd
-rw------- 1 root root 110 Jan 21 06:19 smbpasswd
```

You can use a simple cat to see the contents of the **smbpasswd** database. The sambanobody user does have a password (it is secret).

```
[root@RHEL52 samba]# cat smbpasswd
```

```
sambanobody:503:AE9 ... 9DB309C528E540978:[U        ]:LCT-4976B05B:
```

# 19.5. passdb backend

Note that recent versions of Samba have **tdbsam** as default for the **passdb backend** paramater.

```
root@ubu1110:~# testparm -v 2>/dev/null| grep 'passdb backend'

 passdb backend = tdbsam
```

# 19.6. forcing this user

Now that Samba knows about this user, we can adjust our writable share to force the ownership of files created through it. For this we use the **force user** and **force group** options. Now we can be sure that all files in the Samba writable share are owned by the same sambanobody user.

Below is the renewed definition of our share in smb.conf.

```
[pubwrite]
path = /srv/samba/writable
comment = files to write
force user = sambanobody
force group = sambanobody
read only = no
guest ok = yes
```

When you reconnect to the share and write a file, then this sambanobody user will own the newly created file (and nobody needs to know the password).

# 19.7. practice: first samba user account

1. Create a user account for use with samba.

2. Add this user to samba's user database.

3. Create a writable shared directory and use the "force user" and "force group" directives to force ownership of files.

4. Test the working of force user with smbclient, net use and Windows Explorer.

# 19.8. solution: first samba user account

1. Create a user account for use with samba.

```
useradd -s /bin/false smbguest

usermod -c 'samba guest'

passwd smbguest
```

2. Add this user to samba's user database.

```
smbpasswd -a smbguest
```

3. Create a writable shared directory and use the "force user" and "force group" directives to force ownership of files.

```
[userwrite]
 path = /srv/samba/userwrite
 comment = everyone writes files owned by smbguest
 read only = no
 guest ok = yes
 force user = smbguest
 force group = smbguest
```

4. Test the working of force user with smbclient, net use and Windows Explorer.

```
ls -l /srv/samba/userwrite (and verify ownership)
```

# Chapter 20. samba authentication

# 20.1. creating the users on Linux

The goal of this example is to set up a file share accessible to a number of different users. The users will need to authenticate with their password before access to this share is granted. We will first create three randomly named users, each with their own password. First we add these users to Linux.

```
[root@RHEL52 ~]# useradd -c "Serena Williams" serena
[root@RHEL52 ~]# useradd -c "Justine Henin" justine
[root@RHEL52 ~]# useradd -c "Martina Hingis" martina
[root@RHEL52 ~]# passwd serena
Changing password for user serena.
New UNIX password:
Retype new UNIX password:
passwd: all authentication tokens updated successfully.
[root@RHEL52 ~]# passwd justine
Changing password for user justine.
New UNIX password:
Retype new UNIX password:
passwd: all authentication tokens updated successfully.
[root@RHEL52 ~]# passwd martina
Changing password for user martina.
New UNIX password:
Retype new UNIX password:
passwd: all authentication tokens updated successfully.
```

# 20.2. creating the users on samba

Then we add them to the **smbpasswd** file, with the same password.

```
[root@RHEL52 ~]# smbpasswd -a serena
New SMB password:
Retype new SMB password:
Added user serena.
[root@RHEL52 ~]# smbpasswd -a justine
New SMB password:
Retype new SMB password:
Added user justine.
[root@RHEL52 ~]# smbpasswd -a martina
New SMB password:
Retype new SMB password:
Added user martina.
```

# 20.3. security = user

Remember that we set samba's security mode to share with the **security = share** directive in the [global] section ? Since we now require users to always provide a userid and password for access to our samba server, we will need to change this. Setting **security = user** will require the client to provide samba with a valid userid and password before giving access to a share.

Our [global] section now looks like this.

```
[global]
workgroup = WORKGROUP
netbios name = TEACHER0
server string = Samba File Server
security = user
```

## 20.4. configuring the share

We add the following [share] section to our smb.conf (and we do not forget to create the directory /srv/samba/authwrite).

```
[authwrite]
path = /srv/samba/authwrite
comment = authenticated users only
read only = no
guest ok = no
```

## 20.5. testing access with net use

After restarting samba, we test with different users from within Microsoft computers. The screenshots use the **net use**First serena from Windows XP.

```
C:\>net use m: \\teacher0\authwrite stargate /user:serena
The command completed successfully.

C:\>m:

M:\>echo greetings from Serena > serena.txt
```

The next screenshot is martina on a Windows 2000 computer, she succeeds in writing her files, but fails to overwrite the file from serena.

```
C:\>net use k: \\teacher0\authwrite stargate /user:martina
The command completed successfully.

C:\>k:

K:\>echo greetings from martina > Martina.txt

K:\>echo test overwrite > serena.txt
Access is denied.
```

## 20.6. testing access with smbclient

You can also test connecting with authentication with **smbclient**. First we test with a wrong password.

```
[root@RHEL52 samba]# smbclient //teacher0/authwrite -U martina wrongpass
session setup failed: NT_STATUS_LOGON_FAILURE
```

Then we test with the correct password, and verify that we can access a file on the share.

```
[root@RHEL52 samba]# smbclient //teacher0/authwrite -U martina stargate
Domain=[TEACHER0] OS=[Unix] Server=[Samba 3.0.33-3.7.el5]
smb: \> more serena.txt
getting file \serena.txt of size 14 as /tmp/smbmore.QQfmSN (6.8 kb/s)
one
two
three
smb: \> q
```

# 20.7. verify ownership

We now have a simple standalone samba file server with authenticated access. And the files in the shares belong to their proper owners.

```
[root@RHEL52 samba]# ls -l /srv/samba/authwrite/
total 8
-rwxr--r-- 1 martina martina  0 Jan 21 20:06 martina.txt
-rwxr--r-- 1 serena  serena  14 Jan 21 20:06 serena.txt
-rwxr--r-- 1 serena  serena   6 Jan 21 20:09 ser.txt
```

# 20.8. common problems

## 20.8.1. NT_STATUS_BAD_NETWORK_NAME

You can get **NT_STATUS_BAD_NETWORK_NAME** when you forget to create the target directory.

```
[root@RHEL52 samba]# rm -rf /srv/samba/authwrite/
[root@RHEL52 samba]# smbclient //teacher0/authwrite -U martina stargate
Domain=[TEACHER0] OS=[Unix] Server=[Samba 3.0.33-3.7.el5]
tree connect failed: NT_STATUS_BAD_NETWORK_NAME
```

## 20.8.2. NT_STATUS_LOGON_FAILURE

You can get **NT_STATUS_LOGON_FAILURE** when you type the wrong password or when you type an unexisting username.

```
[root@RHEL52 samba]# smbclient //teacher0/authwrite -U martina STARGATE
session setup failed: NT_STATUS_LOGON_FAILURE
```

## 20.8.3. usernames are (not) case sensitive

Remember that usernames om Linux are case sensitive.

```
[root@RHEL52 samba]# su - MARTINA
su: user MARTINA does not exist
```

```
[root@RHEL52 samba]# su - martina
[martina@RHEL52 ~]$
```

But usernames on Microsoft computers are not case sensitive.

```
[root@RHEL52 samba]# smbclient //teacher0/authwrite -U martina stargate
Domain=[TEACHER0] OS=[Unix] Server=[Samba 3.0.33-3.7.el5]
smb: \> q
[root@RHEL52 samba]# smbclient //teacher0/authwrite -U MARTINA stargate
Domain=[TEACHER0] OS=[Unix] Server=[Samba 3.0.33-3.7.el5]
smb: \> q
```

# 20.9. practice : samba authentication

0. Make sure you have properly named backups of your smb.conf of the previous practices.

1. Create three users (on the Linux and on the samba), remember their passwords!

2. Set up a shared directory that is only accessible to authenticated users.

3. Use smbclient and a windows computer to access your share, use more than one user account (windows requires a logoff/logon for this).

4. Verify that files created by these users belong to them.

5. Try to change or delete a file from another user.

# 20.10. solution: samba authentication

1. Create three users (on the Linux and on the samba), remember their passwords!

```
useradd -c 'SMB user1' userx
```

```
passwd userx
```

2. Set up a shared directory that is only accessible to authenticated users.

```
The shared section in smb.conf could look like this:
```

```
[authwrite]
 path = /srv/samba/authwrite
 comment = authenticated users only
 read only = no
 guest ok = no
```

3. Use smbclient and a windows computer to access your share, use more than one user account (windows requires a logoff/logon for this).

```
on Linux: smbclient //studentX/authwrite -U user1 password
```

```
on windows net use p: \\studentX\authwrite password /user:user2
```

4. Verify that files created by these users belong to them.

```
ls -l /srv/samba/authwrite
```

5. Try to change or delete a file from another user.

```
you should not be able to change or overwrite files from others.
```

# Chapter 21. samba securing shares

# 21.1. security based on user name

## 21.1.1. valid users

To restrict users per share, you can use the **valid users** parameter. In the example below, only the users listed as valid will be able to access the tennis share.

```
[tennis]
path = /srv/samba/tennis
comment = authenticated and valid users only
read only = No
guest ok = No
valid users = serena, kim, venus, justine
```

## 21.1.2. invalid users

If you are paranoia, you can also use **invalid users** to explicitly deny the listed users access. When a user is in both lists, the user has no access!

```
[tennis]
path = /srv/samba/tennis
read only = No
guest ok = No
valid users = kim, serena, venus, justine
invalid users = venus
```

## 21.1.3. read list

On a writable share, you can set a list of read only users with the **read list** parameter.

```
[football]
path = /srv/samba/football
read only = No
guest ok = No
read list = martina, roberto
```

## 21.1.4. write list

Even on a read only share, you can set a list of users that can write. Use the **write list** parameter.

```
[football]
path = /srv/samba/golf
read only = Yes
guest ok = No
write list = eddy, jan
```

# 21.2. security based on ip-address

## 21.2.1. hosts allow

The **hosts allow** or **allow hosts** parameter is one of the key advantages of Samba. It allows access control of shares on the ip-address level. To allow only specific hosts to access a share, list the hosts, separated by comma's.

```
allow hosts = 192.168.1.5, 192.168.1.40
```

Allowing entire subnets is done by ending the range with a dot.

```
allow hosts = 192.168.1.
```

Subnet masks can be added in the classical way.

```
allow hosts = 10.0.0.0/255.0.0.0
```

You can also allow an entire subnet with exceptions.

```
hosts allow = 10. except 10.0.0.12
```

## 21.2.2. hosts deny

The **hosts deny** or **deny hosts** parameter is the logical counterpart of the previous. The syntax is the same as for hosts allow.

```
hosts deny = 192.168.1.55, 192.168.1.56
```

# 21.3. security through obscurity

## 21.3.1. hide unreadable

Setting **hide unreadable** to yes will prevent users from seeing files that cannot be read by them.

```
hide unreadable = yes
```

## 21.3.2. browsable

Setting the **browseable = no** directive will hide shares from My Network Places. But it will not prevent someone from accessing the share (when the name of the share is known).

Note that **browsable** and **browseable** are both correct syntax.

```
[pubread]
 path = /srv/samba/readonly
 comment = files to read
 read only = yes
 guest ok = yes
 browseable = no
```

# 21.4. file system security

## 21.4.1. create mask

You can use **create mask** and **directory mask** to set the maximum allowed permissions for newly created files and directories. The mask you set is an AND mask (it takes permissions away).

```
[tennis]
 path = /srv/samba/tennis
 read only = No
```

```
guest ok = No
create mask = 640
directory mask = 750
```

## 21.4.2. force create mode

Similar to **create mask**, but different. Where the mask from above was a logical AND, the mode you set here is a logical OR (so it adds permissions). You can use the **force create mode** and **force directory mode** to set the minimal required permissions for newly created files and directories.

```
[tennis]
path = /srv/samba/tennis
read only = No
guest ok = No
force create mode = 444
force directory mode = 550
```

## 21.4.3. security mask

The **security mask** and **directory security mask** work in the same way as **create mask** and **directory mask**, but apply only when a windows user is changing permissions using the windows security dialog box.

## 21.4.4. force security mode

The **force security mode** and **force directory security mode** work in the same way as **force create mode** and **force directory mode**, but apply only when a windows user is changing permissions using the windows security dialog box.

## 21.4.5. inherit permissions

With **inherit permissions = yes** you can force newly created files and directories to inherit permissions from their parent directory, overriding the create mask and directory mask settings.

```
[authwrite]
path = /srv/samba/authwrite
comment = authenticated users only
read only = no
guest ok = no
create mask = 600
directory mask = 555
inherit permissions = yes
```

# 21.5. practice: securing shares

1. Create a writable share called sales, and a readonly share called budget. Test that it works.

2. Limit access to the sales share to ann, sandra and veronique.

3. Make sure that roberto cannot access the sales share.

4. Even though the sales share is writable, ann should only have read access.

5. Even though the budget share is read only, sandra should also have write access.

6. Limit one shared directory to the 192.168.1.0/24 subnet, and another share to the two computers with ip-addresses 192.168.1.33 and 172.17.18.19.

7. Make sure the computer with ip 192.168.1.203 cannot access the budget share.

8. Make sure (on the budget share) that users can see only files and directories to which they have access.

9. Make sure the sales share is not visible when browsing the network.

10. All files created in the sales share should have 640 permissions or less.

11. All directories created in the budget share should have 750 permissions or more.

12. Permissions for files on the sales share should never be set more than 664.

13. Permissions for files on the budget share should never be set less than 500.

14. If time permits (or if you are waiting for other students to finish this practice), then combine the "read only" and "writable" statements to check which one has priority.

15. If time permits then combine "read list", "write list", "hosts allow" and "hosts deny". Which of these has priority ?

# 21.6. solution: securing shares

1. Create a writable share called sales, and a readonly share called budget. Test that it works.

```
see previous solutions on how to do this...
```

2. Limit access to the sales share to ann, sandra and veronique.

```
valid users = ann, sandra, veronique
```

3. Make sure that roberto cannot access the sales share.

```
invalid users = roberto
```

4. Even though the sales share is writable, ann should only have read access.

```
read list = ann
```

5. Even though the budget share is read only, sandra should also have write access.

```
write list = sandra
```

6. Limit one shared directory to the 192.168.1.0/24 subnet, and another share to the two computers with ip-addresses 192.168.1.33 and 172.17.18.19.

```
hosts allow = 192.168.1.

hosts allow = 192.168.1.33, 172.17.18.19
```

7. Make sure the computer with ip 192.168.1.203 cannot access the budget share.

```
hosts deny = 192.168.1.203
```

8. Make sure (on the budget share) that users can see only files and directories to which they have access.

```
hide unreadable = yes
```

9. Make sure the sales share is not visible when browsing the network.

```
browsable = no
```

10. All files created in the sales share should have 640 permissions or less.

```
create mask = 640
```

11. All directories created in the budget share should have 750 permissions or more.

```
force directory mode = 750
```

12. Permissions for files on the sales share should never be set more than 664.

```
security mask = 750
```

13. Permissions for files on the budget share should never be set less than 500.

```
force security directory mask = 500
```

14. If time permits (or if you are waiting for other students to finish this practice), then combine the "read only" and "writable" statements to check which one has priority.

15. If time permits then combine "read list", "write list", "hosts allow" and "hosts deny". Which of these has priority ?

# Chapter 22. samba domain member

# 22.1. changes in smb.conf

## 22.1.1. workgroup

The **workgroup** option in the global section should match the netbios name of the Active Directory domain.

```
workgroup = STARGATE
```

## 22.1.2. security mode

Authentication will not be handled by samba now, but by the Active Directory domain controllers, so we set the **security** option to domain.

```
security = Domain
```

## 22.1.3. Linux uid's

Linux requires a user account for every user accessing its file system, we need to provide Samba with a range of uid's and gid's that it can use to create these user accounts. The range is determined with the **idmap uid** and the **idmap gid** parameters. The first Active Directory user to connect will receive Linux uid 20000.

```
idmap uid = 20000-22000
idmap gid = 20000-22000
```

## 22.1.4. winbind use default domain

The **winbind use default domain** parameter makes sure winbind also operates on users without a domain component in their name.

```
winbind use default domain = yes
```

## 22.1.5. [global] section in smb.conf

Below is our new global section in **smb.conf**.

```
[global]
 workgroup = STARGATE
 security = Domain
 server string = Stargate Domain Member Server
 idmap uid = 20000-22000
 idmap gid = 20000-22000
 winbind use default domain = yes
```

## 22.1.6. realm in /etc/krb5.conf

To connect to a Windows 2003 sp2 (or later) you will need to adjust the kerberos realm in **/etc/krb5.conf** and set both lookup statements to true.

```
[libdefaults]
 default_realm = STARGATE.LOCAL
 dns_lookup_realm = true
 dns_lookup_kdc = true
```

## 22.1.7. [share] section in smb.conf

Nothing special is required for the share section in smb.conf. Remember that we do not manually create users in smbpasswd or on the Linux (/etc/passwd). Only Active Directory users are allowed access.

```
[domaindata]
 path = /srv/samba/domaindata
 comment = Active Directory users only
 read only = No
```

# 22.2. joining an Active Directory domain

While the Samba server is stopped, you can use **net rpc join** to join the Active Directory domain.

```
[root@RHEL52 samba]# service smb stop
Shutting down SMB services:                              [  OK  ]
Shutting down NMB services:                              [  OK  ]
[root@RHEL52 samba]# net rpc join -U Administrator
Password:
Joined domain STARGATE.
```

We can verify in the aduc (Active Directory Users and Computers) that a computer account is created for this samba server.

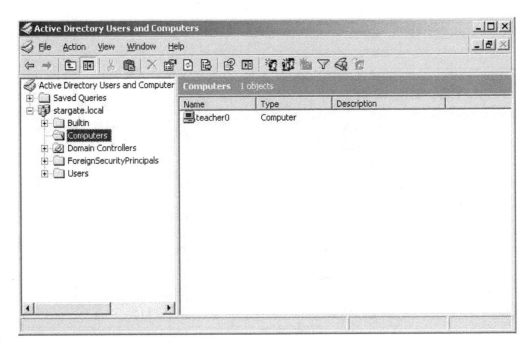

# 22.3. winbind

## 22.3.1. adding winbind to nsswitch.conf

The **winbind daemon** is talking with the Active Directory domain.

We need to update the **/etc/nsswitch.conf** file now, so user group and host names can be resolved against the winbind daemon.

```
[root@RHEL52 samba]# vi /etc/nsswitch.conf
[root@RHEL52 samba]# grep winbind /etc/nsswitch.conf
passwd:     files winbind
group:      files winbind
hosts:      files dns winbind
```

## 22.3.2. starting samba and winbindd

Time to start Samba followed by **winbindd**.

```
[root@RHEL4b samba]# service smb start
Starting SMB services:                          [  OK  ]
Starting NMB services:                          [  OK  ]
[root@RHEL4b samba]# service winbind start
Starting winbindd services:                     [  OK  ]
[root@RHEL4b samba]#
```

# 22.4. wbinfo

## 22.4.1. verify the trust

You can use **wbinfo -t** to verify the trust between your samba server and Active Directory.

```
[root@RHEL52 ~]# wbinfo -t
checking the trust secret via RPC calls succeeded
```

## 22.4.2. list all users

We can obtain a list of all user with the **wbinfo -u** command. The domain is not shown when the **winbind use default domain** parameter is set.

```
[root@RHEL52 ~]# wbinfo -u
TEACHER0\serena
TEACHER0\justine
TEACHER0\martina
STARGATE\administrator
STARGATE\guest
STARGATE\support_388945a0
STARGATE\pol
STARGATE\krbtgt
STARGATE\arthur
STARGATE\harry
```

## 22.4.3. list all groups

We can obtain a list of all domain groups with the **wbinfo -g** command. The domain is not shown when the **winbind use default domain** parameter is set.

```
[root@RHEL52 ~]# wbinfo -g
BUILTIN\administrators
BUILTIN\users
BATMAN\domain computers
BATMAN\domain controllers
BATMAN\schema admins
BATMAN\enterprise admins
BATMAN\domain admins
BATMAN\domain users
BATMAN\domain guests
BATMAN\group policy creator owners
BATMAN\dnsupdateproxy
```

## 22.4.4. query a user

We can use **wbinfo -a** to verify authentication of a user against Active Directory. Assuming a user account **harry** with password **stargate** is just created on the Active Directory, we get the following screenshot.

```
[root@RHEL52 ~]# wbinfo -a harry%stargate
plaintext password authentication succeeded
challenge/response password authentication succeeded
```

# 22.5. getent

We can use **getent** to verify that winbindd is working and actually adding the Active directory users to /etc/passwd.

```
[root@RHEL52 ~]# getent passwd harry
harry:*:20000:20008:harry potter:/home/BATMAN/harry:/bin/false
[root@RHEL52 ~]# getent passwd arthur
arthur:*:20001:20008:arthur dent:/home/BATMAN/arthur:/bin/false
[root@RHEL52 ~]# getent passwd bilbo
bilbo:*:20002:20008:bilbo baggins:/home/BATMAN/bilbo:/bin/false
```

If the user already exists locally, then the local user account is shown. This is because winbind is configured in **/etc/nsswitch.conf** after **files**.

```
[root@RHEL52 ~]# getent passwd paul
paul:x:500:500:Paul Cobbaut:/home/paul:/bin/bash
```

All the Active Directory users can now easily connect to the Samba share. Files created by them, belong to them.

## 22.6. file ownership

```
[root@RHEL4b samba]# ll /srv/samba/domaindata/
total 0
-rwxr--r--  1 justine 20000 0 Jun 22 19:54 create_by_justine_on_winxp.txt
-rwxr--r--  1 venus   20000 0 Jun 22 19:55 create_by_venus.txt
-rwxr--r--  1 maria   20000 0 Jun 22 19:57 Maria.txt
```

# 22.7. practice : samba domain member

1. Verify that you have a working Active Directory (AD) domain.

2. Add the domain name and domain controller to /etc/hosts. Set the AD-DNS in /etc/resolv.conf.

3. Setup Samba as a member server in the domain.

4. Verify the creation of a computer account in AD for your Samba server.

5. Verify the automatic creation of AD users in /etc/passwd with wbinfo and getent.

6. Connect to Samba shares with AD users, and verify ownership of their files.

# Chapter 23. samba domain controller

# 23.1. about Domain Controllers

## 23.1.1. Windows NT4

Windows NT4 works with single master replication domain controllers. There is exactly one PDC (Primary Domain Controller) in the domain, and zero or more BDC's (Backup Domain Controllers). Samba 3 has all features found in Windows NT4 PDC and BDC, and more. This includes file and print serving, domain control with single logon, logon scripts, home directories and roaming profiles.

## 23.1.2. Windows 200x

With Windows 2000 came Active Directory. AD includes multimaster replication and group policies. Samba 3 can only be a member server in Active Directory, it cannot manage group policies. Samba 4 can do this (in beta).

## 23.1.3. Samba 3

Samba 3 can act as a domain controller in its own domain. In a Windows NT4 domain, with one Windows NT4 PDC and zero or more BDC's, Samba 3 can only be a member server. The same is valid for Samba 3 in an Active Directory Domain. In short, a Samba 3 domain controller can not share domain control with Windows domain controllers.

## 23.1.4. Samba 4

Samba 4 can be a domain controller in an Active Directory domain, including managing group policies. As of this writing, Samba 4 is not released for production!

# 23.2. About security modes

## 23.2.1. security = share

The 'Windows for Workgroups' way of working, a client requests connection to a share and provides a password for that connection. Aanyone who knows a password for a share can access that share. This security model was common in Windows 3.11, Windows 95, Windows 98 and Windows ME.

## 23.2.2. security = user

The client will send a userid + password before the server knows which share the client wants to access. This mode should be used whenever the samba server is in control of the user database. Both for standalone and samba domain controllers.

## 23.2.3. security = domain

This mode will allow samba to verify user credentials using NTLM in Windows NT4 and in all Active Directory domains. This is similar to Windows NT4 BDC's joining a native Windows 2000/3 Active Directory domain.

## 23.2.4. security = ads

This mode will make samba use Kerberos to connect to the Active Directory domain.

## 23.2.5. security = server

This mode is obsolete, it can be used to forward authentication to another server.

# 23.3. About password backends

The previous chapters all used the **smbpasswd** user database. For domain control we opt for the **tdbsam** password backend. Another option would be to use LDAP. Larger domains will benefit from using LDAP instead of the not so scalable tdbsam. When you need more than one Domain Controller, then the Samba team advises to not use tdbsam.

# 23.4. [global] section in smb.conf

Now is a good time to start adding comments in your smb.conf. First we will take a look at the naming of our domain and server in the **[global]** section, and at the domain controlling parameters.

## 23.4.1. security

The security must be set to user (which is the default). This mode will make samba control the user accounts, so it will allow samba to act as a domain controller.

```
security = user
```

## 23.4.2. os level

A samba server is the most stable computer in the network, so it should win all browser elections (**os level** above 32) to become the **browser master**

```
os level = 33
```

## 23.4.3. passdb backend

The **passdb backend** parameter will determine whether samba uses **smbpasswd**, **tdbsam** or ldap.

```
passdb backend = tdbsam
```

## 23.4.4. preferred master

Setting the **preferred master** parameter to yes will make the nmbd daemon force an election on startup.

```
preferred master = yes
```

## 23.4.5. domain logons

Setting the **domain logons** parameter will make this samba server a domain controller.

```
domain logons = yes
```

## 23.4.6. domain master

Setting the **domain master** parameter can cause samba to claim the **domain master browser** role for its workgroup. Don't use this parameter in a workgroup with an active NT4 PDC.

```
domain master = yes
```

## 23.4.7. [global] section

The screenshot below shows a sample [global] section for a samba domain controller.

```
[global]
# names
 workgroup = SPORTS
 netbios name = DCSPORTS
 server string = Sports Domain Controller
# domain control parameters
 security = user
 os level = 33
 preferred master = Yes
 domain master = Yes
 domain logons = Yes
```

# 23.5. netlogon share

Part of the microsoft definition for a domain controller is that it should have a **netlogon share**. This is the relevant part of smb.conf to create this netlogon share on Samba.

```
[netlogon]
comment = Network Logon Service
path = /srv/samba/netlogon
admin users = root
guest ok = Yes
browseable = No
```

# 23.6. other [share] sections

We create some sections for file shares, to test the samba server. Users can all access the general sports file share, but only group members can access their own sports share.

```
[sports]
comment = Information about all sports
path = /srv/samba/sports
valid users = @ntsports
read only = No

[tennis]
comment = Information about tennis
path = /srv/samba/tennis
valid users = @nttennis
read only = No
```

```
[football]
comment = Information about football
path = /srv/samba/football
valid users = @ntfootball
read only = No
```

# 23.7. Users and Groups

To be able to use users and groups in the samba domain controller, we can first set up some groups on the Linux computer.

```
[root@RHEL52 samba]# groupadd ntadmins
[root@RHEL52 samba]# groupadd ntsports
[root@RHEL52 samba]# groupadd ntfootball
[root@RHEL52 samba]# groupadd nttennis
```

This enables us to add group membership info to some new users for our samba domain. Don't forget to give them a password.

```
[root@RHEL52 samba]# useradd -m -G ntadmins Administrator
[root@RHEL52 samba]# useradd -m -G ntsports,nttennis venus
[root@RHEL52 samba]# useradd -m -G ntsports,nttennis kim
[root@RHEL52 samba]# useradd -m -G ntsports,nttennis jelena
[root@RHEL52 samba]# useradd -m -G ntsports,ntfootball figo
[root@RHEL52 samba]# useradd -m -G ntsports,ntfootball ronaldo
[root@RHEL52 samba]# useradd -m -G ntsports,ntfootball pfaff
```

It is always safe to verify creation of users, groups and passwords in /etc/passwd, /etc/shadow and /etc/group.

```
[root@RHEL52 samba]# tail -11 /etc/group
ntadmins:x:507:Administrator
ntsports:x:508:venus,kim,jelena,figo,ronaldo,pfaff
ntfootball:x:509:figo,ronaldo,pfaff
nttennis:x:510:venus,kim,jelena
Administrator:x:511:
venus:x:512:
kim:x:513:
jelena:x:514:
figo:x:515:
ronaldo:x:516:
pfaff:x:517:
```

# 23.8. tdbsam

Next we must make these users known to samba with the smbpasswd tool. When you add the first user to **tdbsam**, the file **/etc/samba/passdb.tdb** will be created.

```
[root@RHEL52 samba]# smbpasswd -a root
New SMB password:
```

```
Retype new SMB password:
tdbsam_open: Converting version 0 database to version 3.
Added user root.
```

Adding all the other users generates less output, because tdbsam is already created.

```
[root@RHEL4b samba]# smbpasswd -a root
New SMB password:
Retype new SMB password:
Added user root.
```

# 23.9. about computer accounts

Every NT computer (Windows NT, 2000, XP, Vista) can become a member of a domain. Joining the domain (by right-clicking on My Computer) means that a computer account will be created in the domain. This computer account also has a password (but you cannot know it) to prevent other computers with the same name from accidentally becoming member of the domain. The computer account created by Samba is visible in the **/etc/passwd** file on Linux. Computer accounts appear as a normal user account, but end their name with a dollar sign. Below a screenshot of the windows 2003 computer account, created by Samba 3.

```
[root@RHEL52 samba]# tail -5 /etc/passwd
jelena:x:510:514::/home/jelena:/bin/bash
figo:x:511:515::/home/figo:/bin/bash
ronaldo:x:512:516::/home/ronaldo:/bin/bash
pfaff:x:513:517::/home/pfaff:/bin/bash
w2003ee$:x:514:518::/home/nobody:/bin/false
```

To be able to create the account, you will need to provide credentials of an account with the permission to create accounts (by default only root can do this on Linux). And we will have to tell Samba how to to this, by adding an **add machine script** to the global section of smb.conf.

```
add machine script = /usr/sbin/useradd -s /bin/false -d /home/nobody %u
```

You can now join a Microsoft computer to the sports domain (with the root user). After reboot of the Microsoft computer, you will be able to logon with Administrator (password Stargate1), but you will get an error about your roaming profile. We will fix this in the next section.

When joining the samba domain, you have to enter the credentials of a Linux account that can create users (usually only root can do this). If the Microsoft computer complains with **The parameter is incorrect**, then you possibly forgot to add the **add machine script**.

# 23.10. local or roaming profiles

For your information, if you want to force local profiles instead of roaming profiles, then simply add the following two lines to the global section in smb.conf.

```
logon home =
logon path =
```

Microsoft computers store a lot of User Metadata and application data in a user profile. Making this profile available on the network will enable users to keep their Desktop and Application settings across computers. User profiles on the network are called **roaming profiles** or **roving profiles**. The Samba domain controller can manage these profiles. First we need to add the relevant section in smb.conf.

```
[Profiles]
 comment = User Profiles
 path = /srv/samba/profiles
 readonly = No
 profile acls = Yes
```

Besides the share section, we also need to set the location of the profiles share (this can be another Samba server) in the global section.

```
logon path = \\%L\Profiles\%U
```

The **%L** variable is the name of this Samba server, the **%U** variable translates to the username. After adding a user to smbpasswd and letting the user log on and off, the profile of the user will look like this.

```
[root@RHEL4b samba]# ll /srv/samba/profiles/Venus/
total 568
drwxr-xr-x 4 Venus Venus   4096 Jul  5 10:03 Application Data
drwxr-xr-x 2 Venus Venus   4096 Jul  5 10:03 Cookies
drwxr-xr-x 3 Venus Venus   4096 Jul  5 10:03 Desktop
drwxr-xr-x 3 Venus Venus   4096 Jul  5 10:03 Favorites
drwxr-xr-x 4 Venus Venus   4096 Jul  5 10:03 My Documents
drwxr-xr-x 2 Venus Venus   4096 Jul  5 10:03 NetHood
-rwxr--r-- 1 Venus Venus 524288 Jul  5  2007 NTUSER.DAT
-rwxr--r-- 1 Venus Venus   1024 Jul  5  2007 NTUSER.DAT.LOG
-rw-r--r-- 1 Venus Venus    268 Jul  5 10:03 ntuser.ini
drwxr-xr-x 2 Venus Venus   4096 Jul  5 10:03 PrintHood
drwxr-xr-x 2 Venus Venus   4096 Jul  5 10:03 Recent
drwxr-xr-x 2 Venus Venus   4096 Jul  5 10:03 SendTo
drwxr-xr-x 3 Venus Venus   4096 Jul  5 10:03 Start Menu
drwxr-xr-x 2 Venus Venus   4096 Jul  5 10:03 Templates
```

# 23.11. Groups in NTFS acls

We have users on Unix, we have groups on Unix that contain those users.

```
[root@RHEL4b samba]# grep nt /etc/group
...
ntadmins:x:506:Administrator
ntsports:x:507:Venus,Serena,Kim,Figo,Pfaff
nttennis:x:508:Venus,Serena,Kim
ntfootball:x:509:Figo,Pfaff
```

```
[root@RHEL4b samba]#
```

We already added Venus to the **tdbsam** with **smbpasswd**.

```
smbpasswd -a Venus
```

Does this mean that Venus can access the tennis and the sports shares ? Yes, all access works fine on the Samba server. But the nttennis group is not available on the windows machines. To make the groups available on windows (like in the ntfs security tab of files and folders), we have to map unix groups to windows groups. To do this, we use the **net groupmap** command.

```
[root@RHEL4b samba]# net groupmap add ntgroup="tennis" unixgroup=nttennis type=d
No rid or sid specified, choosing algorithmic mapping
Successully added group tennis to the mapping db
[root@RHEL4b samba]# net groupmap add ntgroup="football" unixgroup=ntfootball type=d
No rid or sid specified, choosing algorithmic mapping
Successully added group football to the mapping db
[root@RHEL4b samba]# net groupmap add ntgroup="sports" unixgroup=ntsports type=d
No rid or sid specified, choosing algorithmic mapping
Successully added group sports to the mapping db
[root@RHEL4b samba]#
```

Now you can use the Samba groups on all NTFS volumes on members of the domain.

# 23.12. logon scripts

Before testing a logon script, make sure it has the proper carriage returns that DOS files have.

```
[root@RHEL4b netlogon]# cat start.bat
net use Z: \\DCSPORTS0\SPORTS
[root@RHEL4b netlogon]# unix2dos start.bat
unix2dos: converting file start.bat to DOS format ...
[root@RHEL4b netlogon]#
```

Then copy the scripts to the netlogon share, and add the following parameter to smb.conf.

```
logon script = start.bat
```

# 23.13. practice: samba domain controller

1. Setup Samba as a domain controller.

2. Create the shares salesdata, salespresentations and meetings. Salesdata must be accessible to all sales people and to all managers. SalesPresentations is only for all sales people. Meetings is only accessible to all managers. Use groups to accomplish this.

3. Join a Microsoft computer to your domain. Verify the creation of a computer account in /etc/passwd.

4. Setup and verify the proper working of roaming profiles.

5. Find information about home directories for users, set them up and verify that users receive their home directory mapped under the H:-drive in MS Windows Explorer.

6. Use a couple of samba domain groups with members to set acls on ntfs. Verify that it works!

7. Knowing that the %m variable contains the computername, create a separate log file for every computer(account).

8. Knowing that %s contains the client operating system, include a smb.%s.conf file that contains a share. (The share will only be visible to clients with that OS).

9. If time permits (or if you are waiting for other students to finish this practice), then combine "valid users" and "invalid users" with groups and usernames with "hosts allow" and "hosts deny" and make a table of which get priority over which.

# Chapter 24. a brief look at samba 4

## 24.1. Samba 4 alpha 6

A quick view on Samba 4 alpha 6 (January 2009). You can also follow this guide http://
wiki.samba.org/index.php/Samba4/HOWTO

Remove old Samba from Red Hat

```
yum remove samba
```

set a fix ip address (Red Hat has an easy GUI)

download and untar

```
samba.org, click 'download info', choose mirror, dl samba4 latest alpha
```

once untarred, enter the directory and read the howto4.txt

```
cd samba-4.0.0alpha6/

more howto4.txt
```

first we have to configure, compile and install samba4

```
cd source4/

./configure

make

make install
```

Then we can use the provision script to setup our realm. I used booi.schot as domain name
(instead of example.com).

```
./setup/provision --realm=BOOI.SCHOT --domain=BOOI --adminpass=stargate \
--server-role='domain controller'
```

i added a simple share for testing

```
vi /usr/local/samba/etc/smb.conf
```

then i started samba

```
cd /usr/local/samba/sbin/

./samba
```

I tested with smbclient, it works

```
smbclient //localhost/test -Uadministrator%stargate
```

I checked that bind (and bind-chroot) were installed (yes), so copied the srv records

```
cp booi.schot.zone /var/named/chroot/etc/
```

then appended to named.conf

```
cat named.conf >> /var/named/chroot/etc/named.conf
```

I followed these steps in the howto4.txt

```
vi /etc/init.d/named   [added two export lines right after start()]
chmod a+r /usr/local/samba/private/dns.keytab
cp krb5.conf /etc/
vi /var/named/chroot/etc/named.conf
 --> remove a lot, but keep allow-update { any; };
```

restart bind (named!), then tested dns with dig, this works (stripped screenshot!)

```
[root@RHEL52 private]# dig _ldap._tcp.dc._msdcs.booi.schot SRV @localhost

; (1 server found)
;; global options:  printcmd
;; Got answer:
;; -HEADER- opcode: QUERY, status: NXDOMAIN, id: 58186
;; flags: qr rd ra; QUERY: 1, ANSWER: 0, AUTHORITY: 1, ADDITIONAL: 0

;; QUESTION SECTION:
;_ldap._tcp.dc._msdcs.booi.schot. IN SRV

;; AUTHORITY SECTION:
.   10800 IN SOA A.ROOT-SERVERS.NET....

;; Query time: 54 msec
;; SERVER: 127.0.0.1#53(127.0.0.1)
;; WHEN: Tue Jan 27 20:57:05 2009
;; MSG SIZE  rcvd: 124

[root@RHEL52 private]#
```

made sure /etc/resolv.conf points to himself

```
[root@RHEL52 private]# cat /etc/resolv.conf
search booi.schot
nameserver 127.0.0.1
```

start windows 2003 server, enter the samba4 as DNS!

ping the domain, if it doesn't work, then add your redhats hostname and your realm to windows/system32/drivers/etc/hosts

join the windows computer to the domain

reboot the windows

log on with administrator stargate

start run dsa.msc to manage samba4

create an OU, a user and a GPO, test that it works

# Part VII. ipv6

# Table of Contents

# Chapter 25. Introduction to ipv6

# 25.1. about ipv6

The **ipv6** protocol is designed to replace **ipv4**. Where **ip version 4** supports a maximum of four billion unique addresses, **ip version 6** expands this to **four billion times four billion times four billion times four billion** unique addresses. This is more than 100.000.000.000.000.000.000 ipv6 addresses per square cm on our planet. That should be enough, even if every cell phone, every coffee machine and every pair of socks gets an address.

Technically speaking ipv6 uses 128-bit addresses (instead of the 32-bit from ipv4). 128-bit addresses are **huge** numbers. In decimal it would amount up to 39 digits, in hexadecimal it looks like this:

```
fe80:0000:0000:0000:0a00:27ff:fe8e:8aa8
```

Luckily ipv6 allows us to omit leading zeroes. Our address from above then becomes:

```
fe80:0:0:0:a00:27ff:fe8e:8aa8
```

When a 16-bit block is zero, it can be written as **::**. Consecutive 16-bit blocks that are zero can also be written as **::**. So our address can from above can be shortened to:

```
fe80::a00:27ff:fe8e:8aa8
```

This **::** can only occur once! The following is not a valid ipv6 address:

```
fe80::20:2e4f::39ac
```

The ipv6 **localhost** address is **0000:0000:0000:0000:0000:0000:0000:0001**, which can be abbreviated to **::1**.

```
paul@debian5:~/github/lt/images$ /sbin/ifconfig lo | grep inet6
          inet6 addr: ::1/128 Scope:Host
```

# 25.2. network id and host id

One of the few similarities between ipv4 and ipv6 is that addresses have a host part and a network part determined by a subnet mask. Using the **cidr** notation this looks like this:

```
fe80::a00:27ff:fe8e:8aa8/64
```

The above address has 64 bits for the host id, theoretically allowing for 4 billion times four billion hosts.

The localhost address looks like this with cidr:

```
::1/128
```

# 25.3. host part generation

The host part of an automatically generated (stateless) ipv6 address contains part of the hosts mac address:

```
paul@debian5:~$ /sbin/ifconfig | head -3
```

```
eth3      Link encap:Ethernet  HWaddr 08:00:27:ab:67:30
          inet addr:192.168.1.29  Bcast:192.168.1.255  Mask:255.255.255.0
          inet6 addr: fe80::a00:27ff:feab:6730/64 Scope:Link
```

Some people are concerned about privacy here...

## 25.4. ipv4 mapped ipv6 address

Some applications use ipv4 addresses embedded in an ipv6 address. (Yes there will be an era of migration with both ipv4 and ipv6 in use.) The ipv6 address then looks like this:

```
::ffff:192.168.1.42/96
```

Indeed a mix of decimal and hexadecimal characters...

## 25.5. link local addresses

**ipv6** addresses starting with **fe8.** can only be used on the local segment (replace the dot with an hexadecimal digit). This is the reason you see **Scope:Link** behind the address in this screenshot. This address serves only the **local link**.

```
paul@deb503:~$ /sbin/ifconfig | grep inet6
    inet6 addr: fe80::a00:27ff:fe8e:8aa8/64 Scope:Link
    inet6 addr: ::1/128 Scope:Host
```

These **link local** addresses all begin with **fe8.**.

Every ipv6 enabled nic will get an address in this range.

## 25.6. unique local addresses

The now obsolete system of **site local addresses** similar to ipv4 private ranges is replaced with a system of globally unique local ipv6 addresses. This to prevent duplicates when joining of networks within **site local** ranges.

All **unique local** addresses strat with **fd...**

## 25.7. globally unique unicast addresses

Since **ipv6** was designed to have multiple ip addresses per interface, the **global ipv6 address** can be used next to the **link local address**.

These **globally unique** addresses all begin with **2...** or **3...** as the first 16-bits.

## 25.8. 6to4

**6to4** is defined in rfc's 2893 and 3056 as one possible way to transition between ipv4 and ipv6 by creating an ipv6 tunnel.

It encodes an ipv4 address in an ipv6 address that starts with **2002**. For example 192.168.1.42/24 will be encoded as:

```
2002:c0a8:12a:18::1
```

You can use the command below to convert any ipv4 address to this range.

```
paul@ubu1010:~$ printf "2002:%02x%02x:%02x%02x:%04x::1\n" `echo 192.168.1.42/24 \
|tr "./" "  "`
2002:c0a8:012a:0018::1
```

# 25.9. ISP

Should you be so lucky to get an ipv6 address from an **isp**, then it will start with **2001:**.

# 25.10. non routable addresses

Comparable to **example.com** for DNS, the following ipv6 address ranges are reserved for examples, and not routable on the internet.

```
3fff:ffff::/32
2001:0db8::/32
```

# 25.11. ping6

Use **ping6** to test connectivity between ipv6 hosts. You need to specify the interface (there is no routing table for 'random' generated ipv6 link local addresses).

```
[root@fedora14 ~]# ping6 -I eth0 fe80::a00:27ff:fecd:7ffc
PING fe80::a00:27ff:fecd:7ffc(fe80::a00:27ff:fecd:7ffc) from fe80::a00:27ff:fe3c:4346 eth0: 56
64 bytes from fe80::a00:27ff:fecd:7ffc: icmp_seq=1 ttl=64 time=0.586 ms
64 bytes from fe80::a00:27ff:fecd:7ffc: icmp_seq=2 ttl=64 time=3.95 ms
64 bytes from fe80::a00:27ff:fecd:7ffc: icmp_seq=3 ttl=64 time=1.53 ms
```

Below a multicast ping6 that recieves replies from three ip6 hosts on the same network.

```
[root@fedora14 ~]# ping6 -I eth0 ff02::1
PING ff02::1(ff02::1) from fe80::a00:27ff:fe3c:4346 eth0: 56 data bytes
64 bytes from fe80::a00:27ff:fe3c:4346: icmp_seq=1 ttl=64 time=0.598 ms
64 bytes from fe80::a00:27ff:fecd:7ffc: icmp_seq=1 ttl=64 time=1.87 ms (DUP!)
64 bytes from fe80::8e7b:9dff:fed6:dff2: icmp_seq=1 ttl=64 time=535 ms (DUP!)
64 bytes from fe80::a00:27ff:fe3c:4346: icmp_seq=2 ttl=64 time=0.106 ms
64 bytes from fe80::8e7b:9dff:fed6:dff2: icmp_seq=2 ttl=64 time=1.79 ms (DUP!)
64 bytes from fe80::a00:27ff:fecd:7ffc: icmp_seq=2 ttl=64 time=2.48 ms (DUP!)
```

## 25.12. Belgium and ipv6

A lot of information on ipv6 in Belgium can be found at www.ipv6council.be.

Sites like ipv6.belgium.be, www.bipt.be and www.bricozone.be are enabled for ipv6. Some Universities also: fundp.ac.be (Namur) and ulg.ac.be (Liege).

## 25.13. other websites

Other useful websites for testing ipv6 are:

```
test-ipv6.com
ipv6-test.com
```

Going to the ipv6-test.com website will test whether you have a valid accessible ipv6 address.

Your internet connection is **IPv6** capable

# 2002:51a5:657d::1

**Telenet**

Address type is

## 6to4

6to4 mapping to IPv4 address **81.165.101.125**

Your internet connection is IPv4 capable

# 81.165.101.125

d51A5657D.access.telenet.be

Going to the test-ipv6.com website will also test whether you have a valid accessible ipv6 address.

# Test your IPv6 connectivity.

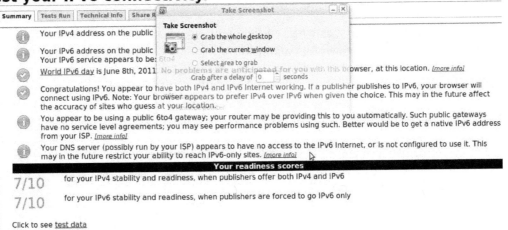

## 25.14. 6to4 gateways

To access ipv4 only websites when on ipv6 you can use sixxs.net (more specifically http://www.sixxs.net/tools/gateway/) as a gatway.

For example use http://www.slashdot.org.sixxs.org/ instead of http://slashdot.org

## 25.15. ping6 and dns

Below a screenshot of a **ping6** from behind a 6to4 connection.

```
81.165.101.125        195.130.131.4        DNS     Standard query AAAA ipv6-test.com
195.130.131.4         81.165.101.125       DNS     Standard query response AAAA 2001:41d0:2:67d1::7e57:1
2002:51a5:657d::1     2001:41d0:2:67d1::7e57:1 ICMPv6 Echo request
2001:41d0:2:67d1::7e57:1 2002:51a5:657d::1  ICMPv6 Echo reply
2002:51a5:657d::1     2001:41d0:2:67d1::7e57:1 ICMPv6 Echo request
2001:41d0:2:67d1::7e57:1 2002:51a5:657d::1  ICMPv6 Echo reply
```

## 25.16. ipv6 and tcp/http

Below a screenshot of a tcp handshake and http connection over ipv6.

| Source | Destination | Protocol | Info |
|---|---|---|---|
| 2002:51a5:657d::1 | 2001:41d0:2:67d1::7e57:1 | TCP | 38036 > http [SYN] Seq=0 Win=5648 L |
| 2001:41d0:2:67d1::7e57:1 | 2002:51a5:657d::1 | TCP | http > 38036 [SYN, ACK] Seq=0 Ack=1 |
| 2002:51a5:657d::1 | 2001:41d0:2:67d1::7e57:1 | TCP | 38036 > http [ACK] Seq=1 Ack=1 Win= |
| 2002:51a5:657d::1 | 2001:41d0:2:67d1::7e57:1 | HTTP | GET /json/addrinfo.php?PHPSESSID=19 |
| 2001:41d0:2:67d1::7e57:1 | 2002:51a5:657d::1 | TCP | http > 38036 [ACK] Seq=1 Ack=708 Wi |
| 2001:41d0:2:67d1::7e57:1 | 2002:51a5:657d::1 | HTTP | HTTP/1.1 200 OK  (text/javascript) |

## 25.17. ipv6 PTR record

As seen in the DNS chapter, ipv6 PTR records are in the ip6.net domain, and have 32 generations of child domains.

```
▷ Frame 46 (132 bytes on wire, 132 bytes captured)
▷ Ethernet II, Src: Apple_5d:2e:52 (00:26:bb:5d:2e:52), Dst: Riverdel_cf:6a:10 (00:30:b8:cf:6a:10)
▷ Internet Protocol, Src: 81.165.101.125 (81.165.101.125), Dst: 195.130.131.4 (195.130.131.4)
▷ User Datagram Protocol, Src Port: 34361 (34361), Dst Port: domain (53)
▽ Domain Name System (query)
     [Response In: 47]
     Transaction ID: 0xcfe3
  ▷ Flags: 0x0100 (Standard query)
     Questions: 1
     Answer RRs: 0
     Authority RRs: 0
     Additional RRs: 0
  ▽ Queries
     ▷ 1.0.0.0.7.5.e.7.0.0.0.0.0.0.0.0.1.d.7.6.2.0.0.0.0.d.1.4.1.0.0.2.ip6.arpa: type PTR, class IN
```

## 25.18. 6to4 setup on Linux

Below a transcript of a 6to4 setup on Linux.

Thanks to http://www.anyweb.co.nz/tutorial/v6Linux6to4 and http://mirrors.bieringer.de/Linux+IPv6-HOWTO/ and tldp.org!

```
root@mac:~# ifconfig
eth0      Link encap:Ethernet  HWaddr 00:26:bb:5d:2e:52
          inet addr:81.165.101.125  Bcast:255.255.255.255  Mask:255.255.248.0
```

```
                inet6 addr: fe80::226:bbff:fe5d:2e52/64 Scope:Link
                UP BROADCAST RUNNING MULTICAST  MTU:1500  Metric:1
                RX packets:5926044 errors:0 dropped:0 overruns:0 frame:0
                TX packets:2985892 errors:0 dropped:0 overruns:0 carrier:0
                collisions:0 txqueuelen:1000
                RX bytes:4274849823 (4.2 GB)  TX bytes:237002019 (237.0 MB)
                Interrupt:43 Base address:0x8000

lo          Link encap:Local Loopback
                inet addr:127.0.0.1  Mask:255.0.0.0
                inet6 addr: ::1/128 Scope:Host
                UP LOOPBACK RUNNING  MTU:16436  Metric:1
                RX packets:598 errors:0 dropped:0 overruns:0 frame:0
                TX packets:598 errors:0 dropped:0 overruns:0 carrier:0
                collisions:0 txqueuelen:0
                RX bytes:61737 (61.7 KB)  TX bytes:61737 (61.7 KB)

root@mac:~# sysctl -w net.ipv6.conf.default.forwarding=1
net.ipv6.conf.default.forwarding = 1
root@mac:~# ip tunnel add tun6to4 mode sit remote any local 81.165.101.125
root@mac:~# ip link set dev tun6to4 mtu 1472 up
root@mac:~# ip link show dev tun6to4
10: tun6to4: <NOARP,UP,LOWER_UP> mtu 1472 qdisc noqueue state UNKNOWN
    link/sit 81.165.101.125 brd 0.0.0.0
root@mac:~# ip -6 addr add dev tun6to4 2002:51a5:657d:0::1/64
root@mac:~# ip -6 addr add dev eth0 2002:51a5:657d:1::1/64
root@mac:~# ip -6 addr add dev eth0 fdcb:43c1:9c18:1::1/64
root@mac:~# ifconfig
eth0        Link encap:Ethernet  HWaddr 00:26:bb:5d:2e:52
                inet addr:81.165.101.125  Bcast:255.255.255.255  Mask:255.255.248.0
                inet6 addr: fe80::226:bbff:fe5d:2e52/64 Scope:Link
                inet6 addr: fdcb:43c1:9c18:1::1/64 Scope:Global
                inet6 addr: 2002:51a5:657d:1::1/64 Scope:Global
                UP BROADCAST RUNNING MULTICAST  MTU:1500  Metric:1
                RX packets:5927436 errors:0 dropped:0 overruns:0 frame:0
                TX packets:2986025 errors:0 dropped:0 overruns:0 carrier:0
                collisions:0 txqueuelen:1000
                RX bytes:4274948430 (4.2 GB)  TX bytes:237014619 (237.0 MB)
                Interrupt:43 Base address:0x8000

lo          Link encap:Local Loopback
                inet addr:127.0.0.1  Mask:255.0.0.0
                inet6 addr: ::1/128 Scope:Host
                UP LOOPBACK RUNNING  MTU:16436  Metric:1
                RX packets:598 errors:0 dropped:0 overruns:0 frame:0
                TX packets:598 errors:0 dropped:0 overruns:0 carrier:0
                collisions:0 txqueuelen:0
                RX bytes:61737 (61.7 KB)  TX bytes:61737 (61.7 KB)

tun6to4     Link encap:IPv6-in-IPv4
                inet6 addr: ::81.165.101.125/128 Scope:Compat
                inet6 addr: 2002:51a5:657d::1/64 Scope:Global
                UP RUNNING NOARP  MTU:1472  Metric:1
                RX packets:0 errors:0 dropped:0 overruns:0 frame:0
                TX packets:0 errors:0 dropped:0 overruns:0 carrier:0
                collisions:0 txqueuelen:0
                RX bytes:0 (0.0 B)  TX bytes:0 (0.0 B)

root@mac:~# ip -6 route add 2002::/16 dev tun6to4
root@mac:~# ip -6 route add ::/0 via ::192.88.99.1 dev tun6to4 metric 1
root@mac:~# ip -6 route show
::/96 via :: dev tun6to4  metric 256  mtu 1472 advmss 1412 hoplimit 0
2002:51a5:657d::/64 dev tun6to4  proto kernel  metric 256  mtu 1472 advmss 1412 hoplimit 0
2002:51a5:657d:1::/64 dev eth0  proto kernel  metric 256  mtu 1500 advmss 1440 hoplimit 0
```

```
2002::/16 dev tun6to4  metric 1024  mtu 1472 advmss 1412 hoplimit 0
fdcb:43c1:9c18:1::/64 dev eth0  proto kernel  metric 256  mtu 1500 advmss 1440 hoplimit 0
fe80::/64 dev eth0  proto kernel  metric 256  mtu 1500 advmss 1440 hoplimit 0
fe80::/64 dev tun6to4  proto kernel  metric 256  mtu 1472 advmss 1412 hoplimit 0
default via ::192.88.99.1 dev tun6to4  metric 1  mtu 1472 advmss 1412 hoplimit 0
root@mac:~# ping6 ipv6-test.com
PING ipv6-test.com(ipv6-test.com) 56 data bytes
64 bytes from ipv6-test.com: icmp_seq=1 ttl=57 time=42.4 ms
64 bytes from ipv6-test.com: icmp_seq=2 ttl=57 time=43.0 ms
64 bytes from ipv6-test.com: icmp_seq=3 ttl=57 time=43.5 ms
64 bytes from ipv6-test.com: icmp_seq=4 ttl=57 time=43.9 ms
64 bytes from ipv6-test.com: icmp_seq=5 ttl=57 time=45.6 ms
^C
--- ipv6-test.com ping statistics ---
5 packets transmitted, 5 received, 0% packet loss, time 4006ms
rtt min/avg/max/mdev = 42.485/43.717/45.632/1.091 ms
```

# Part VIII. Appendix

# Table of Contents

# Appendix A. License

GNU Free Documentation License

Version 1.3, 3 November 2008

Copyright © 2000, 2001, 2002, 2007, 2008 Free Software Foundation, Inc.

Everyone is permitted to copy and distribute verbatim copies of this license document, but changing it is not allowed.

0. PREAMBLE

The purpose of this License is to make a manual, textbook, or other functional and useful document "free" in the sense of freedom: to assure everyone the effective freedom to copy and redistribute it, with or without modifying it, either commercially or noncommercially. Secondarily, this License preserves for the author and publisher a way to get credit for their work, while not being considered responsible for modifications made by others.

This License is a kind of "copyleft", which means that derivative works of the document must themselves be free in the same sense. It complements the GNU General Public License, which is a copyleft license designed for free software.

We have designed this License in order to use it for manuals for free software, because free software needs free documentation: a free program should come with manuals providing the same freedoms that the software does. But this License is not limited to software manuals; it can be used for any textual work, regardless of subject matter or whether it is published as a printed book. We recommend this License principally for works whose purpose is instruction or reference.

1. APPLICABILITY AND DEFINITIONS

This License applies to any manual or other work, in any medium, that contains a notice placed by the copyright holder saying it can be distributed under the terms of this License. Such a notice grants a world-wide, royalty-free license, unlimited in duration, to use that work under the conditions stated herein. The "Document", below, refers to any such manual or work. Any member of the public is a licensee, and is addressed as "you". You accept the license if you copy, modify or distribute the work in a way requiring permission under copyright law.

A "Modified Version" of the Document means any work containing the Document or a portion of it, either copied verbatim, or with modifications and/or translated into another language.

A "Secondary Section" is a named appendix or a front-matter section of the Document that deals exclusively with the relationship of the publishers or authors of the Document to the Document's overall subject (or to related matters) and contains nothing that could fall directly within that overall subject. (Thus, if the Document is in part a textbook of mathematics, a Secondary Section may not explain any mathematics.) The relationship could be a matter of historical connection with the subject or with related matters, or of legal, commercial, philosophical, ethical or political position regarding them.

The "Invariant Sections" are certain Secondary Sections whose titles are designated, as being those of Invariant Sections, in the notice that says that the Document is released under this License. If a section does not fit the above definition of Secondary then it is not allowed to be designated as Invariant. The Document may contain zero Invariant Sections. If the Document does not identify any Invariant Sections then there are none.

The "Cover Texts" are certain short passages of text that are listed, as Front-Cover Texts or Back-Cover Texts, in the notice that says that the Document is released under this License. A Front-Cover Text may be at most 5 words, and a Back-Cover Text may be at most 25 words.

A "Transparent" copy of the Document means a machine-readable copy, represented in a format whose specification is available to the general public, that is suitable for revising the document straightforwardly with generic text editors or (for images composed of pixels) generic paint programs or (for drawings) some widely available drawing editor, and that is suitable for input to text formatters or for automatic translation to a variety of formats suitable for input to text formatters. A copy made in an otherwise Transparent file format whose markup, or absence of markup, has been arranged to thwart or discourage subsequent modification by readers is not Transparent. An image format is not Transparent if used for any substantial amount of text. A copy that is not "Transparent" is called "Opaque".

Examples of suitable formats for Transparent copies include plain ASCII without markup, Texinfo input format, LaTeX input format, SGML or XML using a publicly available DTD, and standard-conforming simple HTML, PostScript or PDF designed for human modification. Examples of transparent image formats include PNG, XCF and JPG. Opaque formats include proprietary formats that can be read and edited only by proprietary word processors, SGML or XML for which the DTD and/or processing tools are not generally available, and the machine-generated HTML, PostScript or PDF produced by some word processors for output purposes only.

The "Title Page" means, for a printed book, the title page itself, plus such following pages as are needed to hold, legibly, the material this License requires to appear in the title page. For works in formats which do not have any title page as such, "Title Page" means the text near the most prominent appearance of the work's title, preceding the beginning of the body of the text.

The "publisher" means any person or entity that distributes copies of the Document to the public.

A section "Entitled XYZ" means a named subunit of the Document whose title either is precisely XYZ or contains XYZ in parentheses following text that translates XYZ in another language. (Here XYZ stands for a specific section name mentioned below, such as "Acknowledgements", "Dedications", "Endorsements", or "History".) To "Preserve the Title" of such a section when you modify the Document means that it remains a section "Entitled XYZ" according to this definition.

The Document may include Warranty Disclaimers next to the notice which states that this License applies to the Document. These Warranty Disclaimers are considered to be included by reference in this License, but only as regards disclaiming warranties: any other implication that these Warranty Disclaimers may have is void and has no effect on the meaning of this License.

2. VERBATIM COPYING

You may copy and distribute the Document in any medium, either commercially or noncommercially, provided that this License, the copyright notices, and the license notice saying this License applies to the Document are reproduced in all copies, and that you add no other conditions whatsoever to those of this License. You may not use technical measures to obstruct or control the reading or further copying of the copies you make or distribute. However, you may accept compensation in exchange for copies. If you distribute a large enough number of copies you must also follow the conditions in section 3.

You may also lend copies, under the same conditions stated above, and you may publicly display copies.

3. COPYING IN QUANTITY

If you publish printed copies (or copies in media that commonly have printed covers) of the Document, numbering more than 100, and the Document's license notice requires Cover Texts, you must enclose the copies in covers that carry, clearly and legibly, all these Cover Texts: Front-Cover Texts on the front cover, and Back-Cover Texts on the back cover. Both covers must also clearly and legibly identify you as the publisher of these copies. The front cover must present the full title with all words of the title equally prominent and visible. You may add other material on the covers in addition. Copying with changes limited to the covers, as long as they preserve the title of the Document and satisfy these conditions, can be treated as verbatim copying in other respects.

If the required texts for either cover are too voluminous to fit legibly, you should put the first ones listed (as many as fit reasonably) on the actual cover, and continue the rest onto adjacent pages.

If you publish or distribute Opaque copies of the Document numbering more than 100, you must either include a machine-readable Transparent copy along with each Opaque copy, or state in or with each Opaque copy a computer-network location from which the general network-using public has access to download using public-standard network protocols a complete Transparent copy of the Document, free of added material. If you use the latter option, you must take reasonably prudent steps, when you begin distribution of Opaque copies in quantity, to ensure that this Transparent copy will remain thus accessible at the stated location until at least one year after the last time you distribute an Opaque copy (directly or through your agents or retailers) of that edition to the public.

It is requested, but not required, that you contact the authors of the Document well before redistributing any large number of copies, to give them a chance to provide you with an updated version of the Document.

4. MODIFICATIONS

You may copy and distribute a Modified Version of the Document under the conditions of sections 2 and 3 above, provided that you release the Modified Version under precisely this License, with the Modified Version filling the role of the Document, thus licensing distribution and modification of the Modified Version to whoever possesses a copy of it. In addition, you must do these things in the Modified Version:

   * A. Use in the Title Page (and on the covers, if any) a title distinct from that of the Document, and from those of previous versions (which should, if there were any, be listed in the History section of the Document). You may use the same title as a previous version if the original publisher of that version gives permission.

* B. List on the Title Page, as authors, one or more persons or entities responsible for authorship of the modifications in the Modified Version, together with at least five of the principal authors of the Document (all of its principal authors, if it has fewer than five), unless they release you from this requirement.
    * C. State on the Title page the name of the publisher of the Modified Version, as the publisher.
    * D. Preserve all the copyright notices of the Document.
    * E. Add an appropriate copyright notice for your modifications adjacent to the other copyright notices.
    * F. Include, immediately after the copyright notices, a license notice giving the public permission to use the Modified Version under the terms of this License, in the form shown in the Addendum below.
    * G. Preserve in that license notice the full lists of Invariant Sections and required Cover Texts given in the Document's license notice.
    * H. Include an unaltered copy of this License.
    * I. Preserve the section Entitled "History", Preserve its Title, and add to it an item stating at least the title, year, new authors, and publisher of the Modified Version as given on the Title Page. If there is no section Entitled "History" in the Document, create one stating the title, year, authors, and publisher of the Document as given on its Title Page, then add an item describing the Modified Version as stated in the previous sentence.
    * J. Preserve the network location, if any, given in the Document for public access to a Transparent copy of the Document, and likewise the network locations given in the Document for previous versions it was based on. These may be placed in the "History" section. You may omit a network location for a work that was published at least four years before the Document itself, or if the original publisher of the version it refers to gives permission.
    * K. For any section Entitled "Acknowledgements" or "Dedications", Preserve the Title of the section, and preserve in the section all the substance and tone of each of the contributor acknowledgements and/or dedications given therein.
    * L. Preserve all the Invariant Sections of the Document, unaltered in their text and in their titles. Section numbers or the equivalent are not considered part of the section titles.
    * M. Delete any section Entitled "Endorsements". Such a section may not be included in the Modified Version.
    * N. Do not retitle any existing section to be Entitled "Endorsements" or to conflict in title with any Invariant Section.
    * O. Preserve any Warranty Disclaimers.

If the Modified Version includes new front-matter sections or appendices that qualify as Secondary Sections and contain no material copied from the Document, you may at your option designate some or all of these sections as invariant. To do this, add their titles to the list of Invariant Sections in the Modified Version's license notice. These titles must be distinct from any other section titles.

You may add a section Entitled "Endorsements", provided it contains nothing but endorsements of your Modified Version by various parties—for example, statements of peer review or that the text has been approved by an organization as the authoritative definition of a standard.

You may add a passage of up to five words as a Front-Cover Text, and a passage of up to 25 words as a Back-Cover Text, to the end of the list of Cover Texts in the Modified Version. Only one passage of Front-Cover Text and one of Back-Cover Text may be added by (or through arrangements made by) any one entity. If the Document already includes a cover text for the same cover, previously added by you or by arrangement made by the same entity you are acting on behalf of, you may not add another; but you may replace the old one, on explicit permission from the previous publisher that added the old one.

The author(s) and publisher(s) of the Document do not by this License give permission to use their names for publicity for or to assert or imply endorsement of any Modified Version.

5. COMBINING DOCUMENTS

You may combine the Document with other documents released under this License, under the terms defined in section 4 above for modified versions, provided that you include in the combination all of the Invariant Sections of all of the original documents, unmodified, and list them all as Invariant Sections of your combined work in its license notice, and that you preserve all their Warranty Disclaimers.

The combined work need only contain one copy of this License, and multiple identical Invariant Sections may be replaced with a single copy. If there are multiple Invariant Sections with the same name but different contents, make the title of each such section unique by adding at the end of it, in parentheses, the name of the original author or publisher of that section if known, or else a unique number. Make the same adjustment to the section titles in the list of Invariant Sections in the license notice of the combined work.

In the combination, you must combine any sections Entitled "History" in the various original documents, forming one section Entitled "History"; likewise combine any sections Entitled "Acknowledgements", and any sections Entitled "Dedications". You must delete all sections Entitled "Endorsements".

6. COLLECTIONS OF DOCUMENTS

You may make a collection consisting of the Document and other documents released under this License, and replace the individual copies of this License in the various documents with a single copy that is included in the collection, provided that you follow the rules of this License for verbatim copying of each of the documents in all other respects.

You may extract a single document from such a collection, and distribute it individually under this License, provided you insert a copy of this License into the extracted document, and follow this License in all other respects regarding verbatim copying of that document.

7. AGGREGATION WITH INDEPENDENT WORKS

A compilation of the Document or its derivatives with other separate and independent documents or works, in or on a volume of a storage or distribution medium, is called an "aggregate" if the copyright resulting from the compilation is not used to limit the legal rights of the compilation's users beyond what the individual works permit. When the Document is included in an aggregate, this License does not apply to the other works in the aggregate which are not themselves derivative works of the Document.

If the Cover Text requirement of section 3 is applicable to these copies of the Document, then if the Document is less than one half of the entire aggregate, the Document's Cover Texts may be placed on covers that bracket the Document within the aggregate, or the electronic equivalent of covers if the Document is in electronic form. Otherwise they must appear on printed covers that bracket the whole aggregate.

## 8. TRANSLATION

Translation is considered a kind of modification, so you may distribute translations of the Document under the terms of section 4. Replacing Invariant Sections with translations requires special permission from their copyright holders, but you may include translations of some or all Invariant Sections in addition to the original versions of these Invariant Sections. You may include a translation of this License, and all the license notices in the Document, and any Warranty Disclaimers, provided that you also include the original English version of this License and the original versions of those notices and disclaimers. In case of a disagreement between the translation and the original version of this License or a notice or disclaimer, the original version will prevail.

If a section in the Document is Entitled "Acknowledgements", "Dedications", or "History", the requirement (section 4) to Preserve its Title (section 1) will typically require changing the actual title.

## 9. TERMINATION

You may not copy, modify, sublicense, or distribute the Document except as expressly provided under this License. Any attempt otherwise to copy, modify, sublicense, or distribute it is void, and will automatically terminate your rights under this License.

However, if you cease all violation of this License, then your license from a particular copyright holder is reinstated (a) provisionally, unless and until the copyright holder explicitly and finally terminates your license, and (b) permanently, if the copyright holder fails to notify you of the violation by some reasonable means prior to 60 days after the cessation.

Moreover, your license from a particular copyright holder is reinstated permanently if the copyright holder notifies you of the violation by some reasonable means, this is the first time you have received notice of violation of this License (for any work) from that copyright holder, and you cure the violation prior to 30 days after your receipt of the notice.

Termination of your rights under this section does not terminate the licenses of parties who have received copies or rights from you under this License. If your rights have been terminated and not permanently reinstated, receipt of a copy of some or all of the same material does not give you any rights to use it.

## 10. FUTURE REVISIONS OF THIS LICENSE

The Free Software Foundation may publish new, revised versions of the GNU Free Documentation License from time to time. Such new versions will be similar in spirit to the present version, but may differ in detail to address new problems or concerns. See http://www.gnu.org/copyleft/.

Each version of the License is given a distinguishing version number. If the Document specifies that a particular numbered version of this License "or any later version" applies to it, you have the option of following the terms and conditions either of that specified version or of any later version that has been published (not as a draft) by the Free Software Foundation. If the Document does not specify a version number of this License, you may choose any version ever published (not as a draft) by the Free Software Foundation. If the Document specifies that a proxy can decide which future versions of this License can be used, that proxy's public statement of acceptance of a version permanently authorizes you to choose that version for the Document.

## 11. RELICENSING

"Massive Multiauthor Collaboration Site" (or "MMC Site") means any World Wide Web server that publishes copyrightable works and also provides prominent facilities for anybody to edit those works. A public wiki that anybody can edit is an example of such a server. A "Massive Multiauthor Collaboration" (or "MMC") contained in the site means any set of copyrightable works thus published on the MMC site.

"CC-BY-SA" means the Creative Commons Attribution-Share Alike 3.0 license published by Creative Commons Corporation, a not-for-profit corporation with a principal place of business in San Francisco, California, as well as future copyleft versions of that license published by that same organization.

"Incorporate" means to publish or republish a Document, in whole or in part, as part of another Document.

An MMC is "eligible for relicensing" if it is licensed under this License, and if all works that were first published under this License somewhere other than this MMC, and subsequently incorporated in whole or in part into the MMC, (1) had no cover texts or invariant sections, and (2) were thus incorporated prior to November 1, 2008.

The operator of an MMC Site may republish an MMC contained in the site under CC-BY-SA on the same site at any time before August 1, 2009, provided the MMC is eligible for relicensing.

# Index

## Symbols

/etc/apache2, 83
/etc/bind/named.conf.local, 133
/etc/exports, 61, 72
/etc/fstab, 62, 72
/etc/hostname, 23
/etc/httpd, 83
/etc/inetd.conf, 69, 209
/etc/init.d/samba, 198
/etc/init.d/smb, 198
/etc/init.d/winbind, 199
/etc/network/interfaces, 16, 40, 43
/etc/nsswitch.conf, 247, 249
/etc/passwd, 256
/etc/protocols, 13
/etc/resolv.conf, 119
/etc/samba/passdb.tdb, 255
/etc/samba/smb.conf, 203, 204, 205, 221, 245
/etc/samba/smbpasswd, 226, 253
/etc/services, 13, 69
/etc/squid/squid.conf, 107
/etc/ssh, 48
/etc/ssh/ssh_config, 48
/etc/ssh/sshd_config, 48
/etc/sysconfig/iptables, 65
/etc/sysconfig/network, 18
/etc/sysconfig/network-scripts/, 18
/etc/sysconfig/network-scripts/ifcfg-bond0, 41
/etc/sysctl.conf, 173
/etc/xinetd.conf, 68
/etc/xinetd.d, 68
/etc/xinetd.d/swat, 209
/proc/net/bonding, 41, 43
/proc/sys/net/ipv4/ip_forward, 173
/sbin, 21
/usr/share/doc, 18
/var/lib/nfs/etab, 61, 72
/var/log/squid, 112
.htaccess, 100
.htpasswd, 90, 97
.ssh, 52
~/.ssh/authorized_keys, 53

## A

A (DNS record), 124
AAAA (DNS record), 124
Alica and Bob, 49
allow hosts (Samba), 238
anycast, 9
apache2, 79
aptitude, 195, 196
arp(1), 24
arp table, 24
atm, 11

authoritative (dns), 128
authoritative zone, 123
axfr, 131

## B

bind, 121
bind(DNS), 147
binding, 39
binding(ip), 38
bonding(ip), 38
bootp, 18, 34
broadcast, 9
browsable (Samba), 239
browseable (Samba), 239
browser master, 253

## C

cahing only name server, 125
chain (iptables), 180
CIFS, 200
Cisco, 11
CNAME (DNS record), 124
create mask (Samba), 239

## D

default gateway, 25
deny hosts (Samba), 239
dhclient, 175
dhclient(1), 23
dhcp, 18, 34
dhcp client, 16, 23
dhcp server, 119
directory mask (Samba), 239
directory security mask(samba), 240
DNAT, 172
dns, 34, 117, 117
dnsdomainname, 123
dns namespace, 120
dns server, 119
domain (dns), 121
domain name system, 117, 117
dpkg, 195
dsa, 49

## E

eth0, 16
ethtool(1), 26
exportfs(1), 61, 72

## F

fddi, 11
filter table (iptables), 180
firewall, 171
fixed ip, 19
fixed ip address, 16
force create mode(samba), 240

www.ingramcontent.com/pod-product-compliance
Lightning Source LLC
LaVergne TN
LVHW060137070326
832902LV00018B/2827